T0305411

Regulation, Governance and Convergence in the Media

Regulation, Governance and Convergence in the Media

Peter Humphreys

Formerly School of Social Sciences, University of Manchester, UK

Seamus Simpson

University of Salford, UK

 Edward Elgar
PUBLISHING

Cheltenham, UK • Northampton, MA, USA

Published by
Edward Elgar Publishing Limited
The Lypiatts
15 Lansdown Road
Cheltenham
Glos GL50 2JA
UK

Edward Elgar Publishing, Inc.
William Pratt House
9 Dewey Court
Northampton
Massachusetts 01060
USA

A catalogue record for this book
is available from the British Library

Library of Congress Control Number: 2018935721

This book is available electronically in the **Elgar**online
Social and Political Science subject collection
DOI 10.4337/9781781008997

ISBN 978 1 78100 898 0 (cased)
ISBN 978 1 78100 899 7 (eBook)

Typeset by Columns Design XML Ltd, Reading
Printed and bound in Great Britain by TJ International Ltd, Padstow, Cornwall

Contents

About the authors

Peter Humphreys was Professor of Politics in the School of Social Sciences at the University of Manchester, where he taught undergraduate courses on media and politics and on European politics and a postgraduate course on media policy. He retired in January 2017. He has published extensively on the theme of comparative media policy and regulation, most recently co-authoring (with Thomas Gibbons) *Audiovisual Regulation under Pressure: Comparative Cases from North America and Europe* (2012, Routledge). He has served as Vice-Chair (2008–2010) and Chair (2010–2012) of the Communications Law and Policy division of the International Communication Association. Also, he served as Vice-Chair (2006–2010) of the Communications Law and Policy section of the European Communications Research and Education Association (ECREA).

Seamus Simpson is Professor of Media Policy in the School of Arts and Media at the University of Salford. He is co-editor (with Manuel Puppis [University of Fribourg] and Hilde Van den Bulck [University of Antwerp]) of *European Media Policy for the 21st Century: Assessing the Past, Setting Agendas for the Future* (2016, Routledge). He was part of the PricewaterhouseCoopers team that undertook the first EU-funded evaluation of the pan-European electronic communications regulator, BEREC, in 2012. He is a past Vice-Chair and Chair of the International Communication Association Communication, Law and Policy Division (2012–2016). He is a Senior Editor of the *Oxford Research Encyclopedia of Communication* (Oxford University Press).

Preface

In 2005 our jointly authored volume *Globalisation, Convergence and European Telecommunications Regulation*, also published by Edward Elgar, explored the transformation of the telecommunications regulatory regime in Europe that had occurred over the previous two decades or so. As the title announced, 'convergence' was already very much a theme in policy discourse. However, as our volume showed, real convergence of telecommunications, electronic media and the emerging online services did not feature in the European Union's framework for the regulation of electronic communications (EUFREC), which we then referred to as the Electronic Communications Regulatory Framework, (ECRF). Among other things, that volume showed how strong demands for the separate regulatory treatment of broadcasting content, as well as a decision to exempt so-called 'information society' or online services from any new regulatory framework resulted in a very modest convergence regulatory framework being agreed by EU Member States in 2002. The EUFREC was convergent only to the extent that it dealt commonly with all network infrastructures and associated services across which electronic content was transmitted. In retrospect, as far as media convergence is concerned, the story we told in that book about emerging convergence policy showed the latter to be more significant for what it omitted than what it included. It essentially remained about telecommunications regulation.

Since that time, our communication research interests have diverged somewhat, whilst at the same time we have both kept our interest in the theme of convergence alive. As this later volume shows, convergence is still elusive to a degree, though it is certainly very much more a practical reality than it was nearly 20 years ago. To be specific, Seamus Simpson's research since 2005 has focused largely on regulatory institutional and infrastructural communications issues, which relate more closely to our earlier work on telecommunications, whilst Peter Humphreys' research has focused on media policy issues, with an emphasis on policy and regulation of media markets (television, the press) and on journalism. Both of us have found these research directions impacted by the new media technologies which provide a context for media convergence in its different forms, in particular, the Internet. This explains the structure of the book. Part I, written by Seamus Simpson, introduces the historical context within which convergence has developed, thereby setting out the core themes of the book. Part II, also written by Seamus Simpson, deals with the governance of three key infrastructural issues: the development of next generation networks, the debate on re-allocating spectrum freed up by digitalisation, and the question of Internet neutrality. Part III, written by Peter Humphreys, looks at three key issues that have to do with media content in a converging communication environment: the controversy and conflicts over copyright enforcement, media concentration, and subsidies for journalism and media content. The Conclusion is co-authored.

The approach of the book is thematic, rather than country-specific or comparative. All chapters cover developments in the USA and Europe, but beyond that our approach ranges over a number of countries. This is partly because of the nature of the themes. Thus, the chapter on next generation networks finds it useful to explore the different approaches taken in the USA, Europe, Australia and South Korea. The chapter on spectrum, because of the importance of the International Telecommunication Union as a forum, contains a global sweep in its discussion. Partly, it reflects the boundaries of our research activity and experience. Thus, the chapters in Part III focus entirely on developments in the USA and Europe. Chapter 7's close attention to the UK case reflects both rationales: the UK policy debate has produced some promising policy proposals on the theme of subsidising public service media in the digital era; and this has been a particular focus of Peter Humphreys' work in recent years. Overall, the book aims to highlight and explain the contradictions, conflicts, and challenges that surround the governance of digital convergence, thereby providing a better understanding of the complexity of the phenomenon, and also to contribute suggestions for the further development of media policy to deal with the challenges of convergence.

Peter Humphreys was Professor of Politics in the School of Social Sciences at the University of Manchester University until January 2017. He would like to acknowledge the support of the Economic and Social Research Council (ESRC) during his academic career, most notably for three substantial grants enabling his research in the communication policy field. Between 1996 and 1999 he was Principal Investigator on a research award (ESRC Ref: L 12625109) for a three-year project 'Regulating for Media Pluralism: Issues in Competition and Ownership', which looked at policies for media ownership regulation in Germany, the UK, and at the EC level. Between 2000 and 2003, he was Co-Investigator on a three-year project, 'European Union as a Medium of Policy

Transfer: Case Studies in Utility Regulation' (ESRC Ref: L 216252001-A). On this project, he was responsible for researching telecommunications, one of the three sectors under investigation. Between 2005 (February) and 2008 (March) he was Principal Investigator on a research project, 'Globalization, Regulatory Competition and Audiovisual Regulation in Five Countries', these being Canada, France, Germany, UK and USA (ESRC Ref: 000 23 0966). Mainly, this project looked at policies for public service television and other television subsidies, but it included a study of the regulation of media concentration in the television sector. The ideas for policy expressed in Part III of this volume represent the culmination of Peter Humphreys' thinking on how the media policy issues identified herein might be addressed, drawing on over three decades of research in the field made possible by this ESRC support.

Seamus Simpson is Professor of Media Policy in the School of Arts and Media at the University of Salford. At the time of writing, he is Co-Investigator on the three-year (September 2015 to August 2018) ESRC-funded project, 'International Professional Fora: A Study of Civil Society Participation in Internet Governance' (Grant no: ES/M00953X/1). Part of the research conducted in this project contributed to the writing of this volume. He would like to acknowledge the support of the Council and express gratitude to project collaborators, Alison Harcourt (University of Exeter – Principal Investigator), George Christou (University of Warwick – Co-Investigator), and Imir Rashid (University of Exeter, Associate Research Fellow).

Peter Humphreys
Seamus Simpson
January 2018

Abbreviations

ABC	American Broadcasting Company (US TV network)
ABU	Asia-Pacific Broadcasting Union
AER	Association of European Radios
AM	Amplitude Modulation (broadcasting transmission)
AOL	America On-Line
APWPT	Association of Professional Wireless Production Technologies
ARD	Association of Public Service Broadcasters in Germany
ARNS	Aeronautical Radio Navigation Service
ARRA	American Recovery and Reinvestment Act
ASBU	Arab States Broadcasting Union
ASMG	Arab Spectrum Management Group
AT & T	American Telephone & Telegraph (company)
AUB	African Union of Broadcasting
BBC	British Broadcasting Corporation
BECTU	Broadcasting, Entertainment, Cinematograph and Theatre Union (UK)
BEIRG	British Entertainment Industry Radio Group
BEREC	Body of European Regulators for Electronic Communications
BIP	Broadband Initiative Program (US)
BNE	Broadcast Networks Europe
BTOP	Broadband Technology Opportunities Program (US)
CBS	Columbia Broadcasting System (US TV network)
CD(s)	Compact Disc(s)
CEPT	European Conference of Postal and Telecommunication Administrations
CITEL	Comisión Interamericana de Telecomunicaciones

CMPF	Centre for Media Pluralism and Media Freedom (EU)
CNN	Cable News Network (US cable and satellite channel)
COICA	Combating Online Infringement and Counterfeits Act (US)
CoM	Council of Ministers (EU)
COSIP	Compte de Soutien à l'Industrie de Programmes (French Cinema and TV production subsidy body)
CPBF	Campaign for Press and Broadcasting Freedom (UK)
DADVSI	Loi sur le Droit d'Auteur et les Droits Voisins dans la Société de l'Information (Law on author's rights and related rights in Digital Agenda for Europe
DCMS	Department of Culture, Media and Sport (UK ministry)
DEA	Digital Economy Act (UK)
DG	Directorate-General (branch of European Commission)
DMCA	Digital Millennium Copyright Act
DPI	Deep Packet Inspection (technology)
DRM	Digital Rights Management
DSL	Digital Subscriber Line(s)
DTT	Digital Terrestrial Television
DTTB	Digital Terrestrial Television Broadcasting
DVD(s)	Digital Video Disc(s)
EBU	European Broadcasting Union
ECC	European Communications Committee
ECHR	European Convention on Human Rights
ECP(s)	End-Use Connectivity Provider(s)
ECRF	Electronic Communications Regulatory Framework (see EUFREC)
EFJ	European Federation of Journalists
EP	European Parliament
EPG	Electronic Programme Guide
EPP	European People's Party (European Parliament)
ESC	European Spectrum Committee
ETNO	European Telecommunications Networks Operators
EU	European Union
EUCD	European Union Copyright Directive

EUFREC	European Union Framework for the Regulation of Electronic Communications
Euralva	European Alliance of Viewers and Listeners Associations
FCC	Federal Communications Commission (US regulatory authority for communications)
FM	Frequency Modulation (broadcasting transmission)
FRAND	Fair and Reasonable and Non-Discriminatory (terms)
GESAC	European Grouping of Societies of Authors and Composers
GSM	Global System for Mobile
GSMA	Global System for Mobile Association
HADOPI	Haute Autorité pour la Diffusion des Oeuvres et la Protection des droits sur Internet (High Authority for the diffusion of creative works and copyright protection on the Internet)
HBO	Home Box Office (US cable and satellite TV network)
HDTV	High Definition Television
IAB	International Association of Broadcasting
ICT	Information and Communications Technology
IMT	International Mobile Telecommunications
IP	Internet Property
IP	Intellectual Protocol
IPPR	Institute of Public Policy Research (UK)
IPR(s)	Intellectual Property Right(s)
IPTV	Internet Protocol Television
ISP(s)	Internet Service Provider(s)
IT	Information Technology
ITN	Independent Television News (UK news provider)
ITU	International Telecommunication Union
ITV	Independent Television (UK)
KEK	Kommission zur Ermittlung der Konzentration im Medienbereich (German Media Concentration Commission)
LLU	Local Loop Unbundling
LTE	Long term Evolution (standard for high-speed wireless)
MPAA	Motion Picture Association of America
MPM	Media Pluralism Monitor (EU)

NABA	North American Broadcasters Association
NBC	National Broadcasting Company (US TV network)
NBN	National Broadband Network (Australia)
NBP	National Broadband Plan (US)
NGN(s)	Next Generation Network(s)
NPA	Newspaper Preservation Act (US)
NRA(s)	National Regulatory Authority (ies)
NTIA	National Telecommunications and Information Administration (US)
NUJ	National Union of Journalists (UK)
Ofcom	Office of Communications (UK regulatory and competition authority for communications)
PACT	Producers Alliance for Cinema and Television
PBS	Public Broadcasting Service (US public service broadcaster)
PIPA	Protect Intellectual Property Act (US)
PMSE	Programme Making and Special Events
PPP	Public Private Partnership
PS	Parti Socialiste (French Socialist Party)
PSB(s)	Public Service Broadcasting -er(s)
PSM	Public Service Media
PSP	Public Service Publisher
PSTN(s)	Public Switched Telephone Network(s)
P2P	Peer to Peer (file sharing)
QoS	Quality of Service
RCC	Regional Commonwealth in the field of Communications (states of former USSR)
RIAA	Recording Industry Association of America
RSPG	Radio Spectrum Policy Group (the 'Lamy group', high level advising the European Commission)
RUS	Rural Utilities Service (US)
SCBG	Satellite and Cable Broadcasters' Group (UK)
SGEI	Services of General Economic Interest
SMP	Significant Market Power
SOPA	Stop Online Piracy Act (US)

TCP/IP	Transmission Control Protocol/Internet Protocol
TV	Television
UHF	Ultra High Frequency
UK	United Kingdom (of Great Britain and Northern Ireland)
UMP	Union for a Popular Movement (French conservatives)
US(A)	United States (of America)
VAT	Value Added Tax
VCR	Video-Cassette Recorder
VoIP	Voice over Internet Protocol
WBU	World Broadcasting Unions
WCT	World Copyright Treaty
WIPO	World Intellectual Property Organisation
WPPT	World Performances and Phonograms Treaty
WRC	World Radiocommunication Conference

PART I

The context of media convergence

1. Media convergence: paths and constructs

INTRODUCTION

Media convergence has a relatively long history and is a multi-faceted phenomenon. In this volume, convergence is viewed as a set of inter-related processes, by this stage significantly well understood by academics to have associated with it a recognisable, if relatively small, body of literature. At the same time, the processes of media convergence and, most particularly, its governance, continue to present many challenging and as yet unanswered policy questions. This opening chapter of the volume has two purposes. First, it maps out the main features of the journey towards media convergence as they have unfolded historically. Second, it explores a range of attempts in the academic literature to characterise media convergence and to understand its governance. The chapter argues that, despite assumptions about the inexorability and inevitability of media convergence as a series of technological and service-based developments, made over a number of decades, the process of media convergence has instead highlighted its fractious, fragmented and protracted character. The chapter argues that this is most clearly evidenced in issues related to the (potential) governance of converging media environments, where key decisions about the allocation of media resources of various kinds are made. A focus on the nature and processes of media convergence governance allows an explanation to be provided for the problematic and incomplete character of media convergence. Furthermore, knowledge of the institutional landscape and communication policy processes in which media convergence issues are considered and (often incompletely) resolved is essential to an understanding of how and why media convergence has developed to date, as well as its future prospects.

A core contention of the volume is that neo-liberal policy agendas, developed and deployed in the communications sector over recent decades, have gone hand in hand with media convergence in many respects. The need to stimulate developments in technology and the new goods and services stemming from them are considered of paramount importance. This, it is argued by its advocates, should be achieved through market-based changes to create competition, alongside developments in governance arrangements to secure reformed market structures promoting competition. Media convergence and neo-liberalism share the common feature of having been propounded as inevitable, inexorable and irresistible. The message that technological changes create new enhanced services in an environment of unparalleled consumer choice has led to arguments that governance structures and media policy arrangements need to change to accommodate and bring to fruition the benefits of convergence that are fundamentally neo-liberal in character. As a corollary, an understanding of the role of neo-liberalism in electronic media environments can explain much of the changes that have occurred within them.

This chapter commences with a brief consideration of key developments in information and communication technologies and services that brought to prominence the idea of a gradual coming together of disparate parts of the communications landscape. It then moves to consider approaches developed in academic work which have understood convergence as an often loosely connected array of commercial and social – including cultural – constructs. From this, the chapter makes the argument that convergence is, thus, a phenomenon in search of an appropriate governance framework and, in so doing, it considers the features of the key path-based approaches to the governance of media convergence that have developed historically. This is illustrated briefly by reference to the EU which has grappled with the challenge of governing media convergence at the international level. The EU's experience exemplifies very well fractious and limited policy efforts to resolve the idiosyncrasies and peculiarities of convergence. These have been generated by the constituent industrial, societal and public policy actors and associated interests that have, in their different ways, advocated the kind of media convergence we witness today.

This opening chapter of the volume thus provides the context within which the salient contemporary issues of governing media convergence selected and explored in the volume – the deployment of upgraded high-speed electronic communications networks, spectrum allocation, Internet neutrality, copyright, media concentration, public subsidies and public service content – can be taken forward.

EVOLVING INFORMATION AND COMMUNICATION TECHNOLOGIES AND MEDIA CONVERGENCE

Historically, the antecedents of what we now recognise as the main technological constituents of media convergence led largely separate lives. The technologies bound up in the main equipment and infrastructure of Information Technology hardware and software, telecommunications, newspaper print and other publishing, and broadcasting displayed little cross-over or common usage.[1] However, a number of key technological and service-level developments enabled convergence. The first and most widely heralded of these was digitisation or, more plainly, the application of computer-based communication technologies to other parts of communication, in the first instance, telecommunications. The much-heralded realisation of telematics in the 1970s took place within, and reinforced, the conceptualisation of a grand process that would lead, for its advocates, to the computerisation of society (Nora and Minc 1980). The convergence of computing and telecommunications was certainly of huge significance for the latter. Advances in electronic (digitalised) switching led to major practical efficiencies but also increased costs in terms of research and development. Through the assistance of modem technology, the ability to connect computer equipment across a communications network expanded the service possibilities open to providers and users. From this point, at least techno-functionally, combinations of voice, data, text and video could be created and delivered across 'standard' telecommunication infrastructure. The extra transmission capacity that this would require, allied to – an albeit putatively perceived – growth in demand for communications services, would be catered for by the development of fibre optic cable technology heralded, even as early as the 1970s, as providing a context for high-speed, content-laden, and interactive networked-based communication. Some 40 plus years later, the complete deployment of fibre optic broadband networks is, of course, a policy aspiration more than an achievement (see Chapter 2). Around the same time, the use of the airwaves for personal, at that stage only voice-based, communication, was vaunted as a possibility and soon became a reality in the shape of an embryonic, by present standards, mobile communications sector (Linge and Sutton 2015). The digitisation of the airwaves soon followed as a convergence-based, partial solution to capacity problems of microwave communication. As significant, it hinted at the possible future use of the airwaves to send more than simply voice signals between two mobile communication handsets (see Chapter 3).

The above developments and their ramifications were felt most resoundingly in an, until then, somnolent telecommunications sector, illustrating both concrete developments in technology and services but, as important, future promises of convergence. However, as telecommunications was changing through technological enablement, so too was traditional broadcasting. The broadening of telecommunications into the so-called enhanced services realm inevitably raised the possibility of (widening the) transmission of audiovisual content through copper and, beyond that, fibre optic broadband networks. The nature of broadcast communication in respect of the content of services with a strongly developed public service purpose, meant, however, that convergence between telecommunication services and broadcasting, whilst technologically feasible, would be the subject of sustained and often controversial debate. This process is, in fact, still ongoing and – as this volume will attest to – provides much of the territory in which policy debates on convergence are taking place.

Nonetheless, technological changes co-terminus with convergence continued apace. In the 1980s, reminiscent of the incorporation of existing microwave technology in a new commercially driven telecommunications service context, the fairly well-established technology of satellite communication, deployed mostly to that point in international communication, was developed and applied to provide domestic television services resulting in an unprecedented increase in network capacity (Collins 1994). Subsequent to this, and arguably much more significant, the digitisation of broadcast communication networks soon gathered pace through the 1990s. The first and most immediate impacts were a 'turbo charging' of the trend towards network capacity expansion (Humphreys and Simpson 2005). Digitalisation in broadcasting affected cable, satellite and terrestrial networks alike. In a remarkably short space of time, a sector noted for its historical capacity limitations now exhibited capacity abundance.

THE EMERGENCE OF THE INTERNET

The above very important developments in new – and adaptions of existing – communications technologies occurred separately from what is now regarded as probably the biggest technological enabler of convergence: the Internet. Emerging from the shadows of network-based communication, by the mid-1990s the Internet was illustrating its power to become the most significant development in mass communication since television technology. With its underpinning objective of enabling communication between users attached to a variety of communication networks and utilising a variety of communication devices, the Internet's communication protocols (TCP/IP) are the essence of technology-enabled media convergence (Ceruzzi 2003). The Internet is interesting in that, although it was developed through the creation of bespoke communication architecture to some extent, for it to realise its full significance, Internet traffic needed to utilise longer established telecommunication infrastructure. Internet communication protocols, assisted by a raft of technical innovations which enabled user-friendly 'point and click' environments, provided both the oil and the glue of media convergence (Simpson 2004).

The Internet's end-to-end principle of communication meant, in its initial years of popularisation, that the power to add new applications and services to its environment lay in the hands of users, commercial and private alike. Those with operational control of network transmission merely provided common carriage services for the growing, increasingly content rich and diverse volume of traffic that Internet communication was giving rise to. As a consequence, the online environment became characterised by the potential to collapse, in a way never before witnessed, the distinction between telecommunication, radio and televisual broadcasting, and journalism and book publishing (Dwyer 2010). In terms of content available, applications through which it might be created and consumed, and services provided in and around its delivery, the Internet provided a convergence landscape in which new and innovated forms of communication have developed, in some cases with exponential growth rates. One of the most significant features of the Internet in the last 10 years has been its development as a site for social networking platforms, most famously Facebook and Twitter. The emergence of so-called social media has a fleeting resonance only with the early ideas of communitarian-based communication. Whilst these are venues within which an enormous mass of information is exchanged between human beings, the environment is heavily underpinned by commerciality. The world of online convergent communication for the vast majority of those taking part in it is the target for experts in marketing and consumer behaviour (Fuchs 2014). The Internet, like no previous communications environment, makes the monitoring of human communicative behaviour and the tailoring of communication services a phenomenon subject to mathematical calculation and algorithmic representation. The Internet is in short, the largest, most dense, and most convergent communications environment in human history.

The emergence of the Internet has created a new focal point for the consideration of internationality in media. Its infrastructural growth (heavily reliant on existing and innovated communications infrastructures), global communicative logic, and increased user friendliness has fuelled expectations of a new, richer, faster, more interactive 24-hour communications environment. The global Internet is often seen as the epitome of media convergence and much, if not all, of the coverage of this volume will relate at least in some part, to its emergence and functioning.

The Internet, at least in its early decades of development, was something of a communications outlier, given that it later became the blazon media convergence (European Commission 1997a). Techno-infrastructurally a product of US research and development money, used in its early years by computer specialists and the academic community, the Internet lay at the margins. However, its end-to-end technical infrastructure pointed towards a decentralisation and democratisation of communicative power to the user; the ability of its communication protocols (TCP/IP) to bring together formerly incompatible communications networks chimed, at least philosophically, with the idea of a convergence in communications of some kind. Those aspects of the Internet that did exhibit features of centralised control (and thus communicative power), most notably its essential Internet Protocol and domain name and addressing system, lay in the hands of the technical community, and were run on a voluntary basis along relatively egalitarian lines. All of this changed with the explosive popular growth of the Internet due to a series of innovations which delivered it as a user-friendly communications environment. Communitarianism, decentredness, and counter-culture soon clashed with proprietisation, centralisation of various kinds perpetrated in commercial and governmental circles, and 'mainstreamism' and increasingly became dwarfed by them whilst not retreating entirely from the Internet's landscapes. As these trends developed, the Internet grew inexorably larger, louder, more colourful and more characteristic of media convergence. A 24-hour, global, interactive multimedia environment where written word and audiovisual content pervade has come to characterise the Internet of the early twenty-first century. The Internet has developed a centrality of social, economic, commercial, cultural and political importance. It is a communications environment of unparalleled variety and, arguably, a communication asset of unprecedented significance. The Internet is now the epitome of media convergence: bold, colourful, interactive, round-the-clock. Yet, like media convergence it is also replete with contradiction, contestation and struggle. These take place in commercial, economic, cultural, political and social environments. Given this kind of importance, the topic of how key aspects of what takes place through the Internet should function and should be governed lies at the heart of any investigation of media convergence.

However, what kind of governance models for the Internet have emerged to date and in what ways might they be deployed to help us understand better the process of media convergence and its governance? As might be expected, the Internet has exhibited a range of governance practices, much of which relates to other quarters of the communications sector and little of which might be characterised as truly revolutionary. Its early origins, as noted above, exhibited a voluntarism and communitarianism in governance. Here, the direct presence of the state was distinctly conspicuous by its absence. However, as the Internet's strategic importance emerged alongside its growth as an international communications asset, strong evidence of the direct and indirect involvement of the state became manifest in debates on Internet governance, particularly in respect of its naming and addressing system and associated assets (see Mueller 2010). The Internet, however, has also displayed hybridity in governance forms between public and private governance, self-governance and what has been described as co-regulation. These forms of governance are not new in themselves. Self-regulation has been a characteristic feature of (particularly broadcast) media governance for many decades. Private interests have also taken a major role in the governance of key aspects of communications media. However, Internet governance has displayed an interesting – and at times novel – variety within these categories.

CONVERGENCE AS AN HISTORICAL SOCIAL CONSTRUCT

Given the broad social significance of convergence, it is no surprise that a debate has arisen around perspectives developed in industrial, governmental, civil society and academic quarters to try to understand and shape its evolution. These perspectives are used to interpret a series of important events that have taken place in the evolution of communication media more broadly. Often, such a process amounts to an *ex post* rationalisation fraught with difficulties. The biggest and most obvious problem though often under-acknowledged in the plethora of confident assertions about convergence emanating from industrial circles, in particular, is the only partially complete, contested and precarious nature of convergence. Such characteristics lead to an uneven and contradictory pattern of development of media convergence. It is important to understand that the coming together of different forms of media, often into a common space, does not automatically lead to their integration.

The historical debate on convergence is particularly salient for media policy makers since conclusions on it can provide the ground for setting a course of action for the future. For media policy academics, an important perennial task is to contextualise – and as a consequence deflate – the hyperbole which often surrounds convergence (see Mansell 2016). The ability to do this effectively and to translate it into clear messages which might be listened to – if not adopted – by national and international policy making communities points towards many of the challenges facing academic research on media. Such an undertaking crystallises much of the debate on the role of media policy and its researchers, whose foundation the administrative and, by contrast, the critical research traditions (Just and Puppis 2012) epitomise.

Differing perspectives on convergence hold serious potential ramifications across a range of cultural, economic, political and social processes. Most often witnessed has been a fairly intellectually blunt, revenue-seeking perspective on convergence with two inter-related elements. The first of these concerns convergence as an inevitable process shaped by technological innovations and commercial development. This view, most vocally articulated in industry circles, can be broadly categorised as a techno-economic determinist perspective on convergence. However, such a perspective has also been evident in the thinking and associated rhetoric of policy makers (European Commission 1994a). The second is a cheerfully optimistic-though-naïve take on media convergence. Here, a range of benefits are seen to be derived from the new array of products and services which convergence provides. These benefits are seen to fall across a wide range of issue areas and to be accruable by all. Most obviously, there is the notion that convergence drives economic development. New networks, hardware, applications and services and content are generators of economic value. They create and grow new markets. They exercise a multiplier effect on local, national and international economic life, in ways such as employment generation. They contribute to individual, corporate, national and international economic welfare.

The inexorable drive of economic growth fuelled by convergence is, however, far from unchallenged. A key issue is the extent to which the benefits of convergence fall (relatively) evenly (Mansell 2017). This has intra-national and as well as international ramifications. A key policy concern is the extent to which the outcomes of the convergence process might be shaped to afford and spread the greatest economic opportunity. This fundamental concern sits at the heart of most of the substance of this volume. At the level of the individual, much thinking on media convergence is underpinned by the notion of the citizen as a consumer. Here, it is argued that a new array of information and communication products and services can be purchased that are discernibly quality of life enhancing. So, new access devices, such as Internet-enabled mobile phones, laptops and tablets provide a high-tech, often colourful entry point to a panoramic array of applications and services which enrich user experience, for those who have the ability to pay. Alongside this is the idea that convergence is enabling. Individuals can communicate with each other more effectively than at any other time in history (Jenkins 2008). Such ideas of convergence enablement are further developed in specific contexts. Social communication has become a richer, more complex process through the use of social media sites (Castells 2013). It is now faster, is 24-hour in nature, and can be achieved orally and aurally, visually and through the written word, all at the same time. For some, convergence-based communication now provides new global reach yet, at the same time, the individual's personal communication environment has never been more immediate. Others, by contrast, point with concern to the mass personalisation of communications services in a context of information farming with packaged personal superficiality (Lovink 2011).

As noted already, media convergence has in technological terms a relatively lengthy history. Viewed in one light, convergence finally delivers the promise of 1970s and 1980s techno-optimists like Toffler (1980) for new flexible working patterns which not only create free space but accommodate the working preferences and lifestyles of busy people with diverse interests. For others, the technologies and services of media convergence have created flexibility whose 'reward' is longer working hours and less fulfilling conditions of employment (Lovink 2011). In particular, there is strong evidence that the distinction between work and non-work activity has blurred to the point of collapse in a converging media environment. Interestingly, this has shed light on the desirability or otherwise of maintaining such distinctions, and how it might be achieved. Concerns of this kind have arisen as a consequence of an 'always on' communication culture where the individual is increasingly assumed to be available constantly in both work and non-work communicative contexts.

Viewed sympathetically, convergence satisfies consumption preferences, empowers in terms of giving new opportunities to express these and other non-consumption-based preferences, and, in the process, liberates individuals and groups. The latter is manifest in new online educational and employment opportunities. In delivering in this way, media convergence saves individuals and groups time, however they might be organised and for whatever purpose. Attendant to this positive view is the environmentally friendly aspect of media convergence – new high-speed, distance-defying ways of communicating negate, or at least reduce significantly – the need for local and long distance international travel. Yet by contrast, the huge infrastructure of cables, wires and hardware in its myriad forms which are the physical manifestation of media convergence place huge question marks over both their recyclability and biodegradability. Added to this, the innate consumer culture of 'upgrading' bound in with 'social status' adds to concerns over sustainability. Furthermore, the development and deliberate release with strategic periodicity of new products and services fuelling the core computing staples of increased capacity and functionality mean a speedy obsolescence rate of equipment, adding further environmental concern to the mix.

In an even broader and equally controversial social context, for its advocates the convergence environment is establishing a new highly pluralistic media space in which access to a panoramically diverse range of information sources with which to assist the conduct and development of our social relations, broadly defined, is manifest. In this interactive environment where a thousand flowers happily bloom, participatory opportunities in terms of opinion giving, deliberation, and argumentation have arisen as never before (Castells 2013). Media convergence is thus, in this view, in the process of delivering a new vibrant information environment, one of whose features is that distinctions between information provider and consumer are often blurred in the context of so-called 'pro-sumerism'. This rich, diverse landscape is a huge enabler of the democratic process domestically and internationally and provides a catalytic context for 'everyday' political change. It also, it is argued, possesses the potential to stimulate radical moments of political development in the direction of democracy in keeping with the principles of the libertarian, liberating convergence communications landscape which is unfolding (Castells 2013). By contrast, a less sanguine view of the communications landscape characterised by convergence posits a somewhat narrower political space, access to which depends on the possession of the requisite educational, technical and economic resources. It is also an environment where political conviction to seek out alternative information (as well as skill in information seeking) is a necessary prerequisite to participation. However, the latter, if not underpinned by an opinion seeking and deliberative open mindedness, can lead to online communicative strait-jacketing.

All this aside, for the majority without such strong political conviction, there is a concern that the Internet's bulk content is only superficially massaged to portray variety, that political content both interfered with to the point of untrustworthiness, and is crowded out in the mainstream by that of an overwhelmingly commercial and populist bent, and that public service information, where available, does not receive the kind of prominence which its importance is arguably due (McChesney 2013). Others point to an Internet-based convergence environment where the communicative behaviour and choices exercised by human beings can be monitored, assessed and categorised for marketing purposes as never before (Heyman and Pierson 2013). Such analyses contrast the façade of superficially welcoming personalisation of online information services on offer with a relentless, high-tech information gathering and processing apparatus taking surveillance of various kinds to a new level, where privacy is either unwittingly compromised or voluntarily surrendered in the interests of security and participation (Humphreys 2013).

Another related feature of the convergence environment has been the growth of user-generated content. In line with ideas of providing communication empowerment for the individual, users can now create their own audiovisual content and post it to online environments. This is most famously illustrated in online audiovisual environments like YouTube. Such content has often generated quite remarkable viewing interest. The increased functionality of mobile phones, many of which now allow high quality picture and video to be shot, has also resulted in users playing a part in the breaking of news stories. Such activity has been bound up in the idea of citizen journalism (Allan and Thorsen 2009), whose development has also gone hand in hand with the growth of online blogging. The emergence to prominence of the microblogging social network site, Twitter, has added a further dimension to this. News is often broken by non-information professionals, through short (originally) 140-character maximum messages. The corollary of this is that Twitter has become a 'go to' site for professional journalists for whom the drive to provide breaking news has been, if anything, intensified in the online environment. The interactive dimension of the online world has thus allowed users to disrupt the linearity of old media in ways never before witnessed. Interactivity is, of course, not a new phenomenon in media: radio and television broadcasters, as well as newspapers, have sought it for many decades. However, the online environment has undoubtedly brought it to new dimensions. Engagement with media content and service providers is now a de rigueur feature of all online platforms, particularly those providing news and audiovisual services.

Underpinning most, if not all, of the development in communication
networks, content and services in the direction of convergence has been
what might be described as a 'culture of speed'. In infrastructural terms,
there appears an ever pressing need to increase the download and upload
speeds of information, something also bound in with the pursuit of
increased network capaciousness. However, the culture of speed runs
much more deeply than this. It has been argued that users have developed
expectations about communication around a culture of instant gratifi-
cation (McQuire 2008). Relatedly, a culture of constant updating of
information has developed with significant time resource implications.
This is no more evident than in social network site environments, such as
Facebook, where updating of personal profiles is part of the fabric of
communication. In professional environments too, the need to update
very regularly is seen as a mark of professionalism, to the extent that
Twitter feeds, with the expectation that they be constantly attended to, are
increasingly embedded in organisational (including individual professional) profiles.

Another key feature of the environment of convergence is mobility.
More than ever before, individuals communicate on the move for both
social and work purposes. Expectations raised among users of the
normalcy of moving around whilst conducting complex communicative
tasks has presented two main challenges. The first concerns the nature
and functioning of the device used to undertake communication. Here,
key developments in IT and telecommunications have combined to
produce end users devices – terminal equipment in telecommunication
parlance – which are increasingly powerful, multi-functional and port-
able. The development of mobility has changed expectations within
organisations about the nature of work and how, where and when it can
be undertaken. The work/non-work rigidities of the Fordist era have
given way to more flexible articulations of work practices, undertaken
remotely from the organisation's premises and, frequently, on the move.
The second challenge in the rise to prominence of mobility in the media
convergence environment relates to network capacity and is a telecommunications and, lately, a broadcasting policy matter. As users'
demand for wireless communication has grown, so too has the demand
for spectrum. As Chapter 3 of this volume illustrates, sophisticated
mobile broadband communication has called forth serious policy considerations of a reallocation of spectrum from digital terrestrial broadcasting to the mobile communication sector. The idea of spectrum as a
public good and how it might best be used in an increasingly commercial
and converging communication environment sits at the core of the debate
on this topic.

The environment of media convergence has also created seismic change in the culture and practices of searching for information. The volume of available written and audiovisual information has grown hugely in the last 20 years. This has provided major opportunities for knowledge acquisition and sharing but has many challenges entailed in taking advantage of it. The relatively new phenomenon of so-called 'big data' has emerged where efforts to discern key patterns in huge volumes of complex information and communication generated electronically has become both an industry in its own right and a topic of study for academics (Mayer Schoberger and Cukier 2013). More mundanely, for the average user, the online environment now contains an often-bewildering panorama of written and audiovisual content. The ability to search and scan effectively has become an essential skill in early twenty-first century social and professional communication environments, in ways – and to an extent – never before witnessed. A culture of scanning, however, raises concerns about pursuit of depth of information and, ultimately, knowledge acquisition. Allied to the possible multiple re-use and re-purposing of the same source information based on both the operational constraints of the information provider and content creator, as well as the need to fill increasingly capacious information environments, a key concern is a move in the direction of what might be considered 'information superficiality' in the convergence environment. This points to the need for prominent and well-resourced public and private information creators and providers (see Chapter 7).

A related issue concerns the feeling of insecurity and uncertainty that the paths to convergence in electronic communication have led to for many users. The mass of information available online makes the assurance of trust in the provision of certain types of media content more important than ever. Whilst a culture of acceptance of inaccuracy – or more specifically the risk of it – has grown in the consumption of online information, the need for reliable sources, well developed in traditional news print and broadcasting – has established itself too in convergent online environments. Alarm at the growth of so-called 'fake news' in online information environments attests to this. More dramatically, assertions of the dawn of a 'post truth era', whilst temptingly headline grabbing, are an unhelpful characterisation of (albeit often problematic) democratic life. They are reflections on the perceived problems of networked media which provide an example of the exaggerated quality of reflections on media convergence environments.

Alongside this, matters of privacy have become prominent in the online environment, in particular. Whilst there is by this stage general acceptance that participation in online communication, particularly that of a commercial character, inevitably involves the relinquishment of some degree of privacy, concerns about secure storage, and use and resale of customer data are some of the most prominent features of the online era. The often (unwittingly) very open communication environments of social network sites, such as Facebook, and concerns about privacy protection attendant to them, stand in contrast to evidence of a growing preference among younger users for the more closed user group social network environments provided by sites such as WhatsApp and Snapchat. Whilst the products of media convergence have enabled an environment in which a mass of information, often homogeneous and bland in character, is freely available, evidence suggests that users are prepared to pay to secure privacy, which has now become, at least in part, commoditised. It is less clear, at this stage, about the degree to which users are willing to pay for online information services that transcend the homogenous, the bland and the superficial.

In this regard, the public service and public interest aspects of the communications sector have been well developed historically in broadcasting, publishing and telecommunication. These are manifest in direct public funding of network infrastructure development, for example. In terms of content creation and production, direct funding of public service broadcasting has been a key feature of media systems in western Europe and beyond for many years. The business of the journalism industry, whether publicly or privately resourced, has held the provision of news, which is considered to be in the public interest, as a prominent goal in its activities. These developmental paths have provided an important set of communications traditions which have now come into a common – though far from integrated – space in the convergent environment of online media (see Chapter 7). Yet, far from dominating this scene, they find themselves dwarfed by the volume of communication services and content with an overwhelmingly commercial purpose in concentrated market environments (see Chapter 6). Whilst this might be viewed as a cause for concern, it could also be considered an opportunity. For information-inundated users online, with often time constrained communication capacity, the need for information which is prominent and sense-making is abundantly clear. This could be balanced and challenging, structured to enable experimental discovery and broadening, and designed and delivered in the public interest.

The paths to convergence trodden by broadcasting, IT, publishing and telecommunication have been characterised by innovation in technology, content creation and service delivery. These paths of continuity de-bunk the hyperbolic myths of discontinuity often promulgated about convergence by commercial players whose interests lie in asserting the path-breaking novelty of convergence content and services. The reality is, happily, less radical, though no less important for human development. A key issue, however, concerns the extent to which, and how, well-established patterns of public provision in electronic and print media can be developed for the convergence environment. What would the main constituent features of such a system look like? What is the likelihood of them being realised and over what timeframe might this reasonably occur? The paths to convergence having been by now for the most part well-trodden; the task is to fashion the convergence environment in the most economically robust and societally valuable way possible. This volume argues that such a task has only begun.

THE EMERGENCE OF MEDIA CONVERGENCE AS A GOVERNANCE CONSTRUCT

The historical approach to the governance of media convergence has been contingent on the traditions and features of its composite parts and, in particular, the propensity for change within them. Perhaps unlike any other sector of the economy, communications displayed historically the greatest degree of structural and operational variety, reinforced by sub-sectoral stability for many years. An important starting point in the mapping of the evolution of media governance in the direction of convergence is a consideration of the role of the state. Given the strategic nature of practically all of the communications sector, this has been unsurprisingly, very significant, though more complicated than a straightforward dichotomy between intervention and laissez faire. The state has in fact manifested itself in three broad ways, some or all of which have been present at any particular time depending on the part of the communications sector under scrutiny: direct ownership of communications assets; operational control of communications markets; and sanctioning of the conditions of governance in the communications sector.

In respect of the first of these, the state's direct presence has been particularly strong in telecommunications in most places apart from the notable exception of the US. In Europe, for example, until the 1980s, the ownership of telecommunications service provision lay in state hands. In the USA by contrast, a private monopoly – AT&T – owned the network and provided telecommunication services. Elsewhere, there have been notable examples of direct state control of broadcasting and newspaper and print publishing. In telecommunications, where the functions of sectoral governance and operation were essentially rolled into one, the state thus had effective operational control of the market. However, by far the most significant development in the role of the state in communications over the last 20–30 years lies in respect of its sanctioning the conditions of governance. This has gone hand in hand with developments in media convergence and is an aspect of the role of the state in the communications that is ongoing, unresolved and thus evolving. It forms a key part of this volume's exploration of the phenomenon of media convergence governance. Yet, the state has been significant in this respect prior to the growth of media convergence. Indirectly, through the passage of laws, it has set the conditions for the structure of the communication sector and its functioning. Thus, laws in libel in publishing, various acts of law related to industry structure, and the creation of regulatory governance bodies for communication all have their roots in state action.

The issue of regulatory governance, in particular, is germane to an understanding of the evolution of communications governance in respect of convergence. Regulation has been an important part of broadcasting for many years. Here, regulatory bodies set in place and policed decisions taken by the state about the structure and functioning of this part of the communications sector. Regulations prescribe and, if necessary, set the conditions for behaviour modification, in broadcasting, where employed. Thus, in the UK, for example, commercial TV broadcasting has been governed by a regulatory body since its inception in 1955. In most of Europe, public service broadcasters were subject to a self-regulatory system to ensure independence from direct state intervention, as was the newspaper press, though the specifics of form and functioning differed markedly in both cases.

However, the most important development in regulatory governance in communications has been underpinned by the broad political–economic project of neo-liberalism. This has been by far the most significant in its quantity and effects in telecommunication, though it has also had profound consequences for broadcasting. Most important of all from the perspective of this volume, the neo-liberal project has been the context for the evolution of a considerable part of the governance of media convergence. In the first instance, this required unprecedented state action to alter the structure and functioning of a large part of the communication sector. In Europe, regulatory governance in telecommunications emerged as an issue of importance gradually from the 1980s onwards. However, like in most parts of the world, it soon became an issue of central importance. Through a process of radical change, private or partially-private ownership replaced traditional state ownership, new differentiated markets were created within the sector and ordered (often not very) competitively. A series of new independent regulatory bodies (National

Regulatory Authorities) policed this unprecedented marketization (Goodman 2006).

In broadcasting too, neo-liberalisation has had a particularly important set of consequences. Network capacity expansion, assisted by a series of techno-organisational changes, set the enabling ground for increased competition to take place between channels. In particular, the use of satellite technology, capacious fibre optic cables and an across-the-board digitalisation of terrestrial, cable and satellite infrastructures created space for new competition to be sanctioned and to take effect. Over the course of at least 25 years, in places where provision was mostly publicly funded, the character of broadcasting systems nationally has taken on a commercial hue. Even where public service broadcasting remains well funded and prominently positioned, the behaviour of public service broadcasters (PSBs) has been recognised as more commercial in orientation (Freedman 2008). Broadcasting systems are now larger in terms of the content available in a multi-channel environment. The huge volume of content has created competition for presence and prominence. Commercial competition for revenues garnered from selling advertising and sponsorship space is fierce. Selectivity has been introduced in a once free-to-air environment through subscription and pay-per-view commercial models. Elite content – manifest in sport of various kinds and film – is more valuable than ever before. Revenue squeezes mean that expensive televisual content is under the inevitable pressure to succeed, even before decisions on its creation have been taken. As a corollary, filling the now spectrum abundant broadcasting landscapes has led to efforts to create a plethora of inexpensive content characterised by homogeneity and blandness, as well as use of repeated content. Interactivity in broadcasting, historically an attractive and important aspect of the medium, has become much more realisable, yet has held within it concerns over fairness and probity, as witnessed in the UK's TV phone-in scandal of the 2006–2008 period (Simpson 2010). All of these changes have occurred as convergence has proceeded and they can be considered part of process, holding within them important policy lessons for the future in governance terms.

At the international level, the pursuit of a governance framework for media convergence has been a subject of interest to the EU for a number of decades. For a complex institution with opportunistic and expansionist policy leanings, media convergence offers considerable scope for action. Convergence presented the promise of a new, open policy agenda, in which the historically well embedded, if not intransigent, traditions of communications could be challenged. Convergence, with the Internet as its forefront, also exudes international potential. This presented scope for the creation of a new policy agenda in which the EU's stake, even as a relatively new actor on the communication policy scene, could have become potentially as important as many, if not most, national governments. Certainly, from an intra-EU perspective, the EU, was a recognisably prominent actor from the mid to late 1980s onwards. As it developed its policy portfolio in telecommunication, a sector hitherto firmly established at the national level, the EU through the European Commission, referred pointedly and repeatedly, to the convergence of computing and telecommunication usually to reinforce the goal of market liberalisation. In the 1990s, as network development proceeded apace and the debate on the utility of continued separate regulatory treatment of broadcasting and telecommunication emerged in the context of convergence, the EU made a controversial policy intervention in the shape of a Commission Green Paper on Convergence. Tactically, the aim at this juncture was to put forward a range of policy options that would down the line emerge as a raft of policy proposals moving the consideration of media convergence to a new international regulatory context. However, the initiative merely illustrated the depth of feeling and controversy around any move to regulate media convergently and at the European level. Strong arguments, emanating nationally, in favour of the separate regulatory treatment of broadcasting content, as well as a decision to exempt 'information society' or online, services from any new regulatory framework resulted in a rather modest convergence regulatory framework being agreed by EU Member States in 2002. Here, the EU Framework for Electronic Communications (EUFREC) agreed was convergent only to the extent that it dealt commonly with all network infrastructures and associated services across which telecommunications content was transmitted. In retrospect, this policy landmark was probably more significant for what it omitted than what it included. However, at the very least, it put in place the idea of regulating electronic communications networks – as opposed to merely telecommunications networks – at the EU level. As network upgrading progressed from this point and policy conversations mutated into a debate on the creation and functioning of new Next Generation Networks (see Chapter 2), the presence of the EUFREC can be viewed as significant.

In a different way, the subsequent policy review of the EUFREC conducted by the EU from 2006, whilst primarily concerned with what is in effect the telecommunications regulatory package, also took on something of a convergence hue in respect of its treatment of Internet services. As noted above, deliberately excluded from the 2002 EUFREC, nevertheless, the inexorable growth in significance of the Internet meant that, by 2006, issues of Internet access and access services were becoming an increasingly important public policy issue. Here, the debate emerged in the context of the review of the EUFREC revisions as a consumer rights matter and developed further policy legs within the burgeoning topic of Internet Neutrality (see Chapter 4). At one point, with the European Parliament as a key political protagonist on the matter, progress on the passage of a revised regulatory hinged on addition of a number of policy measures related to the Internet and consumer rights within it. By this juncture, therefore, policy matters of direct relevance to media convergence were emerging in several distinct quarters of an increasingly inter-related EU policy package for the communications sector. The eventually agreed revised EUFREC contained a number of measures related to standards of Internet access services, though the scope and efficacy of these measures is a subject of debate.

The EU Commission's ongoing concern with convergence policy matters was further manifest in a Green Paper in 2013. Its coverage gave a strong flavour of how the debate on convergence had by that stage shifted to a consideration of the relationship between the traditional and evolving broadcast environment and the online world. The Commission addressed, in particular, the legal implications of continuing media convergence, with particular focus on its Audiovisual Media Services Directive (European Parliament and Council 2010), but also the EU's E-Commerce Directive (European Parliament and Council 2000) and the EUFREC. The Commission argued that, for the benefits of convergence to be accrued, the EU needed to take necessary action to create 'a big enough market to grow, a competitive environment, a willingness to change business models, interoperability and an adequate infrastructure'. Important in this development would be to overcome key barriers, such as the limiting of choice and access, often along national geographic lines. A key issue was a consideration of the need in future to impose *ex ante* regulatory obligations in order to stimulate competition. The Commission also made reference to the continued financing of public service broadcasters, noting its 2009 Communication on State Aid requirement for Member States to conduct *ex ante* tests of the effects of such aid. Rather differently, the ability of manufacturers to thwart application access was noted in respect of the debate on standards in a convergence context. This is an old debate that is arguably more alive now than at any point in the development of ICT and broadcasting. An interesting comment, which pointed to the future, concerned the possible coming together in the shape of hybrid models of on-demand and linear broadcasting, achieved through broadband networks (European Commission 2013a: 11). Yet again, given the complex viewing environment facing consumers, the Commission highlighted the importance of media literacy, which it defined as 'the ability to access the media, to understand and to critically evaluate different aspects of the media and media contents and to create communications in a variety of contexts' (European Commission 2013a: 12). The Commission also raised to be fundamental in the future the media policy staples of the editorial role of service providers, parameters of access and prominence in online environments, variety and the ability to move between platforms to exercise choice.

NEO-LIBERALISM AND THE GOVERNANCE OF MEDIA CONVERGENCE

As noted above, the idea of regulated competition was not new in media. However, it is its renewed force of presence under the neo-liberal ideological and policy drive which has been remarkable. Such developments led to the assertion that a new 'regulatory state' (Moran 2003) had developed of which sectors like communications are exemplary. This was even asserted to have cross-national dimensions in certain parts of the world – the arrival of the European regulatory state was heralded in a burgeoning time of regulatory capitalism (see Majone 1996). Underpinning these developments was the philosophical assumption of the superiority of the market as an organisational form and attendant series of social relations. A key policy assumption was that where competition did not exist, it should be introduced and in places where it was only weakly evident, it should be intensified. Competition, as the policy adage produced by successive UK governments would have it, realised better quality of products and services, would speed innovative breakthroughs in technology and would result in price reductions and, more generally, an environment in which prices would approximate as closely as possible to actual costs of production. This alluring neo-liberal political roster had one further attraction: implementation flexibility and adaptability. As long as the pursuit of competition as the prime form of social relations was in evidence, neo-liberal capitalism could flourish in many operational varieties. This flexibility has contributed to its remarkable powers of durability – that the neo-liberal model has survived (despite having been central to) the near collapse of the global financial system in 2008 is surely its greatest testament in this respect. In communications, the neo-liberal blueprint was thus evident at least to some extent in all continents of the world. It has set the context for the evolution of the communications sector over the last 20 years. It has also provided the ground for its intellectual exposition and critical examination by the academic community, as well as support and opposition by advocates and detractors, respectively.

A key element of the agenda of neo-liberal marketization has been its internationality. Going hand in hand with ideas of developing economic globalisation, neo-liberalisation has prompted strong efforts at global trade liberalisation. This has been in evidence across communications, in telecommunications especially but also in respect of the audiovisual sector in a more limited way. However, the international agenda has been developed much more deeply than this in the media sector, stretching to the cultural, political and social realm. This is in key respects not a new phenomenon. In the 1970s, the New World Information and Communications Order addressed the consequences of the international spread of audiovisual products. For many decades, the need to facilitate international telecommunication resulted in a series of traffic management agreements between national carriers, negotiated in the International Telecommunication Union. Debates on the economic, cultural and social consequences of internationalising media are thus nothing new.

Freedman defines media governance as 'the sum total of mechanisms, both formal and informal, national and supranational, centralised and dispersed, that aim to organise media systems according to the resolution of media policy debates' where the latter are sites of contested and continual 'development of goals and norms leading to the creation of instruments that are designed to shape the structure and behaviour of media systems' (Freedman 2008: 14). Here, in a neo-liberal era, legally founded regulation of various kinds has played an increasingly important role. Policy debates on media convergence and the governance arrangements that have emerged as a consequence of them reflect much of the neo-liberal thinking that has dominated international political and economic life over the last 40 years, as well as challenges to it.

Neo-liberal policy agendas in the communications sector through time have gone hand in hand with media convergence, in many respects. The need to stimulate developments in technology and the new goods and services stemming from them, as this chapter has argued, is considered of paramount importance. The message that technological changes create new enhanced services in an environment of unprecedented consumer choice has led to arguments that governance structures and regulatory measures need to reform to accommodate and bring to fruition the benefits of a media convergence. From this underpinning perspective, an analysis of neo-liberalism can explain many of the changes that have occurred within the constituent parts of the communications sector. Telecommunication has been transformed radically along neo-liberal lines. Already characterised by modest regulatory governance and commercialism in part, broadcasting has become a radically commercialised sector. The Internet too, from its communitarian and social libertarian origins has developed into a deeply commercialised landscape. A discourse of imminent media convergence has been a core aspect of the evolution of each of these parts of the communications sector, which have nevertheless developed along separate evolutionary paths, mostly incremental, occasionally radical, in character.

Yet, as this volume will argue, a study and understanding of neo-liberalism also reveals the contradictions of – and limitations to – media convergence. These are most luminescent in the realm of media policy and governance, since this activity refers to control over the levers of a considerable part of the productive power in media systems. Specifically, the impediments that this volume will highlight in respect of the movement towards what might be described as a deeply embedded, integrative form of media convergence can be explained by the inability of neo-liberalism to accommodate non-market-based solutions into a new media convergence paradigm. Instead, conflicts and struggles have ensued which have resulted in only shallow, partial and paradoxically segmented media convergence to this point. Despite the elsewhere recognised flexibility of neo-liberalism – for example in the varieties of capitalism literature – this innate neo-liberal myopia in the media convergence governance context exhibits an intransigence that is inhibiting the development of enriched cultural and social understandings of convergence that might be both facilitated and architected through new governance structures and media policies. The character of shallow media convergence is evident in the remaining chapters of the book.

THE STRUCTURE OF THE BOOK

Following from this opening chapter, Part II of the volume contains three chapters which explore key aspects of the broad governance of communications infrastructures in an environment of converging media. A key contention of this volume is that to understand better the topic of media convergence, it is essential to explore in depth governance and policy issues of communications infrastructures, as well as the content and services delivered through them. The chapters in this section have a number of recurring themes. They show how media convergence is a far from complete process. They illustrate how it has been characterised by multiple and persistent sites of contestation. Ultimately, they provide evidence of the need to give consideration to the role and position of public service issues amidst an environment of media convergence dominated by issues of commercial priority. Chapter 2 explores policy efforts to create high-speed broadband network environments, or so-called Next Generation Networks (NGN). In analysing recent developments in network evolution in a range of national contexts, as well as the international environment of the EU, a key theme of the chapter concerns the role of public sector involvement in network refurbishment and upgrading. The chapter shows how, since the financial crash and global economic recession of 2008, states have exercised what might be termed developmental governance activity through major investments in electronic communications network upgrade. The underlying assumption here is that investment in NGN can provide economic growth and renewal through creating the infrastructural context necessary for the content creation and service delivery synonymous with positive visions of media convergence. The chapter argues that the range and extent of such public intervention should, however, be contextualised. The scale of the task at hand has meant that the neo-liberal model which has characterised electronic communications infrastructural development since the late 1980s still predominates.

Chapter 3 of the volume turns its attention to the changing governance of airwave spectrum in a context of media convergence. Spectrum has historically been viewed as an invaluable, scarce communications resource governed with strong public interest principles in mind. The digitalisation of the airwaves provided capacity-saving benefits, as well as an enabling infrastructure for content-rich media services, a classic feature of media convergence environments, to be sent and received wirelessly. However, ironically, this so-called digital dividend has whetted the appetite of commercial players from the mobile broadband sector to secure increased spectrum to intensify their service provision at the expense of incumbent terrestrial TV broadcast players. The chapter illustrates how what is effectively a turf war over spectrum exemplifies much of the tensions between media with a public service function and sensibilities and those which are out and out commercial in nature. It provides further illustration that processes of technology-enabled media convergence are merely partial in character since they provoke deeply contested, messy and unresolved debates on the future governance of communications.

Chapter 4 of the volume explores the controversial issue of Internet Neutrality in a media convergence context. In one respect, Net Neutrality is about the conditions according to which users are afforded access to infrastructures of information and communication. However, the Net Neutrality debate is also about how users are treated in their use of the infrastructure. Thus, in this way, the chapter shows how the Net Neutrality topic connects issues of infrastructure with service delivery and user experience. If articulated beyond its historically narrow techno-economic rationality, Net Neutrality can lead to an exploration of communications rights and public interests in an environment of converging media on the Internet. The chapter undertakes a critical exploration of the incompletely understood idea of neutrality. In so doing, it shows the reality of long-standing and persistent intervention in Internet traffic flows. However, careful consideration and development of the idea of intervention can allow expansive and progressive understandings of the capacities for – but also the necessary limitations of – non-neutral intervention in the converging communications environments of the Internet to be developed.

The chapters in Part III of the book concern governance issues bearing on media content and journalism in the converging media environment and Internet era; these being copyright, media concentration, and media subsidies. The three chapters all have themes that interconnect. All three point to the scale of the challenge posed to effective regulation along traditional lines by the new media, whilst at the same time arguing the continuing need for regulation in the converging, new media environment. Another interconnecting thread of the chapters is discussion of how the challenge can be met by adapting existing policy approaches, but changing the main thrust of policy away from negative regulation, namely restrictions and prohibitions that are hard to implement, towards positive regulation, concentrating on subsidizing quality, professional media content and what might be termed 'public service journalism' in the digital and online environment. Relatedly, all three chapters raise the question whether new Internet intermediaries (ISPs, Google, YouTube and so on) should be considered as simple conduits, deserving of regulatory exemption from much responsibility for content, or whether they should be subjected to greater responsibility for the content they distribute (or if it is preferred, 'host') online through stricter external supervision and the imposition of a levy in order to cross-subsidize those media that produce the content that supports their businesses. Above all, all three chapters depart from the neo-liberal perspective that market-led solutions can be relied upon and that state intervention generally impedes desired outcomes by distorting the market. As far as the issue of the future of quality media content and journalism is concerned, active intervention is required, otherwise convergence will lead to a hyper-commercial and self-cannibalising media environment in which quality media is produced in diminishing quantity.

Chapter 5 explores the challenge presented to copyright by digital convergence and the Internet. It takes issue with scholars who, by an arguably one-sided over-emphasis on the alleged exploitation of copyright law by powerful corporate copyright holders to maximise their control of the media industries and their profits, rather play down the issues of copyright 'piracy' (illegal) and 'free-riding' (legal, see Levine 2011) on a scale that threatens to undermine the business models that underpin the creative industries, from the recorded music business through to traditional newspapers. By exploring how copyright reform has been debated, and to some extent positive change introduced, in the United States and in Europe, it reveals a marked hesitancy on the part of government to legislate and a reliance on a mix of legal process and inter-industry agreements in the US in comparison with a somewhat more active policy making and legislative approach in Europe. Here, policy makers at EU level and in certain European countries appear more minded to defend their culture industries by making technology companies much more responsible for what their users upload. However, as of yet, in Europe as in the United States, neo-liberal thinking and inhibitions about the need to promote new technologies (and defer to the new technology companies) has seen a concern for 'the free market' generally prevail over cultural and culture–industry interests, though this is far from being the whole story.

Chapter 6 considers the issue of media concentration, arguing that it continues to be a major policy issue even in the Internet environment. First, it considers why media concentration per se is a serious content issue not least because of the importance of ensuring a multiplicity of voices in the media for underpinning democracy. The chapter explains why the media are particularly prone to economic pressures towards concentration. Then, it explores trends in media concentration and its regulation, first by exploring the US case, then the European. The chapter shows how the universal trend has been the progressive de-regulation of sector-specific structural rules designed to limit media concentration, the ideological force for which has been a neo-liberal policy turn from the 1980s on and the principle argument against them being that they are no longer appropriate in a converging new media environment where markets are fluid, where it is difficult to determine the 'relevant market' for determining concentration, and where essentially the same media output can be distributed over a number of media vectors or platforms. Next, the chapter turns to the debate between Internet celebrants and sceptics about the pluralising impact of the Internet, showing that, in the converging media and Internet environment, concentration still needs addressing through policy and regulation. The chapter concludes by suggesting pointers towards policies that might be adopted, which are further discussed in the book's conclusion. One of the chapter's conclusions is that, given the decreasing purchase of sector-specific anti-concentration regulation, an important policy for promoting media pluralism in the new media and Internet era should be a new approach to subsidy, a theme that is taken up in the next chapter.

Chapter 7 explains how new media, lifestyle changes and generational change have combined to present a powerful challenge to traditional quality journalism and news media. First, the chapter examines the challenge to journalism and traditional media organisations represented by the changing technological and market environment they function in. Then, the chapter explores the theme of subsidy, first as a policy mooted to confront what has been seen as a crisis of journalism in the United States, then as a tried and tested policy in Europe with respect both to supporting the press and especially broadcasting. The chapter shows how the UK has always been a generous subsidiser of public service broadcasting and how the policy debate continues to produce highly interesting ideas for innovation. Its main argument is the need to rethink policy for the public subsidy of journalism in the Internet era, where old technology-specific approaches having been rendered increasingly anomalous by digital convergence of the media and the Internet. The chapter explores how public policy might instead support in a technology neutral manner media, public or private, which provide 'public service journalism'. Echoing a conclusion of Chapter 6, it argues that public service broadcasters (PSBs) should continue to be generously supported, not least to allow them to become public service media (PSM). However, it also suggests that there is a case for a new institution to be developed tasked and funded specifically to support public service content in the digital, online environment, along the lines of the 'public service publisher' concept mooted by UK regulator Ofcom as a policy to support plurality of public service broadcasting in the digital era, but doomed by a combination of corporate vested interests and a neo-liberal concern on the part of policy makers about the market distortion that such an innovation implied. The chapter suggests how this could be funded through a number of different possibilities for industry levies, so as not to damage established PSB/PSM institutions.

In the fourth part of the volume, we present our conclusions to the analysis of the governance of media convergence presented in the volume. Whilst the preceding chapters of the volume highlight a problematic and challenging picture in considerable part, this notwithstanding, a central argument of Chapter 8 is that convergence, due to its incomplete nature, presents considerable opportunities. The chapter argues that media governance and policy can set the context for a more inclusive and progressive process of convergence to unfold. A series of potential media policy solutions to the current impediments to convergence are presented in the core areas of coverage of the volume's preceding chapters. The chapter puts forward an agenda for future work that can lead to a richer understanding of the significance and capacity of digital convergence.

Overall, the convergence in media that we witness and experience at the time of writing is a product of different traditions, practices and cultures. This has the unsettling consequence that the picture of convergence is still complex and contradictory – and thus indistinct and incomplete – in much of its character. To understand better why and how this is the case requires a detailed exploration of the core aspects of media convergence and its governance. It is to this task that the remainder of this volume addresses itself.

NOTE

1. There were some exceptions to this pattern. For example, copper cable was used extensively in telecommunication and less frequently in cable broadcasting, particularly where terrestrial broadcast technologies were impractical because of topography.

PART II

The infrastructures of media convergence

2. Next generation networks: providing a sustainable convergence platform

INTRODUCTION

Much of the work of this volume focuses on the governance of communicative activity which arises from the introduction and use of an array of new applications and services with characteristic features of media convergence. However, without an appropriate technical infrastructure, none of this activity could take place. Put simply, convergence applications and services require ample capacity. To work effectively they require high-speed transmission. They often benefit from being as international in reach as possible. All this points to the requirement to refurbish and upgrade traditional electronic communication networks to provide high-speed, capacious environments international in scope. Yet the task of achieving this is daunting in terms of investment cost, the physical process of putting new network infrastructure in place, and the need to achieve this as quickly as possible. The process of network upgrade to higher quality broadband infrastructure – what have been called NGN – is thus a strategic communication policy priority given the stakes attendant in its (non) realisation.

This chapter explores the subject of broadband network upgrade as a strategic goal in the process of media convergence through the lens of media governance, broadly defined. Given the size of the job at hand, it has a number of themes which articulate the role of the state and the private sector, respectively, in the formidable journey to widespread NGN. These are: the degree and types of state intervention in the process of NGN development; the actors involved in upgraded network roll out from the private sector and the roles they are adopting; market structures and NGN development; and the governance balance between liberal market and strategic industrial policy approaches to NGN. The online environment is now for many an integral part of daily life. However, within that context, access to and opportunities within this environment vary considerably. Strover and McDowell (2014: 51) argue that 'we have moved on from an era prescribing the significance of the Internet to one assuming its operational availability. This quality of being "taken for granted" highlights digital divide concerns'. For Preston and Cawley (2008: 817), meanwhile, the significance of new network infrastructure lies in no less than the fact that, 'broadband offers access not just to entertainment but also to new communicative abilities, information, ideas, education and abilities in conducting relationships with family, friends, peers, and the public sphere'.

THE HISTORIC IMPORTANCE OF NETWORK INFRASTRUCTURE

The development of network infrastructure has sat at the heart of the evolution of the electronic communication sector since its inception, though it is often less high profile in nature than issues to do with network services and content, possibly due to its 'back end' nature. The challenge of network roll out has shaped many of the core values and practices of the communication sector. This was particularly strong historically in telecommunications and mass communication broadcasting. In the former, the need to build the components and lay out a complex network was a costly feat of research and engineering. These technical requirements and cost parameters were influential factors in the governance arrangements and market structure which developed in the sector. In the US, for example, AT&T was given private monopoly privileges in return for assurances, to a powerful independently established regulator in the shape of the Federal Communications Commission (FCC), to roll out the network to realise progressively universal service. Across Europe, a similar goal pertained, pursued through different means, based on ideological persuasion. Here, monopoly market structure was established through the creation of a state-owned service provider which, unlike the US arrangement, combined operational and regulatory governance functions. The goal in most cases, was twofold: realisation of universal service through progressive network roll out and tariff re-balancing to provide a relatively uniform price structure which did not operate according to a consumer group costs recovery model (Simpson 2017). In broadcasting too, issues of network development and roll out related directly to regulatory governance in respect of decisions taken which determined market structure, for the most part. Here, the by now long-gone situation of limited network capacity was balanced with social goals to result in an independently regulated system into which market entry was tightly controlled and publicly funded self-regulating public service broadcasters took their place. As network capacity broadened with the use of satellite and cable technology in tandem with terrestrial systems, this network expansion led broadcasting markets in general to become more commercially ordered, though still firmly regulated (Flew, Iosifidis and Steemers 2016).

Aside from the differences in free market and state centrist approaches to communication, the above arrangements point up clearly the long-standing important relationship between network infrastructure development, political decision-taking and media governance. Moving forward to the late twentieth/early twenty-first century and an era dominated by the Internet, much of the same kind of relationships pertain, though the circumstances vary considerably. As explored in detail in Chapter 1 of this volume, a considerable part of the debate on media convergence centres on the development of communication through the Internet. Whilst through it many users are able to access a plethora of media services with convergence characteristics, a number of key concerns exist about the ability of the Internet to deliver widely the kind of content-rich, high-speed, interactive communications environment much vaunted by proponents of convergence in commercial and governmental quarters. Many of these concerns relate either directly or indirectly to the quality of network infrastructure and access to it. In other words, network infrastructure matters are as important now as they ever have been in the history of electronic communication. The two key issues in terms of functionality concern network capacity and content download and upload speeds. It is important to understand that an unsatisfactory user experience due to inadequacies in respect of each, whilst a network issue, manifests itself for the consumer at the service level. Thus, the 'long arm' of network governance and development stretches directly to the point of service consumption. It is this stark realisation that should promote a detailed and judicious scrutiny and planning of network development in policy and governance terms. As a consequence, there is strong evidence of a public sector led push to secure network upgrade. In considering state intervention, Picot and Wernick (2007: 664) argue that 'the more sunk costs are involved and barriers to market entry are built up, the more an incumbent can exert market power, making public intervention necessary'.

That the state has formed a key interest in wholesale network upgrade presents an interesting turn in the recent development of electronic communication networks and in certain respects is reminiscent of an earlier era in communication eschewed and even condemned until lately in a sector which had become a blazon of international neo-liberal capitalism. However, there is strong evidence that in recent years, among other things, states viewed broadband networks as a way of attracting inward investment (Falch and Henten 2010) and a means of promoting the forward-looking nature of a country, more broadly. Strategic approaches to network development provide an interesting mix of adherence to the neo-liberal model of regulated markets, direct public investment in network upgrades, as well as a distinct industrial policy orientation towards NGN which harks back to a previous era in network communication that in some respects is reminiscent of the old monopolistic systems of telecommunications. A key recent trend has been direct government financial support for the construction of NGN, not least as a way to counteract the global economic downturn which set in after 2008 (Falch and Henten 2010). Feijoo, Gomez-Barroso and Bohlin (2011: 791) regard this as nothing less than an 'enormous shift' which can be accounted for in considerable part by the success of public interventions aimed at developing broadband infrastructure in some parts of the Asian region.

The approaches witnessed to the development of NGN public investments are related to a considerable extent to technologies available. Telecommunications operators historically ran so-called Public Switched Telephone Networks (PSTNs) with a focus on digital subscriber lines (DSL). Yet, broadband cable and wireless have become increasingly important technologies and development of wireless broadband technology (see Chapter 3 of this volume) has been described by Falch and Henten (2010: 498) as an 'open game' in terms of competitor entry. Falch (2007: 246–7) discerns three kinds of public policies for broadband which he terms direct intervention, regulation and facilitation. The latter aims to 'ensure a good environment [in] the market for broadband services without direct intervention in the market'. Ruhle et al. (2011: 797–8) cite various state justifications for interventions in the development of broadband. These include enhancing economic and social progress, as in the cases of Australia, New Zealand and Germany; provision of public access and service as in Finland; promotion of health and education, as in Sweden; regional policy purposes as in France; the improvement in international league tables and public safety as in the case of the US; and, more generally, the development of international leadership in telecommunications technology exports.

APPROACHES TO THE REALISATION OF NGN IN EUROPE

The pursuit of better quality communications can be regarded as something of an ongoing policy goal, such that the term 'next generation networks' amounts to a misnomer if considered as a static idea relevant only to a particular historical time period. The term has acquired particular significance in the last decade in Europe due to the efforts of the European Union (EU) to put together a policy package aimed at securing what are considered to be the manifold benefits of an upgraded electronic communication network infrastructure. These efforts have a considerable – though not entirely distinguished – history. The characteristic feature through various phases has been the articulation of bold (and probably deliberately unrealistic) policy goals. Failure to attain the set targets has been posited in part as a reason for the launch of a successive phase, often couched in the context of heightened risks to the welfare of the EU's citizenry, alongside stiff competition and comparatively better progress in other regions of the world. For example, as far back as the early 1990s, the consideration by a group of techno-industrial elites of the so-called Information Society and how to achieve it was articulated in the Bangemann report (European Commission 1994a). The highly predictable steer to policy makers emanating from the group was to instigate telecommunication market liberalisation as quickly and as extensively as possible. From the mid-1990s onwards, neo-liberal regulatory capitalism became strongly embedded in Europe in communications, though, somewhat ironically, the period did also result in a successive series of publicly funded Information Society policy initiatives by the EU's Member States through the EU budget under the successive monikers of the Information Society, e-Europe, i-Europe and, since 2010, the Digital Agenda for Europe. The problem for these initiatives was that they were comparative tokens amidst the sea of market making, market liberalisation and market harmonisation which gripped Europe (and beyond) from the 1990s to the present.[1]

The Digital Agenda for Europe policy phase was heavily influenced by the global economic slump and attendant enormous Member State budget deficits which have dogged Europe since 2008. These curtailed heavily the public-sector spending power required to realise – by 2020 – a set of ambitious communication policy goals which were directly or indirectly premised on the creation and widespread availability of high- or very high-speed broadband networks. Unsurprisingly, most of these goals were shaped around the Internet. For example, all EU Internet users should, by 2020, have access to download speeds of at least 30 MBps (with an initial estimated investment cost €38–58 billion), with half of these experiencing speeds of 100 MBps (with an estimated investment cost €181–268 billion) (European Commission 2010a). The aim was to provide an appropriate infrastructural context for the realisation of a number of other varied policy goals such as digital literacy, climate

change, healthcare and ageing (European Commission 2010b). The EU
was able to claim a significant, though in the context of NGN only
modest, policy success with the availability of basic broadband to all EU
citizens by 2013 (European Commission 2017b). The EU also, in 2010,
introduced policy measures aimed at encouraging public and private
investment in high-speed infrastructure, the liberalisation of access to
NGN, and the more intensive deployment of radio spectrum for communication services (European Commission 2010b).

Nevertheless, by 2010, a discernible shift in EU communication policy
was beginning to be detectable in respect of the role of public investment.
This manifested itself earliest in EU policy statements on broadband,
such as the contention from the European Commission that societal
benefits from NGN creation were 'much greater' than incentives presented to the private sector to invest in these networks (European
Commission 2013b: 3). However, rather than injecting clarity into EU
thinking on NGN policy, this development has served to illustrate the
tensions and possible contradictions at the heart of an NGN policy
couched in the rhetoric and belief systems of the neo-liberal era on the
one hand, but pointing, on the other, however reluctantly, to the prag-
matic recognition of the need for public investment in difficult economic
circumstances. A key policy question around the time of the launch of the
Digital Asset Exchange (DAE) and a number of other specific measures
for NGN infrastructural development (see below) was the extent to which
the EU might be hidebound by its – by that stage comprehensively
established – marketisation agenda. Another key policy issue concerned
the efficacy of any new orientation in EU policy in the direction of public
investment should this be discernible. Some early analysis of the initiative was sceptical of the EU's ability to operate in any meaningful way
outside the parameters of a neo-liberal mindset (Simpson 2012). Other
analysis suggested that policy contradiction, underpinned by public
investment responses to the economic crisis in Europe, have come to
characterise EU communication policy (Michalis 2016).

In 2016, the EU developed significantly its 2020 DAE goals through
the launch of a raft of initiatives as part of a *Connectivity for a European
Gigabit Society* strategy where availability and take up of very high
capacity networks might enable the widespread use of products, services
and applications in the Digital Single Market (European Commission
2017a). An important aspect of this was the continuation of its broadband
development strategy. With a target date of 2025, it is proposed that all
households across the EU will have network access affording download
speeds of at least 100 MBs with all major roads and railways offering 5G
wireless broadband access. Separately, the EU launched, in 2013, a 5G

public–private partnership (PPP) project with a range of companies in communication manufacturing, telecommunications network operation and service provision and research institutions across Europe. The goal of the 5G PPP is to 'deliver solutions, architectures, technologies and standards for the ubiquitous next generation communication infrastructures' for wireless broadband (European Commission 2017b). All schools, transport hubs and main public service providers should have access to download and upload speeds of 1GBs.

The European Commission collates, through *Broadband Europe*, information about the state of development of upgraded broadband infrastructure at the national level. This latest phase of policy in pursuit of NGN is, according to the Commission, complemented by an ongoing review of the EU legislative framework in electronic communications. The EUFREC has been the cornerstone of the development of regulated competition in EU Member State telecommunications sectors since the late 1980s (for a review of this, see Simpson 2017).

Alongside EU efforts to launch specific public sector led international policy initiatives to improve network quality, the EU has also used extensively its legal and regulatory policy power to take action aimed at securing NGN developments. These measures do not entail the disbursement of financial resources but are an interesting indicator of the extent to which the EU has grown in influence in the communication sector in recent decades. The legal remit in question in the case of NGN is a generic one: the EU's role in approving or otherwise proposed state aid at the national level. In the case of regulation, the remit is sector specific in the form of a broad regulatory framework for electronic communication which has been developed at the EU level since the late 1980s. Neither of these NGN policy levers is without problems.

Articles 87 and 88 of the EU Treaty refer directly to state aid and Article 86(2) to what are termed Services of General Economic Interest (SGEI), which covers the provision of public services. The EU created a specific measure for SGEI through Article 16 of the Treaty of Amsterdam complemented by a specific European Commission-created SGEI framework. The perspective taken by the EU by dint of its legal remit involves a consideration of the permissibility of proposed state aid measures by Member States. A relatively restrictive legal environment persists, where a set of cumulative conditions for state aid to be permitted have to be met according to Article 87. In addition to providing clear economic benefits to parties in receipt of it, each proposed measure must be not competition-distorting in its actual or potential effects. Article 86 of the Treaty refers to the application of state aid measures as public services (European Commission 2001) and is read alongside the 2003 Altmark

Ruling which focused on SGEI. For a measure to lie outside the scope of Article 87, thereby avoiding a negative Commission decision, four criteria must be met: the state must have entrusted formally the provision of a service to the recipient of intended resources with a clear statement of the latter's obligations; a transparent system must exist to calculate an appropriate figure to compensate the provider of the SGEI before the transferral of resources to it; compensation much not be excessive; and if any system does not operate along clear competitive procurement lines, the determination of appropriate compensation must happen by calculating costs of service provision plus a reasonable surplus margin (European Commission 2009a: 5–6).

In 2014, the EU passed a directive aimed at reducing the cost of implementation of high-speed electronic communications networks. Implemented in Member States since July 2016, this directive addresses procedures: to allow public network providers to access physical infrastructure – principally ducts, poles and masts – to allow them to install their networks; to ensure coordination of civil engineering works in this regard; to create clear and equitable permit granting procedures; to enable network operators to access so-called in-building infrastructure in the installation of their networks (European Commission 2017b). Article 3 of the directive requires Member States to 'ensure that every network operator has the right to offer undertakings providing, or authorised to provide, electronic communications networks, access to its physical infrastructure with a view to deploying elements of high-speed electronic communications networks' (European Parliament and Council 2014: 9). Article 5 of the directive states that network operators performing civil work, either fully or partly financed by public means, must meet any reasonable request from any provider of a public electronic communications network for coordination of such work. Article 9 of the directive states that 'any holder of the right to use the access point and the in-building physical infrastructure meets all reasonable requests for access from public communications network providers under fair and non-discriminatory terms and conditions' (European Parliament and Council 2014: 13).

Preston and Cawley (2008: 813) argue that much of the EU's broadband policy has naively assumed that 'once adequate infrastructure is in place, socially useful – and usable – applications and services will follow'.

Falch and Henten (2010) note the rise of public–private partnerships (PPP) in initiatives designed to promote and deliver NGN. For them, PPP 'refers to private sector entities carrying out assignments on behalf of public sector entities and fulfilling public policy goals or public sector activities helping private sector entities' (Falch and Henten 2010: 497). It is possible to create new private organisational entities, to utilise existing private companies, or to involve non-governmental bodies with community-based goals. The debate on NGN has focused for the most part on the role that public investment can assume in developing communications infrastructure in unprofitable areas for the private sector. Examples in Europe are networks for research and education; rural and socio-economically disadvantaged networks; and city-based networks. The motivation for the public sector may be money saving, where investment may be more cost effective in the long run than leasing private provider capacity; a lack of private sector interest or a political motivation to provide users with a free service connection (Falch and Henten 2010: 499).

Across the EU's Member States, different national approaches to the realisation of NGN have been adopted. Some examples include local and regional government partnerships developed in Ireland; loans to operators in chosen areas of Spain; subsidies to private sector players in Sweden; pilot project funding in the UK; and PPPs in Austria and Greece (Picot and Wernick 2007: 665). The French utilised a public bank to fund municipal networks and, in 2010, launched the National Ultra-High-Speed programme funded with €2 billion, with the aim of ensuring all of France has broadband coverage by 2025 (Ruhle et al. 2011: 800). Whilst infrastructural upgrade is important, Cawley and Preston (2006: 260) caution against the subordination of content innovation to network access regulation that has been practised widely in Europe. The inclusion of broadband in a designated universal service package is also a policy option (Ruhle et al. 2011: 800).

Sweden launched a network infrastructure creation programme as early as 2000, whose broader strategy emphasised public sector intervention and which provided €400 million for all aspects of infrastructure development. The Swedish government built an alternative network to that of the incumbent operator, Telia. It also emphasised the middle layer of the network to create open regional and local networks in areas with limited competition where network upgrading was a funding priority (Eskelinen, Frank and Hirvonen 2008). By contrast, Finland's strategy, launched in 2003, focused on a technologically neutral, market-based approach. The strategy aimed initially to have 40 per cent of Finnish households with access to broadband by 2005. The plan contained as many as 50 action points which emphasised the promotion of competition, content provision on networks, and strengthening demand for broadband. However, local authorities were given power to subsidise infrastructure investments with both public service and competition stimulating goals in mind. In both

Sweden and Finland, the decision on broadband subsidy was made by a local authority (Eskelinen, Frank and Hirvonen 2008). In Sweden, public intervention had an immediate effect in lowering consumer prices for broadband. Interestingly, Finland's strategy of promoting competition, over a longer term led to lower prices and increased broadband penetration. Overall, Eskelinen, Frank and Hirvonen (2008: 420) conclude that 'the contrasting policy approaches in Sweden and Finland have not led to any major differentiation in terms of the final policy aim, that is, broadband use' but note that the condition of the networks upon which broadband policies are largely taken forward is an important factor in determining their course of development.

THE ROAD TO NEXT GENERATION NETWORKS IN THE USA

The USA has in recent years undertaken landmark policy action to stimulate and bolster the creation of upgraded broadband network infrastructure. Underpinning this state-led investment drive was the economic crisis of 2008 and subsequent severe economic downturn. The 2009 American Recovery and Reinvestment Act allocated as much as $7.2 billion to broadband investment measures of various kinds. This led to the creation of two significant programmes: the Broadband Technology Opportunities Program and the Broadband Initiative Program. In 2010, after a consultation, the US Federal Communications Commission (FCC) issued 'Connecting America: The National Broadband Plan' (NBC) (FCC 2010) which amounted to no less than a broad-ranging policy statement on the need to upgrade the US electronic communication environment using broadband and how to achieve it.

The US case is particularly interesting, since it has been probably the arch advocate of the neo-liberal agenda in electronic communications since the 1980s. To a considerable extent, the latter represented an extension of the US model for telecommunications developed since the early part of the twentieth century. Unlike Europe and elsewhere, the US system was one of regulated service provision through the private sector, though with very little competition in the market. Attempts to marketise the US sector, through break up of the incumbent and market liberalisation have produced mixed results, at best. Despite this, it would be incorrect to assume that US communication policy has eschewed public intervention. As LaRose et al. (2014: 53) point out 'U.S. communication policy has historically produced a dual strategy: reliance on private sector investment complemented by regulatory and other public policies intended to overcome the shortcomings of market forces'.

So, the recent focus by the US on next-generation networks can, in fact, be seen as consistent in outline with past agendas and overall policy approaches. Nevertheless, the media convergence agenda has added a layer of complexity into the latest phase of advanced communication infrastructure development. A reason for this is the different regulatory contexts faced by the main network owners and operators. Specifically, the principle of common carriage which underpinned traditional tele-communication provision was absent among cable service operators. A number of legal and regulatory decisions in respect of the delivery of new services with convergence characteristics moved regulation in the light touch direction, that is, away from the more stringent common carriage tradition. In 2002, the FCC classified cable modem services as infor-mation, rather than telecommunications, services. Several years later, a similar approach was taken to the regulation of digital subscriber lines (DSL), wireless broadband and broadband over power lines (LaRose et al. 2014).

The BIP and BTOP programmes aimed to address broadband provision at the community level through assisting those places which were either unserved (with less than 10 per cent penetration rate) or under-served (with less than 40 per cent penetration rate) with a rather modest 768 KBps defined as the minimum download speed. The BIP program provided a combination of grants and loans to established broadband providers, whereas BTOP assigned grants to new and established service providers. Both schemes aimed at creating choice and competition in broadband services in designated areas. The schemes between them focused on infrastructure creation, establishment of public facilities and adoption projects with a public benefit goal (LaRose et al. 2014: 54). BTOP and BIP (administered respectively by the National Telecommuni-cations and Information Administration and the Rural Utilities Service) concluded in 2013. The National Broadband Plan set a somewhat more ambitious, though still essentially conservative, 4 MBps minimum down-load speed for broadband.

LaRose et al. (2014) sketch the main features of US broadband policy since the mid-1990s. An important juncture was the passage of the 1996 US Telecommunications Act, one of whose broad thrusts was the opening up of local communications markets in the US to competition. Another important policy measure has been the E-Rate programme which, since 1996, has given funds to create high-speed Internet connections for schools and libraries. The US Rural Utilities Service has, since 2002, through the Community Connect programme provided resources for projects whose goal has been to improve quality of life through online connectivity. In 2011, the NTIA initiated the first National Broadband Map, updated on a twice-yearly basis. In the same year, the FCC allocated 500 MHz of spectrum to mobile data transmission and a Wireless Innovation Fund was launched to stimulate investment in mobile technologies and services. Yet again, in 2011, the FCC created the Connect America Fund which revised the then existing Universal Service Fund with a particular focus on broadband. The fund declared the goal of connecting all rurally located Americans to broadband by 2020. Within these schemes a range of measures has been deployed targeting network roll out and deployment and market coordination, as well as public–private partnerships. At federal level, the provision of grants to fund infrastructural development, and subsidisation of public Internet connections in community locations, such as schools and libraries, has occurred.

The National Broadband Plan can be regarded as a significant landmark in recent US communication policy history. Six long-term goals were set out. Four of these were general in nature relating, respectively, to establishing the US as the world leader in mobile communication, securing universal access to broadband; creating a high-speed network to shore up public safety; and to develop a cleaner energy economy through online communication. The remaining two were more specific: first, to ensure that at least 100 million homes had access to at least 100 MBs download speed and 50 MBs upload speed by 2020. Second, to ensure that every US community had access to 1 GBps broadband service for the running of community institutions such as schools, hospitals and government buildings.

The plan made a strong statement about its financial affordability. The auctioning of 500 MHz of spectrum would generate significant revenue to off-set the costs of funding to be devoted to public safety, deployment and adoption initiatives in under-served areas. Elsewhere, it was argued that the 'vast majority of recommendations do not require new government funding; rather, they seek to drive improvements in government efficiency, streamline processes and encourage private activity to promote consumer welfare and national priorities' (FCC 2010: xv).

The FCC described broadband deployment as '*the* great infrastructure challenge of the early 21st century' (FCC 2010: 3) where broadband was now 'essential to opportunity and citizenship' (FCC 2010: 3). Its articulated goals were broad and ambitions large. The plan addressed what it described as the 'entire broadband ecosystem – networks, devices, content and applications' (FCC 2010: xi). In 2011, the FCC established the Connect America Fund which extended universal service funding to the provision of broadband access. It is important to note that the first set out priority of the plan was the establishment of competition policies, the clear message being that private sector activity will deliver the necessary improvements for the most part, government's role being to create policies of a facilitating nature in furtherance of this goal. The plan specifically noted that it addressed 'actions government should take to encourage more private innovation and investment' (FCC 2010: 5). Activities, such as information gathering and benchmarking, alongside more specific measures related to wholesale competition rules, the reallocation of spectrum, data roaming, the set-top box market and consumer privacy were set out in the plan. The FCC noted particular challenges faced by the US. It does not possess a nationwide incumbent fixed link telecommunication provider, its population density varies and is thin in large areas and the US has a strongly developed federal political system.

A key part of the plan addressed infrastructural issues with a recommendation to free up 500 MHz of spectrum for broadband communications within 10 years. Spectrum was acknowledged as a public resource in that the federal government, under the auspices of the FCC and the NTIA, holds the property rights to it. Related to this, was the proposal to incentivise the re-purposing of spectrum, achieve greater transparency in its allocation and an exploration of innovative ways to access it. In terms of fixed link infrastructure, the plan addressed rental rates for access to poles, rights of way management, and effective and efficient construction of new infrastructure through 'dig once' policies. A key issue was the regulation of wholesale markets, the FCC noting that 'while networks generally have been converging to integrated, packet mode, largely IP networks, regulatory policy regarding wholesale access has followed the opposite trajectory' (FCC 2010: 47). The plan recommended the establishment of measures that would make better use of the US's existing infrastructure, such as reasonable rental rates for pole attachments, and reform of the dispute settlement process of infrastructure access. The importance of ensuring maximum impact from federal government expenditure was asserted. Here, any newly financed road and bridge construction projects should allow simultaneous work on infrastructure conduit deployment; the setting of fees for access to federal rights of way and the possible introduction of 'dig once' legislation should apply to federally funded projects along rights of way; and the creation of master contracts for the placement of wireless towers on federal government buildings was set out (FCC 2010: 109). It was estimated that running fibre through an existing duct was three to four times cheaper than creating a new aerial conducting facility (FCC 2010: 114).

Another major component of the plan concerned developing a universal availability and adoption of a set of policies and actions for broadband. Here a raft of measures was presented. Notable amongst these was the aforementioned Connect America Fund. The aim was to provide at least 4 MBs broadband download speed to under-served and unserved users, for which the plan advocated shifting $15.5 billion from the already established Universal Service Fund. Other proposed measures were a mobility fund for 3G mobile services and a reform of inter-carrier compensation to address the privileged position held by telephone companies. The plan also resolved to create affordable broadband services for low-income citizens and to provide educational opportunities for the attainment of digital literacy through the establishment of a national digital literacy corps.

Recent analysis by the Pew Center has shown that a rapid increase in the number of US adults with domestic access to high-speed broadband occurred between 2000 and 2010 but since then 'adoption growth has been much more sporadic' (PEW 2017). According to Horrigan and Duggan (2015), 'cost is the chief reason that non-adopters cite when permitted to identify more than one reason they do not have a home high speed subscription', with the availability of wireless broadband services through smartphones also important. In contrast to this, Downes (2015) dismisses price of broadband as a barrier to uptake, noting that 'non-users are more likely to identify a perceived lack of relevance of broadband Internet in their lives as the main reason not to adopt'. Whatever the reason, in terms of the goal of securing universality of access to – and usage of – upgraded broadband services, Pew Center research (2017) has found that as many as 50 per cent of those in the US without broadband are in what they describe as a 'hard to reach' category, making them unlikely to become subscribers quickly.

An assessment by Kruger (2013) of the first three years of the NBP's implementation presented a mixed picture. Here, whilst the US appeared to be making broadband available, ensuring its widespread adoption was more challenging. Similarly, the attainment of target network download speeds appeared to be more achievable than those related to upload speed. Related to both these concerns was the finding that the cost of broadband services to the customer was high. It was noted that, at the local level, the number of so-called Community Anchor Institutions with very high-speed connections was comparatively low. Concern was also expressed about the uptake of wireless broadband by US consumers despite the strong position of the US in wireless technology innovation. Large roll out programmes like the NBP will inevitably generate differences of opinion. The goal of ensuring that 100 million households have access to 100 MBs speeds has been 'criticized for endorsing an evolution of broadband deployment that could leave rural areas without the next generation broadband service that urban and suburban areas might enjoy' (Kruger 2013: 12).

A 2015 assessment of the plan's achievements was, however, more optimistic. Here, it was claimed that the 'plan's audacious goal of encouraging private investments to provide 100 million homes access to the Internet at speeds of 100 MBs by 2020 now appears to be a foregone conclusion … [where] … an even bigger surprise has been the construction of networks delivering 10 times the plan's milestone speed of 100 MBs' (Downes 2015). The picture regarding spectrum release for mobile broadband was less optimistic, however, where 'the plan's projections have proven conservative, requiring even more aggressive measures to feed the continuing mobile revolution' (Downes 2015). By the end of 2016, the US FCC was able to report that the maximum advertised cable broadband service speed had risen from 20–30 MBs in March 2011 to 100–300 MBs by September 2015. Importantly, it was also found that the actual speeds experienced by customers were in line with, or even exceeded, the advertised speeds (FCC 2016).

NATIONAL APPROACHES TO BROADBAND NETWORK UPGRADE IN AUSTRALIA AND SOUTH KOREA

In their analysis of the characteristic features of national broadband policies, Ruhle et al. (2011: 799) emphasise the importance of four measures: direct government investment; so-called investment facilitation actions; policies to promote construction work; and demand (tax benefits) and supply-side measures (roll out subsidies). Tax relief has been a prominent measure in the USA, France, South Korea and Japan. Of these, Japan and South Korea have displayed strong state-led ICT strategies. Large publicly funded network expansion has also been prominent in Australia and France (and less so in Germany and the UK). Structural or functional separation has been used as a regulatory tool to encourage network development in the UK and New Zealand.

Australia followed the liberalisation path initiated by most countries from the late 1980s. All but 10 per cent of the incumbent Telstra's shares were sold by 2006 (Given 2010). In 2007, the then Australian Prime Minister, Kevin Rudd, declared the aspiration that 98 per cent of

Australian homes would be connected to an upgraded national broadband network by 2020. In 2009, a plan was created to invest AU$43 billion over eight years to create a nationwide broadband network. The expectation was that it would provide fixed link network access giving 93 per cent of the population download speeds of 100 MBps (the remaining 10 per cent of users would get wireless access with download speeds of 12 MBps). Target online access speeds of 1 GBps were also envisaged (Li 2012). The aim was to establish a majority owned public company to build the network with an initial outlay of AU$4.7 billion, with the remainder to come from private sources and the issuance of government bonds. It was intended that this would result in an open wholesale access network with separation of infrastructure and services. The intention of the government was to reduce, through gradual scaling down, its ownership of the company from 51 per cent (Falch and Henten 2010: 499). However, the initiative soon encountered serious organisational challenges. The partly privatised Australian telecommunications incumbent, Telstra, initially envisaged as a leading player in the roll out of the network, opted out of involvement in its construction due to a clash with the Australian telecommunications regulator, the Australian Communications and Media Authority, over competitor network access arrangements. This led the government to create a new company, called NBN, to deliver the initiative. Progress with the roll out of the NBN has been described as 'slow, sporadic and expensive' (Marshallsea 2017). A key controversial moment occurred in 2013, when the new Liberal–National coalition government decided to use less expensive, but slower, copper wire, rather than fibre optic cable, for last mile connections to consumer premises. A key area of concern has been the high retail cost of capacity for service providers, which, it has been suggested, has led to under-purchase of capacity vis-à-vis peak time customer requirements, leading to complaints about quality of service and a lack of confidence and take up among consumers in the NBN (Remeikis 2017). It has been argued that the 'smaller players are in danger of being squeezed out of the market through complex and expensive NBN wholesale offerings' (Budde 2016).

In commenting on the decision to make this very large investment in broadband, Given (2010: 543) argues that because 'the state had never quite vacated telecommunications, it was not so large a step for it to contemplate a return when concerns about broadband became widespread'. In Australia, the public–private partnership approach was developed aimed at 'restoring public finance and goals to a recently privatized sector where commercially motivated finance and expertise are thought to have delivered a less-than-publicly-acceptable outcome' (Given 2010:

545). This amounted to a 'dramatic re-entry into public telecommunications investment, a reassertion of power' by a state which 'not long ago
could not give it away quickly enough' (Given 2010: 545). Li (2012: 221)
described the NBN company as a 'business-like government entity'. She
argues that four factors lie behind the growth of such PPPs: first, the need
to identify accurately social and economic goals; second, the need to
match better resources and capabilities; third, the need to deal with often
difficult topographical issues; and, finally the need to match services to
expected demand more accurately.

The initial Australian proposal came with plans for regulatory reform
to ensure the structural separation of its incumbent, Telstra. The latter
responded in 2010 with an agreement with NBN Co, for Telstra to make
its infrastructure available to NBN Co and an agreement to migrate its
customers over time to NBN Co's network. Given (2010) argues that
whilst, on the surface, the plan could be seen as a government-led
initiative to create an alternative network to the incumbent, in reality the
aim of the plan was to create some kind of enforced compromise with
Telstra. In June 2011, Telstra signed definitive agreements with the
Australian government and NBN Co (Li 2012). In March 2011, an NBN
Access Bill was passed which, inter alia, put in place a measure which
would prevent ISPs implementing their own high-speed Internet to
undercut the NBN Co before its network roll out was complete. On the
other hand, the bill severely restricted NBN Co's ability to discriminate
against retail service providers, which was only permitted where the
latter were proven to be uncreditworthy.

The NBN initiative has been the subject of strong criticism. Li (2012)
argued that, at the outset, it assumed only minimal growth in the wireless
broadband market in the medium- to long-term future. She argues that
the plan can be seen in part as motivated by the desire to 'reconstruct'.
She is critical of the lack of consideration of an appropriate pricing
model for the network which meant that the cost of bandwidth-heavy
audiovisual content consumption likely to characterise increasingly future
consumption patterns in media convergence contexts, will be borne
primarily by the consumer. The issue of Points of Interconnect on the
network has also been raised. A proposal to increase these from 14 to 120
in 2010 held significant implications for overall network running costs
(and thus retail prices to be charged to consumers) for network services
(Li 2012: 229). Marshallsea (2017) cites data suggesting that, since the
announcement of the project in 2007, Australia's average Internet speed
international league table position has actually fallen. Smyth (2017)
reported a view from business leaders that 'Australia's biggest infrastructure project ... has become an object lesson in how not to pursue a

national building plan ... [with] ... political interference, poor technology choices and inadequate delivery'.

South Korea has had a long-standing information society development policy stretching back to 1987, which yielded considerable success. In 1994, its National Information Society Agency launched a Korean Information Infrastructure Initiative to create, ultimately, a national broadband fibre network. Plans have included the Broadband Convergence Network and IT839 programmes, which also address content and services issues (Falch and Henten 2010: 500). Towards the end of the 1990s, the government provided loans to create local access networks worth more than US$150 million as well as rural infrastructure aid. Beyond this, initiatives to provide government, domestic business and private users, and universities and research institutes with high-speed broadband by 2005 were created. The South Koreans also included Internet literacy programmes as part of this activity (Picot and Wernick 2007: 669).

The regulatory environment in South Korea was a significant factor in broadband development. Here, distinction is made between cable and telecommunications operators. The latter comprise three groups: facilities-based service providers; specialised service providers (for example, IP telephony); and value-added service providers (for example, those offering broadband Internet connection). The South Korean Ministry of Information and Communications also acts as the telecommunications regulator. The Korean Broadcasting Commission regulates the cable industry with the MIC, which sets technical standards and issues licences. Platform competition between telecommunications and cable operators in South Korea was crucial in falling price levels, according to Picot and Wernick (2007: 672). The introduction of local loop unbundling (LLU) in 2002 increased service-based competition and dampened tendencies to create alternative telecommunications infrastructures. South Korea's supply- and demand-side actions, competition regulation in DSL and the imposition of open access requirements on cable network operators have been important, helped by a favourable geography and housing structure across the country. Falch (2007: 253) notes that 'demand has been stimulated through extensive educational programmes in IT involving all tiers of the society'.

By as early as 2010, download speeds of 100 MBs were available in South Korea. The estimated cost of the initiative was US$24.6 billion with government support amounting to as much as US$1 billion (Falch and Henten 2010: 500). Falch (2007: 247) argues that it is not necessarily the case that those countries with high income levels will witness highest levels of broadband penetration, as exemplified by South Korea, which had at the time of writing 'the second highest penetration rate in spite of a comparatively low income level'. It is interesting to note that Germans and Italians have higher per capita incomes than South Koreans but with considerably lower broadband penetration rates (Falch 2007).

The South Korean BcN consortium was created in 2004 and comprised the then Ministry of Information and Communication alongside telecommunications firms, such as Korea Telecom and Hanaro Telecommunications. The project was designed with three phases, the third of which commenced in 2008 with the overall aim of achieving a blurring of distinctions between media services, content and applications in broadband networks with no restrictions on place, time or devices. The initiative also had the goals of developing collaboration between government, and the private and third sectors with a view to securing greater efficiency, transparency and productivity (Menon 2011). According to Menon (2011: 282) 'the dramatic growth in the broadband market in South Korea is the culmination of appropriate government policy, growing demand and fierce market competition based on responsive supply'.

It was expected that the BcN would be the site of convergence between telecommunications, Internet and television networks (Shin and Jung 2012). Between 2000 and 2002, the number of broadband subscribers in South Korea rose by 200 per cent and household penetration levels increased from 27 to 69 per cent. Yet, evidence suggests that its broadband operators did not prosper in this environment. In 2003, Thrunet and Onse, the third and fourth largest companies respectively, went into receivership yet at the same time 'bolstered by an eager and technology savvy-market, a highly urbanized and dense population, and extensive government support, broadband services reached 72% of all households ... a level of penetration three times higher than the U.S. and more than six times what many European countries' (Shin and Jung 2012: 585) experienced. Broadband mobile access is extensive in South Korea and covered 97 per cent of the population as early as 2009 (Shin and Jung 2012: 582). In South Korea, the pattern of services provision and consumption has developed through time from online trading of shares, educational services and interactive games initially, to music downloading and gaming, through to online consumption of broadcast services, e-commerce and e-learning applications (Shin and Jung 2012: 583).

Whilst recognising the magnitude of the BcN initiative, Shin and Jung (2012: 579), argue that it has weaknesses in terms of what they describe as its 'ontologically bounded accountability ... [which] ... characterises the BcN as a public good, or public utility'. Specifically, these authors contend that the network was 'designed primarily to serve the demands of the major corporate suppliers and industries at the expense of the public interest' and also that the technical aspects of network design have pervaded (Shin and Jung 2012: 580) over and above social aspects.

CONCLUSION

This chapter has shown that, in recent years, public funding of key parts of electronic network communications, not least in respect of infrastructure, has emerged alongside the very strong neo-liberal predilections and policies which dominated the previous two decades. Evidence exists of market failure in the neo-liberal model which the features of media convergence set out in Chapter 1 of this volume have served to illuminate strongly. Important among these are price and service quality disparities, slow network and service growth and thwarted demand due to consumer digital under-literacy.

Given the chosen policy approaches, public intervention amounts only to a small part of the resources needed to deliver fully upgraded broadband next generation networks. Delivering this infrastructure will be left predominantly in the hands of private actors. This realisation holds very significant risks and challenges from a public policy and governance perspective since the infrastructure forms the basis upon which the various aspects of media convergence explored in detail in much of this volume, will unfold. Jock Given (2010) argues that the public–private initiatives witnessed in the development of broadband policies in a number of nations provide evidence of three trends. First, and most obvious, is a shift away from the liberalisation and privatisation paradigm of the last 30 years plus in telecommunications. Second, it is clear that there is a widely held belief in the power of broadband to deliver broad social and economic goals and that, to realise these, a high-grade wholesale fixed network infrastructure is a necessary condition to be fulfilled. Third, this activity can be viewed as a consequence of the global economic recession which hit towards the end of the last decade and is still exercising its impact.

However, how radical have the changes been in reality? Given (2010: 547) argues that '"interplay" seems the right word to describe the kind of negotiation that is occurring'. A key issue in the debate is a consideration of the state's enabling and, by contrast, rule-making roles and the degree to which broadband networks are viewed as public goods (Picot and Wernick 2007: 663). In the EU, a strong technological determinism has been in play where policy has been 'too focused on supply-side infrastructure and technology and neglectful of the demand side, applications and social learning processes by which new technological systems are adopted by society' (Preston and Cawley 2008: 814). Ruhle et al. (2011: 798) conclude that 'especially in European countries where there is a stronger focus on creating framework conditions (instead of public spending), the development in terms of penetration and availability is slower than in those countries where public institutions courageously have acted as first movers'. It is interesting to note that mobile broadband companies may be able to cater more quickly and flexibly for broadband customer demands into the future than the fixed link network investors (see Chapter 3 of this volume). Other challenges for PPP initiatives are decisions on where to roll out the networks first, how to convince consumers of the desirability of migration to broadband networks and how to develop a relationship with the incumbent telecommunications operator. South Korea is an interesting case of success in broadband. Shin and Jung (2012: 587) argued that the 'clear difference between the Korean BcN and the broadband networks of other countries is that the Korean government has actively engaged in the entire process from the planning stage to the actual implementation stage in coordination with the business sector'. Given the interplay between market-based and publicly stimulated network investment, it is clearly difficult to determine with accuracy the specific impacts of each kind of development on the evolution of the electronic communications network infrastructure. However, realisation of next generation broadband networks still remains very much a work in progress globally.

NOTE

1. For a detailed discussion on the growth of regulation in European telecommunications, see Humphreys and Simpson (2005).

3. The future is (still) mobile: spectrum governance issues in a converging media environment

INTRODUCTION

The features of media convergence discussed in Chapter 1 of this volume have exercised significant impact in the important arena of the governance of spectrum and are the focus of this chapter. The chapter shows how debates on – and changes to – the pattern of spectrum governance provide an important example of the disruptive, contested and only partially complete nature of media convergence, a recurring theme of this volume. At the core of the spectrum debate is a struggle over the scarce and valuable communication capacity of the airwaves. The chapter shows how growth in demand for audiovisually-based mobile communication – one of the motifs of convergence – has created pressure from commercial interests in mobile communication to secure increased spectrum capacity, in this case at the expense of broadcasting interests. Rather than spectrum illustrating a smooth path of convergence between broadcasting and mobile communication, the picture is one of perceived incursion on the one hand, and intransigence, on the other, leading to open, sustained policy contestation.

The chapter shows how, paradoxically, digitisation of the airwaves, a key technological facilitator of convergence, provided the initial context for this pressure through its capacity saving, so-called 'digital dividend'. Spectrum policy change became widely manifest in the movement from analogue to digital terrestrial broadcasting: the 'digital switchover'. Yet digitisation has merely provided a context for interest contestation, rather than the development of a space for new converged mobile audiovisual services. An added media convergence ingredient in this complex and often fraught milieu has been the (potential) growth in capacity of cable-based Next Generation Networks (see Chapter 2), which has led to the view in certain quarters that IP-based communication can become the basis for much, if not all, broadcasting currently delivered through digital terrestrial means. The chapter illustrates how what is effectively a turf war over spectrum exemplifies much of the tensions between public service and commercial media that is evident elsewhere in this volume (see Chapters 6 and 7, in particular). It provides further illustration that processes of technology-enabled media convergence are merely partial in character since they provoke deeply contested, messy and unresolved debates on the future governance of communications.

MEDIA CONVERGENCE AND THE PRIORITISATION OF SPECTRUM: CONTENT-RICH SERVICES CONSUMPTION AND MOBILITY

The airwaves have served as a vital resource with which to conduct communication for well over a century. Airwave spectrum capacity is a scarce resource and therefore the governance arrangements specifying its allocation to a range of different users have been particularly important. Here, ensuring the allocation of sufficient capacity to the security and emergency services and public health service providers is a priority. Other key users of spectrum have been commercial and public service terrestrial television and radio broadcasters, satellite communication service providers, and, in recent decades, mobile communication service providers. Given the international significance of much of the communication conducted through the use of spectrum, efforts to coordinate and develop its use were undertaken at the global institutional level through the International Telecommunication Union (ITU 2017).

Two key developments, both hallmarks of media convergence, have led to a rise in prominence of spectrum matters up media policy agendas nationally and internationally: the rise of mobile communication and the growth of the Internet. The growth in consumption of Internet services has two dimensions; consumption of these services using mobile communication handsets or so-called 'smartphones' and the growth in accessing the Internet wirelessly through laptops and tablets in domestic environments and public spaces using WiFi frequencies.

Developments in mobile communications and consumption patterns of Internet services occurred around the same time as important changes in broadcasting in the form of digitisation of the airwaves. The two soon became inextricably linked. The Ultra High Frequency (UHF) band (below 1 GHz) occupied, historically, in significant part by broadcasters, is attractive since it affords broad coverage and good reception using relatively small antennae. The ability to digitise terrestrial broadcasting afforded bandwidth savings through the transition from analogue to digital terrestrial television (DTT). This so-called 'digital dividend' potentially freed up spectrum around the time when demand for it was growing from expansive commercial mobile communications companies wishing to deliver high quality mobile broadband services to customers, the latter keen, in particular, to consume Internet-based services on the move. Changes in broadcasting and mobile telecommunications on the surface thus seemed to coincide in a serendipitously complementary fashion, the latest staging post on the inexorable journey to media convergence. However, like much of the story of the development of convergence, such an assumption ignores the idea that technological developments take place in institutional contexts, where established perspectives, patterns of behaviour, interests and preferences are often slow to develop and are oppositional and conflictual in nature. The functional 'inevitability' of technology is distorted by human preferences expressed through institutional contexts, in other words. The case of international policy change to spectrum allocations provides an apposite example of this.

THE GLOBAL GOVERNANCE OF SPECTRUM AND CHANGING NATIONAL POSITIONS

The ITU has been the global institutional forum for policy decisions on use of the airwaves for communication since the International Radio Telegraph conference held its first meeting in 1906. The World Radiocommunication Conference (formerly the World Administrative Radio Conference) of the ITU, held every three to four years, has the task of reviewing the ITU's Radio Regulations, an intergovernmental agreement between members for the governance of radio spectrum and geostationary and non-geostationary satellite orbit.[1] As digitalisation of the airwaves became increasingly commonplace, a key moment occurred at WRC 2007 when a compromise definition of the 'digital dividend', spectrum that could be vacated by broadcasters as a result of digitalisation, was reached. In ITU Region 1 (comprising Europe, the Middle East and Africa), this was defined as 790–862 MHz (known as the 800 MHz band) whereas in ITU Regions 2 (Americas, Greenland and eastern Pacific Islands) and 3 (Asia and Oceania), the definition was broader, comprising 698–806 MHz (the 700 and 800 MHz bands).[2]

Ala Fossi and Bonet (2016) argue that whilst the policy objective of the USA at WRC in 2007 was to see the global release of the 700 MHz band to the mobile communications sector, for most European countries, the outcome was important in that it both encouraged the development of the mobile communications industries and simultaneously allowed protection of long established and strategically important domestic terrestrial broadcasting. However, pressure continued post WRC-07 for a further reallocation of the 700 MHz band from broadcasting to mobile communications. At the WRC held in 2012, the adopted resolutions 232 and 233 established the two most controversial agenda items for the succeeding WRC-15. Resolution 232 declared that states in ITU's region 1 (Europe, Middle East and Africa) should allocate the 694–790 MHz frequencies (known as the upper 700 MHz band) for mobile communications on a co-primary basis with broadcasters, to become effective immediately after the WRC-15. Agenda item 1.1 of WRC-15 called on states to identify additional frequency bands for allocation to mobile services on a primary basis, in line with Resolution 233 of WRC-12 (ITU, 2015). The focus here was on the sub-700MHz band, deep in the spectrum territory of digital terrestrial broadcasters.

NATIONAL POSITIONS ON SPECTRUM CHANGE IN THE SUB-700 MHZ BAND AT WRC-15

The US National Telecommunications and Information Administration (NTIA) is responsible for US participation at the WRC. The Radio Conference Subcommittee (RCS) of the US Interdepartmental Radio Advisory Committee (IRAC) works to provide recommendations for preliminary positions to be taken by the NTIA in advance of WRCs. NTIA and the FCC liaise to produce draft US preliminary views and proposals for approval by the State Department. These positions are sent to the Inter-American Telecommunication Commission Permanent Consultative Committee II on Radiocommunications (CITEL PCC II) for its regional preparatory meeting or are sent direct to the ITU. Prior to WRC-15, the NTIA made clear its wish to ensure 'U.S. manufacturers have sufficient harmonized international spectrum to realize economies of scale for emerging technologies' (NTIA 2015).

In the lead up to WRC-15, the US position continued to argue strongly for the release of spectrum for mobile broadband purposes. In its proposals for the conference, the US cited the 'acute need for additional spectrum' for mobile broadband, noting how the situation was particularly pressing in developing countries where 'mobile wireless is often the only means to achieve ubiquitous broadband access'. Noting the 'unique propagation characteristics' of spectrum in the range below 1 GHz, the US argued that high coverage at relatively low investment cost could be achieved (US Government 2015: 1). Nevertheless, the US was keen to point up the continuing and likely future importance of broadcasting as a community service and that 'broadcast television continues to evolve to keep pace with technological and marketplace changes' (US Government 2015: 1). Drawing on ideas of convergence, it noted evidence that 'television broadcasters now adopt a three-screen approach, sharing their programming online and on mobile services, in addition to providing it over the air'. The US stressed that 'providing mobile access to broadcast television content is a compelling factor in the future DTTB systems' (US Government 2015: 1). Using this convergence perspective, as well as citing examples of current DTT research projects ongoing in its territory, which have the pursuit of mobility in consumption of broadcast content as a goal, provided the US with a platform to argue for bringing together broadcasting and mobile broadband interests as co-users of the same spectrum range. Recognising the need to take action to combat interference, particularly in cross-border contexts, the US advocated the adoption of WRC specification 9.21 which would mandate the putting in place of a coordination agreement in the event of sharing of spectrum space between mobile communication players and broadcasters.

US preparations for WRC-15, like those of other states, provided evidence of the differing positions of the mobile broadband and broadcasting constituencies of interest. The FCC's WAC Informal Working Group 2 submitted a non-consensus recommendation with two opposing views, 'one backed by the National Association of Broadcasters, CBS and Fox, the other by Alcatel-Lucent, AT&T, Ericsson, Intel, Motorola Mobility, Nokia, Samsung, Sprint-Nextel, Telecommunications Management Group and Verizon' (Standeford 2014a: 2). Despite this, the US draft position was in favour of the co-primary allocation[3] of the 694/698–890 MHz band with an identification for International Mobile Telephony. It also proposed that this band be retained as the primary spectrum allocation for broadcasting which should be explicitly protected (Standeford 2014a). In familiar terms, mobile players cited the growth of – and unsatisfied demand for – mobile broadband services. By contrast, broadcasting players noted an under-addressing of the likely international interference problems that would ensue in a co-primary allocation situation. The continued use of the airwaves by cable and satellite systems was also cited as a rebuttal to the assertion that over the air viewing was in decline in the US. The broadcasting view also argued that its research on next generation TV systems, broadcast content's economic contribution to US exports and the role of broadcasters as first informers in emergencies had been dismissed in the non-consensus recommendation (Standeford 2014a).

In summary, the US argued for a solution that would 'preserve and protect broadcasting and other services in the UHF range … facilitate the development of future broadcasting systems and … allow administrations flexibly to address the mobile spectrum shortage consistent with their domestic requirements'. Its proposed solution to securing this balancing act was a change to the 'Radio Regulations that would add an allocation to the mobile services and identification for IMT in the range 470–694/ 698 MHz except for 608–614 MHz band in Region 2'. In what might be viewed as a gesture of reassurance to broadcasting interests, it was proposed that broadcasting should retain primary allocative rights in the broader 470–890 MHz range, that rule 9.21 would be applied on a mandatory basis to ensure the avoidance of interference between services and that, in this process, broadcasting would have what was termed 'super-primary coordination priority' (Standeford 2014a: 2). Key US players, such as FCC Chair Tom Wheeler, emphasised the importance of allocating the sub-700 MHz band to mobile through a global allocation in order to achieve the global economies of scale available. The US Coordinator for communications and information policy, Daniel Sepulveda, argued that securing agreement on spectrum was a key test of the effectiveness of the ITU (Youell 2015a).

The Arab Spectrum Management Group (ASMG) established by the Arab Ministerial Council for ICT to prepare for WRC-15 and comprising 22 Arab states supported setting the lower limit of spectrum band reallocation to the mobile communication sector to 694 MHz. In a draft position in advance of WRC-15, the Regional Commonwealth in the field of Communications (RCC) representing states from the former USSR (comprising Russia, Azerbaijan, Armenia, Belarus, Kazakhstan, Kyrgyz Republic, Moldova, Tajikistan, Turkmenistan, Uzbekistan and the Ukraine) declared its decision not to support 'consideration of the 470–694 MHz band or part of this band for allocation to MS [mobile service] on a primary basis and its identification for IMT [international mobile telephony], taking into account current and future spectrum requirements for terrestrial broadcasting' though it went on to argue that 'implementation of the mobile service in the entire frequency band 694–790 MHz in RCC countries is possible' (RCC 2013: 1–2). In its final position, the RCC made it clear that it supported 'identification of additional frequency bands for IMT on the condition of optimizing the use of already identified frequency bands' and that 'protection of other services that have allocations within the subject bands and adjacent bands should be ensured and the necessity of their development be taken into account when determining possibilities and conditions for allocation of frequency bands to the MS and their identification for IMT' (RCC

2015: 1). In its final position, the RCC declared, in respect of the 470–694 MHz band, that its administrations 'object[ed] to the primary allocation to the MS and identification for IMT systems ... due to intense use by incumbent services and possible unacceptable interference' (RCC 2015: 2). In respect of the 694–790 MHz band, the RCC declared its view that the use of this band for broadcasting should continue where national administrations deemed it necessary. It also stated that 'the lower edge of the allocation to the mobile service ... shall not be lower than 694 MHz' and that a decision on allocation in this band should be taken on the basis of 'defining the protection conditions of the terrestrial TV broadcasting and ARNS [Aeronautical Radio Navigation Service] systems'. The RCC was clear that 'imposing restrictions or application of additional requirements for the BS [broadcasting service] shall not be allowed' (RCC 2015: 3). Similar protections were asserted for ARNS and broadcast and programme-making ancillary services (Services Ancillary to Broadcasting/Programme making (SAB/ SAP)).[4]

The positions of the countries of the Americas prior to WRC-15 illustrated a difference of opinion on the future of the 470–698 MHz band. Canada, the US and Costa Rica expressed a preliminary preference for opening up the band to IMT, whilst Argentina, Brazil, the Dominican Republic, Ecuador, Nicaragua and Panama were against such a move (Youell 2014a). Those against any move presented the familiar argument that the process of realising the so-called digital dividend was still in train in many states and underscored the importance of free-to-air DTT. An indication of the tense nature of the negotiations on the future of the sub-700 band was the decision of the WRC-15 Chair, Festus Daudu, to take negotiations 'out of the hands of formal committees' and to create an 'informal inter-regional committee' (Youell 2015b: 2) to encourage flexibility beyond re-statement of positions. At WRC-15, the Comisión Interamericana de Telecomunicaciones (CITEL)[5] found itself in the position (unlike the other regional bodies whose position was for no change in the 700 MHz band) of presenting two multi-state proposals that reflected a split on the future use of the band in the region (Youell 2015b).

At WRC-15, the broadcasting community proved especially well organised in its efforts to ensure maintenance of the 694–790 MHz band in its hands. Evidence of the generation of a strong vanguard to protect the status quo position emerged in 2014, with a report produced by Aetha Consulting, commissioned by a wide group of broadcast network equipment firms, and broadcasters.[6] The evidence presented in the report might be viewed as an attempt to counter previous studies which had asserted the economic benefits of mobile broadband services. The report argued that allowing co-primary use of the 700 MHz band would be likely to damage DTT. It estimated that the cost of DTT migration as a necessary set of actions required of the service provider and consumer would amount to €38.5 billion. The report went on to provide estimates of the net benefit of the use of the band by the mobile communication sector, concluding that 'even in the most aggressive traffic forecast the potential use of the band for broadcasting was worth four times as much for mobile broadband' (Youell 2014b: 5).

As many as 630 organisations located across the world produced a joint document arguing for maintenance of the status quo. These organisations were represented collectively by regional level bodies such as the Asia-Pacific Broadcasting Union (ABU), the Arab States Broadcasting Union (ASBU), the African Union of Broadcasting (AUB), the European Broadcasting Union (EBU), the International Association of Broadcasting (IAB), the North American Broadcasters Association (NABA) and Broadcast Networks Europe (BNE). In the submission, the groups claimed that DTT was 'the most widely used platform for television viewing' and 'the central pillar of the cultural and creative sector' with broad economic and employment impact (BNE et al. 2015: 2).

The free-to-air aspect of DTT was emphasised, as well as its dual public service/commercial service character. It was argued that DTT encouraged content creation and was a key disseminator of information and education. Here, DTT 'preserves and encourages [f]reedom of expression and [i]nformation which underpins social cohesion, and ensures that news, major events and a diversity of general entertainment are available to all in society' (BNE et al. 2015: 2). The report cited evidence from several studies which argued that there would continue to be a demand for DTT, which itself was developing along a technological pathway aimed at delivering so-called ultra HDTV.

The report made a particular plea in respect of DTT infrastructure development in ITU regions 1, 2 and 3, arguing that loss of the 490–694 MHz band would thwart DTT development in Africa, in particular. The submission also made strong claims in respect of the economic value of DTT. It was argued that broadcasters and consumers had made a cumulatively huge investment in networks and equipment associated with DTT delivery and consumption. The report also argued that DTT had been a key enabler of the growth of local TV stations through providing a low-cost delivery platform, thus enabling local content production. DTT was argued to be 'the most reliable and efficient way to deliver TV to mass audiences'. It was noted that DTT broadcasters were also investing in the provision of hybrid (linear–non-linear) services and needed regulatory surety about their future in order to do this effectively. Demand for linear TV was high and would remain so; demand for non-linear services was growing rapidly but was closely related to – and reliant upon – a strong linear DTT environment. The report argued that DTT had already proved a good neighbour in the 494–690 band with users such as the radio astronomy and aeronautical radio navigation communities and that clearance of the band for use by IMT would also effect negatively these constituencies.

In a different way, the report questioned predictions about the future growth of the mobile communication industry on which the demand for the release of spectrum in its direction was based. It also argued that there were technical solutions that could be pursued by the mobile communications sector to use more efficiently spectrum already allocated to it, citing the use of small cells. The broadcast constituency also argued that it was the unlicensed spectrum environment of WiFi which would address consumer demand for mobile data services. Finally, the report made the interesting point that, in the case of two neighbouring countries which had taken the decision to use a single band for DTT and IMT respectively, effectively sharing the band in this way would prove difficult technically (BNE et al. 2015: 2–3).

The UK collective body, DigitalUK, argued that re-allocating 470–694 MHz would in the UK 'expose terrestrial broadcasting to unreasonable commercial uncertainty' (DigitalUK 2015: 3). It put forward ten reasons to make no change to the allocation in this band, citing the economic and social value of DTT, noting its established benefits in sharing with other users, asserting its ability to develop new services like catch up TV alongside linear services and calling into question the need for extra spectrum for mobile communications through reallocation of the 470–694 band. It cited the increasing importance of WiFi technology and noted existing limitations of IP networks as means of providing mass audience broadcast services (DigitalUK 2015).

The intense and detailed preparation of the broadcasting lobby in advance of WRC-15 appeared to have been successful. In relation to the sub-700 MHz band (470–694 MHz) in Region 1, states decided to preserve the frequencies exclusively for broadcasting. The re-allocation of this band will not be part of the WRC-19 agenda, while a review of the whole UHF band was scheduled for the WRC in 2023 (EBU 2015). It is likely that any change of policy regarding the sub-700 MHz band may not be set in place until the subsequent WRC, set to take place in 2027.

In the aftermath of WRC-15, the World Broadcasting Unions organisation, comprising regional representative bodies from the Asia-Pacific,

Arab, African, Caribbean, European, North American and Central American and South American areas, noted that the outcome of WRC-15
'ensures a harmonised use of the band for terrestrial broadcasting and
creates favourable conditions for the continuous development of digital
terrestrial television' (WBU 2015: 1). The WBU went on to note how the
concerted coordination pursued by broadcasters worldwide in advance of
WRC-15 had paid dividends in that it 'successfully demonstrated the
universal importance of terrestrial broadcasting and supported the
national administrations throughout the WRC-15 negotiations' (WBU
2015: 1). The Wider Spectrum Group, a diverse collective organisation
comprising civil society, employee, and business interests in broadcasting, also welcomed the outcome of WRC-15 as it provided 'long
term regulatory security for broadcasting spectrum' (WSG 2015: 1).

By contrast, the Next Generation Mobile Networks (NGMN) group
published in 2015 a paper on the roll out of 5G mobile services which
highlighted the need to utilise those parts of the spectrum below 1 GHz
and to ensure that this occurred in a globally harmonised, overwhelmingly licensed (as opposed to unlicensed spectrum sharing) fashion
(Youell 2015c). Concern has been expressed about the effect of a
piecemeal stage by stage reallocation to the mobile business in terms of
coordinated roll out of services and networks (Watson 2012). The GSMA
– an international representative body for mobile communication operators, equipment manufacturers, software and Internet companies –
argued that the 2014 Aetha Report ignored the need to address the growth
in mobile communications flexibly. With clear media convergence under-
tones, its senior director of spectrum policy, Wladimir Bocquet, argued
that future demand patterns, with technological efficiencies in terms of
spectrum use and greater use of the Internet for accessing TV, meant that
regulators needed co-primary allocations of spectrum in place to allow
them to respond quickly and flexibly to such developments (Youell
2014b). The GSMA has also emphasised that the sub-700 MHz band
offered consumers located in rural areas and dense urban environments
the opportunity to access high quality mobile broadband services due to
the reach and penetration characteristics of the band (Yip 2015). In the
lead up to WRC-15, when it became clear that the EU would oppose any
move to co-primary allocation of the 490–694 MHz band, the director of
government and industry relations at Ericsson argued that the decision
'put innovation on hold in mobile connectivity' (cited in Youell 2015d:
4). Nokia has argued that in the future there will be a converged
broadcast and mobile network. In the process leading to this outcome,
changes in viewing habits are likely to create capacity in spectrum in
different states at different times (Standeford 2014b).

Elsewhere, the GSMA praised the decision taken at WRC-15 to harmonise globally the higher 694–790 MHz band to allow mobile broadband use. It noted that it 'particularly commends the vision shown by many countries' which wanted to open the sub-700 MHz band to mobile broadband use, noting that this band 'is now available for mobile in markets covering more than half the population of the Americas' and several markets of the Indian sub-continent (GSMA 2015). In the lead up to WRC-15, GSMA also criticised what it saw as the spreading of misinformation by broadcasters (Youell 2015d). Despite undoubted opposition, the assessment of mobile communications players of the outcome of WRC-15 was not entirely negative. Ericsson noted 'the above decision to make additional spectrum available for mobile broadband as a step towards achieving the full potential of a Networked Society' (Ericsson 2015) but according to its Chief Technology Officer, Ulf Ewaldsson, 'Beyond 2020 ... additional spectrum will be needed to support the wide range of 5G-enabled uses, such as the Internet of Things' (Ericsson 2015).

CONVERGENCE, SPECTRUM POLICY CONTESTATION AND THE EU

In the 1980s, Europe developed global leadership in mobile communication systems, through its Global System for Mobile development under the coordinative aegis of the European Conference of Postal and Telecommunications Administrations (CEPT). In 1987, the EU bolstered these efforts through its GSM directive which created harmonisation of frequencies used for GSM services across its Member States. An important juncture in the development of spectrum policy occurred with government decisions to auction new tranches of spectrum. This departed from the previously utilised strategy of so-called beauty contests. Drawing on US practice and unsurprisingly pioneered in the EU by the UK, auctions proved lucrative revenue generators for states, though the financial outlays required from mobile communications operators would later place in jeopardy their network and service investment plans and, in some cases, their commercial viability. It is important to note that reliance on DTT across the 28 (soon to be 27) EU Member States varies considerably, even between as much as 5 and 90 per cent (Youell 2014c). Low use contexts, such as the BENELUX countries and Germany, are likely to pre-dispose the regulatory authority in question towards advocating flexible use of the 470–694 MHz band, since primary allocation could inhibit the ability of potential new services to be provided by mobile broadband operators.

In 2002, the EU created the European Spectrum Committee and Radio Spectrum Policy Group through its telecommunications framework directive (European Parliament and Council 2002a). The establishment of these bodies meant that work in preparation for future World Radio Conferences would be coordinated with the pan-European, 48-member European Conference of Postal and Telecommunications Administrations (CEPT). Within Europe, the European Communications Committee (ECC) of the CEPT signed a Memo of Understanding with the European Commission. The EU's Radio Spectrum Decision (European Parliament and Council 2002b) sets out the relationship with the CEPT, which primarily involves information and advice giving. According to Ala Fossi and Bonet (2016), through the work of the ESC, the EU provides a mandate to the CEPT's ECC which it is required to address in a specified time period. This facilitates ESC decision taking which leads to the adoption of a position by the European Commission, which is then presented to the European Parliament and Council. The EU and the ECC aims to ensure coordination of their respective work programmes through membership and liaison in each other's committees, such as the ECC's Steering Group and the EU's Radio Spectrum Committee and Radio Spectrum Policy Group (ECC 2017).

However, differences of policy approach have characterised the evolution of the EU's relationship with CEPT. For example, in advance of the 2007 WRC, CEPT did not wish to change any of the existing allocations of spectrum in the UHF band occupied by broadcasting (470–862 MHz), whereas the European Commission wished to open the band up to the mobile industry on a co-primary basis. Some Member States, notably the UK, had already decided to reallocate the 800 MHz band away from broadcasters and towards the mobile sector (Ala Fossi and Bonet 2016). The EU is in a precarious position in respect of WRCs. The CEPT puts together common European proposals for each conference and the European Commission prepares EU positions through communications. However, the EU has no voting rights in WRCs, which sit entirely with national Member States given the intergovernmental character of the ITU. The CEPT noted that the WRC-15 decision to make no change to the allocation of spectrum in the 490–694 band and to review use of the band at WRC-23 was 'fairly consistent with the CEPT position on the topic' (CEPT 2015: 1). The CEPT supported the allocation of the 694–790 MHz band to the IMT sector on a primary basis.

In 2012, the EU launched its Radio Spectrum Policy Programme which was premised on releasing the 800 MHz band for use by the mobile communication industry by 2013 across all EU Member States. The WRC-12 decision, whilst providing flexibility for states, was something of a tipping point in that, for example, where two countries shared a land border, use of the band for mobile communications, in one case, and DTT, in the other, would not be feasible due to technical interference which would likely drown out the mobile communication signal (Sims 2012). Ala Fossi and Bonet (2016) note that the Commission's desire to be given authority to assess the technical efficiency of spectrum alloca- tion in Member States, with the goal of finding more possible capacity for mobile communication, raised concerns at the national level and the proposal was omitted from the final version of the programme ratified in 2012. WRC-12 proved particularly controversial from an EU perspective. Here, no European proposals were tabled to change the then current allocation, yet there was mixed opinion on the African and Arab proposal to have the 700 MHz band reallocated to the mobile sector after consideration at the subsequent WRC in 2015. In the aftermath of WRC-12, Finland declared its intention to reallocate the 700 MHz band to the mobile sector on a primary basis from 2017. This was followed in 2014 by similar decisions from Sweden and Germany.

In the interim, acutely aware of the risk of a series of uncoordinated national policy decisions on the 700 MHz band across Member States, the European Commission set up a high-level group, led by Pascal Lamy, on the matter. The Lamy Group's main constituents were from the broadcasting and mobile communications sectors and its deliberations reflected the strong divergence of opinion that exists between the two quarters on the future allocation of spectrum. Reporting in 2014, the Lamy Group was unable to reach a consensus position on a way forward. Asserting that its goal was to achieve a 'win–win situation for both the mobile sector and the broadcasting sector' the report nevertheless claimed that 'linear TV viewing will remain dominant for the foreseeable future' (Lamy 2014: 3). It went on to argue for the importance of DTT as a free at the point of access service. It made a clear statement on the limited extent to which media convergence had occurred to date noting that 'terrestrial broadcasting and mobile broadband platforms are likely to co-exist for a long time'. Lamy asserted: 'I conclude that convergence of both platforms is not on the practical policy agenda yet' (Lamy 2014: 4).

Instead, Lamy proposed a so-called 20-25-30 model. Here, the 700 MHz band would be released for mobile communications by 2020; the sub-700 MHz band would be retained for broadcasting until 2030 and that this position would be asserted in WRC-15. However, given the unpredictability of technological and service developments, a review of the decision taken by the EU post-Lamy would occur in 2025. Given variations in the market share of DTT across the different states of the EU, the Report proposed a flexibility option which would 'study EU-harmonized scenarios allowing co-existence of traditional broadcasting services in the 470–694 MHz band with other downlink-only (i.e. unidirectional) electronic communications services, in cases where there is no or declining demand for DTT at national level' (Lamy 2014: 8–9). The intention was that this option could be used to provide innovative services by 'mobile or any future convergence operators' (Lamy 2014: 8–9).

Reactions to the Lamy Report reflected how deeply contested the spectrum issue was across different interests in the media sector. ARD, the German cooperative of regional public service broadcasting companies, emphasised the need for careful cross-border coordination in changes to spectrum allocation across EU Member States and asserted its understanding that its agreement to the possible release of the 700 MHz band to the mobile sector was done 'under the pre-condition of securing' the sub-700 MHz band 'as the exclusive core audiovisual band' (ARD 2015: 8). In respect of the flexibility option recommended by the Lamy Report, which would give Member States the discretion to use specific parts of the 470–694 MHz band for flexible downlink only use by the mobile broadband sector, ARD argued that the concept of flexibility was poorly understood, should not be introduced in a way that would constrain current DTT functioning or impede the future development of the platform (ARD 2015: 14). The ARD urged the EU to adopt a 'no change' position to current allocation in the band at WRC-15.

The radio sector, in the shape of the Association of European Radios (AER), the pan-European trade body for commercially funded radio stations, argued that reallocation of the 470–694 MHz band 'could have indirect dire consequences on radio' since the displacement of broadcast services might see them occupying space planned for broadcast radio (AER 2014: 4). The British Entertainment Industry Radio Group (BEIRG) stated its opposition to any change in the 470–694 MHz band, and argued in rebuttal of the flexibility option that LTE wireless broadband was a 'notoriously bad sharer of spectrum' (BEIRG 2015: 19). The European Alliance of Viewers' and Listeners' Associations (Euralva) extolled the social, political and cultural importance of DTT and asserted its strong opposition to change in the band and its view that there should be 'intensification of efforts to use non-UHF bands [for mobile broadband], since these will be less disruptive to European viewers and will not threaten the valuable public interest services that the DTT platform supports' (BEIRG 2015: Euralva, para. 2.6). Discerning a 'strong bias' towards mobile communications players in the evolution of spectrum policy over a decade, Mediaset, the largest commercial broadcaster in Italy, made the point that commercial DTT delivers an economic multiplier in the specific respect of the knock-on revenue generation which accrues from purchases as a result of advertising that takes place through the medium, estimating that every euro spent on DTT advertising generated between five and nine euros in the economy (Mediaset 2015: 11–14).

As might be expected, reactions to the Lamy Report's recommendations were rather different from the telecommunications sector. In advance of WRC-15, the European Telecommunications Network Operators (ETNO) body argued strongly for a co-primary allocation in the 490–694 MHz part of the spectrum (Standeford 2015a). British Telecom (BT) from the UK supported the proposed downlink flexibility option. It argued that waiting until 2025 to review possible introduction of a co-primary allocation in the 470–694 MHz band was 'far too late' and recommended 2022 to do this instead (BT 2015: 4). Teleindustrien (TI), representing the Danish telecommunication industry also found the 20-30-25 model 'too unambitious' in that 'a co-primary allocation would allow countries less dependent on the use of terrestrial TV to move forward faster when it comes to roll out of mobile broadband' (TI 2015: 7). DIGITALEUROPE argued for flexibility to allow 'introduction of additional capacity mobile broadband on a case-by-case basis'. Reflecting the lack of concrete developments in respect of media convergence in the spectrum case, it noted that 'in a possible converged scenario ... cooperative spectrum sharing or service cooperation could be envisaged' (DIGITALEUROPE 2014: 19). ETNO – the European telecommunications network operators collective body – argued unequivocally that the co-primary allocation of the 470–694 MHz band should occur at WRC-15 (ETNO 2015). The mobile operator Orange argued that it was 'too early for the EU to give up on sub700' as part of its strategy for spectrum harmonisation (Orange 2015: 4). It went on to argue for a two-step approach which would involve ensuring co-primary allocation in the band at WRC-15 to be followed by a process, to take place between 2020 and 2023, to achieve Europe-wide harmonisation of spectrum use in the band.

Unlike broadcasters, the mobile player Nokia argued for an ambitious approach to be adopted in the face of the uncertainty around future service developments. Co-primary allocation in the 470–694 MHz band would, in its view, be a 'future looking action' to enable the EU 'to act in a flexible way, if and when needed' (Nokia 2015: 7). In a similarly ambitious reference to a convergent media future, the Spanish telecommunications operator, Telefonica, referred to itself as a 'Digital Telco' providing 'mobile connectivity and audiovisual services'. It envisaged vacation of a large part of the sub-700 MHz band by DTT and a licensing of new players in EU Members States. It argued that the Report's recommendation on flexible downlinking in the sub-700 MHz band 'should be considered only as a temporary solution during the transition to a more ambitious technology and service neutral licensing regime' (Telefonica 2015: 25). The UK satellite broadcaster, Sky, was notable as a voice from the broadcasting community which advocated the opening up of the UHF bands to use by players from outside broadcasting. In line with its membership of the Dynamic Spectrum Alliance, Sky argued that the Lamy Report's flexibility downlink only recommendation was modest in nature and urged increased efforts to explore the possible increased usage of unlicensed white spaces in UHF bands, traditionally utilised as interference buffers between spectrum users (Sky 2015).

Lamy himself argued that the 20-25-30 model put forward was the 'backbone of EU Spectrum policy' (cited in Youell 2015e: 5). In respect of the 700 MHz band, the Commission was in favour of mandating licensing conditions for the reassignment, though looser coordinating measures were opted for eventually. This may have had something to do with the EU's experience of reassigning the 800 MHz band, where half the EU's Member States missed the initial deadline (Youell 2015f).

The WhiteSpace Alliance, an international organisation comprising players from electronics equipment and memory device manufacturing, and private ICT research and database providers, among others, was motivated to see what it described as 'opportunistic use of licensed spectrum by unlicensed cognitive radios … [through] … the development, deployment and use of standards based products and services as a means of providing broadband capabilities via WhiteSpace spectrum' (WhiteSpace Alliance 2015: 2). WhiteSpace spectrum refers to those bands which are used as buffers between different users in order to ensure the avoidance of radio wave interference. These spaces have been used effectively by companies from broadcasting, for example, to test the efficacy of electronic equipment. In a resource-scarce spectrum landscape, the Alliance expressed the view that white space spectrum can be opened up effectively to greater usage through the development and use of appropriate technical standards, without causing technical interference between users. The Alliance also argued, radically, for 'Licence-exempt usage of the spectrum from 470 MHz to 698 MHz while creating no interference to existing DTT services' (WhiteSpace Alliance 2015: 4).

A subsequent consultation on the Lamy Report also reflected a strong difference of opinion between the mobile broadband and broadcasting constituencies. It has been claimed that the main reason the Lamy Group was unable to reach a consensual position was that broadcasters and mobile communications operators dissented to a coordinated approach at

WRC-15. There was concern among broadcasters that a 2020 deadline to move out of the 700 MHz band would not give enough time to certain broadcasters and consumers in terms of required network and equipment changes. The EBU, in support of Swedish broadcasters, was critical of what it saw as the haste in the Swedish decision, taken in 2014, to reallocate the 700 MHz band to mobile players by 2017 (Watson 2014). On the other hand, mobile broadband players were keen to see not only the 700 MHz band allocated for their use, but also re-allocation of the sub-700 MHz band on a co-primary basis (Standeford 2014b). In 2015, the RSPG produced an opinion which endorsed the assignment of the 700 MHz spectrum for mobile broadband and the maintenance of the 490–694 MHz band for broadcasting until at least 2030, though interestingly raised the possibility of allowing wireless broadband communications in this band for downlink communication (RSPG 2015).

In 2015, the European Commission presented a proposal for a council decision which asked Member States to agree to 'reject the co-primary allocation to the mobile service of the band 470–694 MHz in Europe' (European Commission 2015: 2) at WRC-15. This move aimed at shoring up national Member State positions ahead of WRC-15 and deviated clearly from the procedure employed to that point of articulating a joint EU position in advance of a WRC through non-legally binding Council of Ministers conclusions. This proposed move was rejected by a large number of Member States (Ala Fossi and Bonet 2016). Nevertheless, as noted above, the decision taken at WRC-15 to open the upper part of the 700 MHz band to the mobile communications sector on a co-primary basis but to institute no change to the current allocation in the lower part of the band (470–694 MHz) until at least the WRC scheduled to take place in 2023, was in line with the agreed European position prior to the conference and one voted for by all EU Member States bar Finland at WRC-15. The experience of the Finnish action at WRC-15 motivated the European Commission to instigate legal proceedings against the European Council of Ministers for not agreeing to vote on a decision to legally bind Member States' positions in advance of WRC-15. This decision illustrates how crucial the Commission viewed developing an international coordinated position of its Member States on the future of spectrum but was also couched more broadly in the fragile political economic environment pervading the EU at the time.

The EBU, a collective body for broadcasters at the pan-European level, as might be expected, lobbied strongly for no change to occur to the allocation of spectrum in the 470–694 MHz band until 2030 at least and strongly endorsed this position held by the EU's RSPG on the matter. Drawing on the view of Lamy that DTT was the 'backbone of the

European audiovisual model', the EBU went further in asserting that, in respect of the 700 MHz band, 'notwithstanding the view that the urgency for such a release for providers of wireless broadband services remains unfounded, the EBU believes that a release by 2025, rather than 2020 or 2022 would provide the necessary time for EU Member States to fully complete a complex frequency coordination and transition process' (EBU 2015: 2).

The EBU went on to argue for the core benefits of DTT as a means of delivering free-to-air public service broadcasting; a flexible, reliable and cost-effective way of delivering broadcast content to mass audiences; an insurer of diversity and choice in content; and a means to deliver competition to cable and satellite TV platforms (EBU 2015). The UK convergence regulator Ofcom has argued that it will be impossible to consider switching off DTT before 2030, due to the evolution of alternative IP and satellite platforms. Unsurprisingly, this position was strongly backed by DigitalUK and the EBU (Standeford 2014c).

The views of the programme making and special events community sat in strident opposition to the allocation of the 694–790 MHz band to the mobile industry on a primary basis. The Association of Professional Wireless Production Technologies (APWPT) argued the band was heavily used by the Programme Making and Special Events (PMSE)[7] community which it represented, noting that the alternative bands proposed by the Commission for PMSE (823–832 MHz and 1785–1805 MHz) were 'grossly inadequate in terms of both quantity and quality' and as such the initiative risked 'serious damage to the cultural and creative industries and to publicly fund[ed] cultural institutions which are not able to operate without wireless production equipment' (APWPT 2014: 1). The APWPT went further in arguing that the reallocation of the 694–790 band would be 'tantamount to a restriction of press freedom' given that the consequent shortage of frequencies would restrict the ability of 'camera and radio broadcast teams to report live from sporting, political, social or cultural events' (APWPT 2014: 1).

The Wider Spectrum Group in a direct submission to the President of the European Commission, Jean-Claude Juncker, asserted its view that spectrum was:

> [a] live issue, not ... a binary technical debate ... [where] an approach that pitches industries against each other and portrays the issue as a choice to make between mobile telecommunications and Terrestrial TV Broadcasting Services gives at best an incomplete picture of the role of spectrum allocation policy and its impact, notably towards creative and cultural industries.

It emphasised its view that there was a 'strong socio-economic case for co-existence' between terrestrial broadcasting and mobile broadband communications' (WSG 2015: 1). Praising the Lamy Group's conclusions as 'balanced proposals that respect Europe's realities and unique audio-visual model', it went on to criticise a reported draft communication from the Commission which it argued 'appears not to make the connection between spectrum allocation and local creative and cultural jobs, media pluralism and diversity' (WSG 2015: 1). In 2015, France and Germany undertook auctions to allocate tranches of spectrum in the 700 MHz band, garnering just short of €4 million in revenue in the process (Youell 2015g).

Subsequent to WRC-15, the European Commission produced a proposal aimed at creating a more coordinated EU spectrum policy. In 2017, the European Parliament, European Council of Ministers and the European Commission reached a political agreement on the future allocation of the UHF spectrum. Here, Member States were required to commit to a reallocation of the 700 MHz band for use by the mobile communications sector by 2020, unless there were justifiable reasons for not doing so, in which case up to an extra two years might be utilised to effect the change (European Parliament and Council 2017). It was also agreed to maintain the sub-700 MHz band for use by broadcasting until at least 2030. However, according to the Commission, the agreement 'is balanced with the opportunity for each Member State to take a more flexible approach to alternative spectrum use – such as advanced mobile multimedia services – according to different levels of digital terrestrial television (DTT) take-up' (European Commission 2016: 1).

CONCLUSION: SPECTRUM, PUBLIC POLICY AND MEDIA CONVERGENCE

This chapter has illustrated how moves in the direction of media convergence have created major policy battle lines between the broadcasting and mobile broadband communications constituencies in respect of allocation and use of spectrum. More than 160 states were represented at WRC-15 where, despite evidence of a desire to re-allocate spectrum away from broadcasting and towards mobile broadband provision, the policy talk at the end of the WRC-15 debate was of co-existence and development of a hybrid approach (in the case of evolving DTT). This is clearly a long way away from full convergence around IP for broadband telecommunications and broadcasting. However, DIGITALEUROPE, an industry body representing a range of companies from IT, telecommunications and consumer electronics recently put forward the interesting view that the 470–690 MHz band 'should preserve the current and future deployments of DTT'. However, this perspective appeared to be motivated by a desire to see co-primary usage of the band, all the while ensuring that 'potential licensees must not interfere with legacy DTT receiver installation and that re-planning additional DTT deployments or redeployment of the latter must be possible without additional constraints for DTT on a national or international level (DIGITALEUROPE 2014: 2). This conciliatory approach also argued that technological development of DTT systems could serve to release spectrum. In respect of the 694–790 MHz band, the view was similarly concessionary. Whilst overall, the organisation's view was in favour of 'repurposing the band the band for MBB [mobile broadband]' (DIGITALEUROPE 2014: 6) it wished to ensure that in the process there was no disruption to the DTT service and its consumers.

Similarly, in 2014, the EBU produced an interesting report on the possible use of mobile LTE networks to deliver broadcast TV content. Whilst noting that its research had concluded that 'free-to-air delivery could in principle be enabled by LTE eMBMS ... further development is required'. The report also cautioned that 'regulatory constraints, business and operational models including free-to-air, costs and availability of user equipment need to be better understood to finally judge on the viability of delivering broadcast content via LTE' (EBU 2014: 4).

In a report on the future use of the UHF band, the European Communications Committee (ECC) predicted that 'for the coming years, coexistence is feasible between broadcast and mobile downlink networks whereas coexistence between mobile uplink and broadcasting or mobile downlink is difficult and challenging' (ECC 2014: 4). The report also predicted that 'linear viewing will remain the main way of viewing TV content for the foreseeable future' and that whilst viewing on handheld devices would grow, most of it would occur via larger screens. The introduction of HDTV and ultra HDTV was foreseen with interactive services. In terms of convergence, it was argued that 'hybrid broadcast-broadband services will become commonplace, possibly including a wireless broadband element, to allow increased access to non-linear as well as linear content' (ECC 2014: 2).

From a media policy perspective, it is important to note that determining the social value of spectrum is more difficult than calculating its economic value; the latter can be the reason that regulators, such as Ofcom in the UK, have focused on a market-based approach to calculating spectrum's worth (Watson 2007). By contrast, in 2015, the UK

Department of Culture, Media and Sport produced a report entitled 'Incorporating Social Value into Spectrum Allocation'. This referred to benefits from the use of spectrum, such as promotion of political freedom, diversity and national culture (Barwise et al. 2015). However, the extent to which social value issues figure primarily in decisions on whether or not to reallocate spectrum is open to question (Standeford 2015b).

The market regulatory approach, evident in many of the ways communications has evolved in recent decades, set an underpinning perspective that militates against conclusions that would argue strongly for the maintenance of spectrum in the hands of broadcasters. The current position is that the existing strategy is a transitory one that will end after 2030, if not sooner (should technological change and market development proceed faster than expected). All of this is buttressed ideologically on the dubious assumption of the inevitability of technological change creating conditions for the deepening marketisation of communications. The convergence narrative sits very much at the heart of this and is in many respects one of its key drivers. What is clear is that spectrum will continue to be a crucial, contested communication infrastructural resource into the future as media convergence proceeds.

NOTES

1. See: http://www.itu.int/en/ITU-R/conferences/wrc/2015/Pages/default.aspx (accessed 23 March 2018).
2. The terms '700' and '800' MHz bands are abbreviations to cover a frequency range within the specified band.
3. Co-primary allocation refers to a situation where more than one user group or class is provided first access user rights to a particular tranche of spectrum on an equal basis.
4. Services Ancillary to Broadcasting (SAB) support the activities of broadcast service companies carried out in the production of their programme material. Services Ancillary to Programme making (SAP) support the activities carried out in the making of 'programmes', such as film making, advertisements, corporate videos, concerts, theatre and similar activities not initially meant for broadcasting to general public. Source: https://www.apwpt.org/terminologies-q-z/sab-sap/index.html (accessed 4 January 2018).
5. CITEL coordinates telecommunications-related mandates of the Organisation of American States (OAS).
6. The group comprised Abertis (Spain), Télédiffusion de France (French radio and TV transmission company) (TDF) (France), Arqiva (UK), the British Broadcasting Corporation (BBC), Broadcast Networks Europe and the European Broadcasting Union.
7. Programme Making and Special Events equipment is used to support broadcasting, cultural (including sporting) and trade-related events.

4. Access and opportunity online: the debate on Internet neutrality and converging media

INTRODUCTION

In a relatively short time span, the Internet has developed into an essential communications infrastructure for domestic and international communication. As well as being a medium of communicative exchange, the Internet is also a hugely significant source of information. Established forms, such as 'traditional' websites and email are now supplemented by a variety of constantly updated information and communications resources, most notably in the shape of social media platforms like Facebook, WhatsApp, SnapChat and Twitter. More than any other development in communications over at least the last century, the Internet has become the embodiment of media convergence.

The more burgeoning and complex the Internet has become, the greater have been the demands on its infrastructural resources. Equally, as the Internet has become a huge globalising communication environment underpinned predominantly by commercial principles and practices, the greater has been the pressure to create a variety of information products and services for a growing range of markets, differentially priced accordingly. As communications of all kinds have converged across the Internet's landscapes, a range of key issues has arisen about current and future delivery of what is now a veritable panorama of Internet content and associated services. One of the most important and hotly disputed matters is whether ISPs should be allowed (or even required) to intervene in the flow of traffic traversing the Internet. A core aspect of this has been the consideration of whether differential *access* to Internet services, in terms of speed, should be allowed to particular users based on the price they pay for the service. Another is whether ISPs should be able to prioritise certain types of content and websites over others. This would amount to a challenge to the traditional Internet principle of non-discrimination between services provided to Internet users by ISPs. The ensuing debate around the degree to which Internet communication actually is, and should, remain 'neutral' and undifferentiated in this way in an era of developing media convergence also raises a raft of thorny economic, social and, ultimately, regulatory governance matters. The Net Neutrality debate, as it has come to be known, and its implications for media convergence, constitute the focus of this chapter.

The chapter explores Net Neutrality as a governance matter, in the process pointing up a number of the core themes of this volume. First, it argues that whilst the Internet in theory is *the* key site of the most extensive and expansive expressions of media convergence, Net Neutrality as a governance construct and set of practices, has only been narrowly and modestly articulated. This is the case because thinking on Net Neutrality is illustrative of the fractious, conservative and only conservatively developed understandings of media convergence discussed in the opening chapter of this volume. The chapter illustrates how the pursuit of neutrality has been viewed defensively and unrealistically as non-intervention and argues that Net Neutrality, like the broader media convergence context in which it is developing, has fallen into the 'neo-liberal trap'. Here, an ideological aversion to the idea of intervention has created two problems. The first arises from a failure to recognise and understand fully the complexities of intervention in Internet communication. This leads to the second problem which, like in the case of media convergence more broadly, is an unwillingness and failure to embrace the potential of selective intervention to broaden our understanding of the idea of 'neutrality', which can lay the ground for socially enlightened media policies for the Internet in a converging media environment of the kind explored in the concluding chapter to this volume.

The chapter begins with a brief overview of the historical origins and main policy features of Net Neutrality. In this process, the differences between the communicative origins of the Internet and its associated principles, compared with those of the currently evolving commercial context, come into sharp focus. The chapter then explores the development of regulatory governance approaches to Net Neutrality, in the process comparing the EU with the US. These cases are chosen since the US was the source – and remains the policy epicentre – of the Net Neutrality debate. The EU, by contrast, has exemplified international media policy efforts on Net Neutrality within a policy discourse which has advocated strongly the realisation of media convergence. The implications of these approaches to Net Neutrality are explored in the context of a consideration of possible regulatory routes forward for the consideration of Net Neutrality in an environment of media convergence.

THE CONTEXT OF NET NEUTRALITY

Net Neutrality has its origins in the US where it was coined as the principle that all information services should enjoy equal access online. At the heart of the consideration of Net Neutrality is the relationship between telecommunications network operators that provide Internet access, content and application service providers and Internet users (Belli 2013). Specific articulations of Net Neutrality stretch back only to the early part of the last decade (see Wu 2003), though the ideas under-pinning them sit at the core of any media policy consideration of the role and function of electronic communication in the social world. Lentz (2013) provides a detailed account exploring the terminology used in the development of Net Neutrality regulation in the US from the conceptual perspective of inter-textuality. She sources its origins as far back as the mid-1960s and the first of the three US Computer Inquiries which tackled crucial definitions of what are now termed information services and which, in the mid-1980s, featured a particular debate on the term 'neutral' (Lentz 2013: 574). More broadly, ideas of neutrality can also be related to the communitarian and libertarian origins of the Internet, which eschewed both state and big business involvement in the Internet, in equal measure.

The Internet – much like telecommunications and postal services, though in functionally very different ways – initially created a communi-cation infrastructure unconcerned with the content delivered through it. Here, its characteristics of layering and 'end-to-end' are central. The former separated the functions of addressing and routing of information from the end point function of processing and presentation of content. The latter meant that networks and their operators undertook only network, not end point tasks (McDiarmid and Shears 2013: 27). The essence of Net Neutrality is that ISPs should treat equally traffic of a broadly similar kind and should not engage in blocking of applications without the approval of the user. The 'end to end' architectural principle of the Internet meant that it did not discriminate between types of content (see Marsden 2017). In the USA, the historic telecommunications com-mon carriage principle is akin to this idea. Routing on the Internet occurred in a non-discriminatory way. Users could create new services, applications, protocols and devices without any consultation with net-work operators. Network operators all had the opportunity to interconnect with each other (Center for Democracy and Technology 2006). Viewed thus, ISPs should treat all legal Internet data equally, not discriminating –

including by price – in favour of any particular user, content, application, communication service or platform.

Thus, broadband providers would be prevented from creating 'fast lanes' for privileged users (more high value customers) on the Internet and from blocking or slowing down certain Internet traffic. Despite this, in practice Internet communication was anything but neutral, in its purest sense. To understand why, it is important to distinguish between the different reasons why ISPs might manage their network traffic. Some traffic management has to occur to enable ISPs to cope with problems such as network congestion. They may prioritise certain 'specialised services' that require a particular quality of support, Internet Protocol television (IPTV) being a good, relatively early, example. ISPs also have to fulfil regulatory obligations, such as blocking access to illegal content.

The real controversy over Net Neutrality, however, has largely centred on the issue of the deepening commercial interventionism of ISPs, in particular the extent to which they should be permitted in regulatory terms to levy additional charges, beyond access and usage fees, on both end user and content providers. Net Neutrality was described as 'the single most important communications policy issue – at least within the United States' (Peha, Lehr and Wilkie 2007: 709). It is interesting to consider the extent to which it has emerged as a response to perceived problems in the evolving delivery of Internet services to customers, rather than being enshrined as a tenet and functional imperative of the Internet as its popularisation proceeded. This should come as no surprise: the history of the development of communications technologies evidences the efforts of social and political actors working in 'recovery mode' to protect and promote social freedoms around communicative practice. Such actors, in the case of Net Neutrality, included no less than former the US President, Barack Obama, who expressed strong support for it.

THE NATURE OF INTERVENTIONS IN INTERNET TRAFFIC

Despite assumptions that the Internet is a communications environment whose (unclearly defined) neutrality is in need of protection, it is the case that intervention in Internet traffic has been commonplace, in three key areas. The first area can be broadly defined as quality of service. This has concerned ISP intervention that may slow down the speed of Internet traffic, known as throttling or degradation, the blocking of access to certain websites, and the prioritisation of certain services according to data source and type. Relatedly, focus has occurred on the particularly controversial practice of access tiering, where access providers give 'priority, at a price independent from Internet access fees to applications, service and content providers that are willing to pay for quality of services' (DLA Piper 2009: 12). ISPs can also apply restrictions on the running of certain applications and equipment on the Internet by users.

A key aspect of intervention in Internet traffic concerns blocking. This might occur through partial or complete restriction of access to certain online services or websites. Part of this involves the practice known as throttling, where a service provider degrades a certain kind of traffic in order to manage the system better and minimise congestion at key times. Whilst this can be done for the positive reasons of securing network efficiency and performance, it is also possible for degrading to occur by network operators in respect of the services provided by a competitor. Filtering is a technique that involves direct intervention by an ISP to ascertain the nature of data traffic across the network and remove it before it reaches an intended destination. This holds considerable resonance for security issues, on the one the hand, but also privacy and data protection, on the other.

The second area of intervention is underpinned by the desire of ISPs to exploit commercial advantage. ISPs can be key players in what economists refer to as a two-sided market, since they hold a privileged position between content producers and consumers. The ISP is thus able to exploit its knowledge of both parties to extract maximum economic rents from them. Consumers are in a particularly weak position, even in a competitive ISP market, due to a potential lack of knowledge about what is a technically complex service offering.

The pursuance of non-neutral network behaviour is also very much evident in certain traffic management practices undertaken by service providers. Historically, access provision took place on the basis of so-called 'best effort' service provision, where there was no specific guarantee made to users about quality of service. As the Internet has matured, traffic management to provide certain services at a guaranteed level of quality has become increasingly important and, at the same time, controversial. This has involved the creation of new network control processes that prioritise certain kinds of data over others. The picture is also complicated by the existence of vertical integration, where network ownership may be integrated with service provision and even content creation. According to Brown and Marsden (2013: 140) 'all major consumer ISPs are vertically integrated to some extent with proprietary video, voice, portal and other services' making things more complex for the consumer. In these cases, players may have an incentive to charge competitors as much as possible for network usage. In 2011, the

European Commission (2011) highlighted three key types of non-neutral behaviour: packet differentiation, IP (Internet Protocol) routing and filtering. Packet differentiation occurs where a network operator treats various kinds of communications traffic differentially. These tend to be high bandwidth services whose quality would most likely be otherwise degraded, such as real-time live streaming or VoIP. IP routing occurs where ISPs send IP packets through different pathways to reduce congestion in a particular route. The consequence of this may be a slowing down of a service, though arguably this is better than it stalling completely.

Marsden (2010: 54) provides a neat encapsulation of the Net Neutrality problem for governments and regulatory authorities where:

> [W]e are in the era of settled incumbents in mobile and fixed broadband. Their networks are public communications, though no longer common carriage. The rights and responsibilities they maintain towards their end users are being redefined for the broadband era. To the extent that they are creating new innovative means of accessing the Internet, their influence is beneficial, and the positive net neutrality that would prevent their charging discriminatory pricing would be both intrusive and disproportionate. Where they are rationing and degrading existing applications and services, their influence is less benign.

The third major area of intervention concerns matters of security. A key issue is the emergence of Deep Packet Inspection (DPI) technologies where filtering and censoring by file type and content provider can occur. The inspection of 'packets' of information has two broad aspects to it. Each packet contains a data section which holds the data to be sent as well as a header section which provides information related to the source and destination of the packet. In the process of routing of packets, the header section is inspected to complete the task. This kind of inspection can also be used to filter content. DPI can thus allow higher or lower priority to be given to data from a particular source or blocking of data destined for a particular source. Inspection of the data section of a packet can be used to protect the security and integrity of the network by tackling viruses, spam and other illegal material. It can also be utilised to undertake highly detailed traffic monitoring and shaping and data gathering about network usage down to the level of the individual subscriber (DLA Piper 2009: 6). In the process, there is at least the potential for DPI to raise concerns over privacy. In so doing, MacDonald, Cannella and Ben-Avie (2013: 51) note that ISPs have the potential to transgress Article 8 of the European Convention for the Protection of Human Rights and fundamental Freedoms (ECHR) and Articles 7 and 8 of the Charter of Fundamental Rights of the EU. DPI confronts the originally established operational end-to-end principle of Internet communication. Whilst it may be considered an affront to free communication and innovation on the Internet, on the other hand it is also viewed a necessary tool to combat a number of key negative externalities that have arisen from Internet communication. This is, of course, nothing new. Technology has long been an enabler and, at the same time, an arbiter of communication. However, this realisation should underpin the need to put in place a robust and adaptive public policy system to cope with its challenges. Until recently, bar important work by regulators in the USA, the governmental and communications policy communities have manifestly under addressed the raft of Net Neutrality policy issues pertinent to private citizen and commercial actor alike.

US PERSPECTIVES ON NET NEUTRALITY

In the US, Net Neutrality has been considered particularly important for the simple reason that – unlike in Europe – there is little competition in the provision of Internet access. Prior to 2002, telephone companies, which provided most Internet access, but also cable television companies, who also provided access, were required by the Federal Communications Commission (FCC) to fulfil the common carriage requirement enshrined in Title II of the Telecoms Act. By the end of the 1990s, although the number of telephone companies was fast shrinking as a result of the deregulatory 1996 Telecommunications Act (for a highly critical account of which, see Aufderheide 1999), the number of ISPs had mushroomed, and Internet access was a highly competitive market. However, the Internet represented an obvious threat to the future business of telephone and cable television companies, which were powerful lobbies in Washington. Thus, McChesney (2013: 111–12) notes how, in 2002,

> very quietly, with no debate or public hearing and scarcely a scintilla of news media coverage ... the Bush administration's FCC reclassified cable modems as an information service, rather than a telecommunication service ... This change allowed cable to escape the common-carrier provisions ... Shortly thereafter, the FCC reclassified the phone companies' Internet access services as information services, so they, too, could avoid the open-access requirement.

The rather dramatic result was that broadband competition 'collapsed' as nearly all independent ISPs went out of business. In 2013, McChesney (2013: 112) claimed that as many as 96 per cent of US households were confronted with merely a duopoly for fixed broadband access made up of the local monopoly telephony service provider and a cable company. Media convergence was providing a significant context for (cross) market concentration in wireless Internet access services, where a 'handful of old telephone companies ... gobbled up spectrum and transitioned to becoming the dominant cell phone and wireless ISP providers' where four companies controlled around 90 per cent of the US wireless market with AT&T and Verizon (with 60 per cent wireless market share) being particularly dominant.

Since the 1990s, there has been an often intense debate in the US about whether Net Neutrality should be required by law. In 2004, the then Chair of the FCC, Michael Powell, set out what came to be known as the four Internet Freedoms: to access content; to attach technical devices to the network of one's choosing; free use of applications; and rights to obtain information on service plans. Marsden (2010) argues that a key moment in US telecoms policy occurred in 2005 with a Policy Statement which established the principle that competition was to be realised in an inter-network, as opposed to intra-network, fashion. This ruling alongside the 2002 ruling on cable modem service providers set the ground for further rulings which, according to Lentz, (2013: 588) 'freed providers of broadband over wireline, wireless, and electrical power lines from stricter common carriage requirements'. Between 2005 and 2012, no fewer than five attempts to enact Congressional bills containing neutrality provisions all failed. The FCC's regulatory jurisdiction has also been under regular challenge in the US courts, principally from network infrastructure owners and operators keen to ensure that they are able to exercise flexibility over the functioning of their networks. Important here was the successful challenge launched in 2010 by Comcast Corporation, the US cable incumbent, in respect of the FCC's authority to create and impose Net Neutrality measures at all. This legal action was in response to an earlier FCC ruling in 2008 that upheld a complaint that Comcast had discriminated against users of the BitTorrent file-sharing software across its broadband infrastructure. The defeat precipitated the FCC's efforts to re-establish its position in Net Neutrality regulation. In December 2010, it agreed a compromise position, one which still, however, split Democratic and Republican Commissioners. The Open Internet Order declared a differentiation between fixed link and wireless Internet service provision and instructed ISPs not to block or interfere with any type of Internet traffic that did not harm the system. An exception, however, lies in respect of what is termed loosely as reasonable network management (Wyatt 2013). Here, whilst fixed line providers could not block or discriminate unreasonably against websites and applications, mobile providers are permitted to manage their networks more flexibly, though this activity must be declared and be subject to regulatory scrutiny. Significantly though, the regulations did not explicitly ban faster access through payment and were severely criticised by US civil liberties groups.

Around this time, a proposal for Net Neutrality was produced jointly by the mobile operator Verizon and Google, which itself excited considerable controversy. Whilst being supported by major telecommunications carriers like AT&T, Internet content providers and the increasingly influen tial Facebook expressed opposition. The essence of the proposal was that Net Neutrality rules should accommodate the creation of so-called paid fast lanes where Internet content providers would have to pay for faster access to their websites or services being afforded to customers of the infrastructure provider in question. The Google–Verizon proposal also argued that future online services that were not public in nature should also allow for differential access arrangements to be put in place. In 2011, the US House of Representatives approved a measure to block the FCC's Net Neutrality measures deeming them to be beyond the scope of its authority. This further brought into focus the partisan positioning of the main US political parties on Net Neutrality, where the Democrat-controlled US Senate was in favour of the FCC's proposal. Interestingly, both parties accused the other of supporting big business – Republicans large communications incumbents, Democrats large Internet technology companies – in taking their opposing views (Wyatt 2011). In January 2014, the US Court of Appeals for the District of Columbia ruled in favour of a challenge to the Oxford Internet Institution (OII) brought by the telecoms company Verizon. The next development, in May 2014, appeared to see the FCC reverse its former stance by producing draft rules that would have allowed ISPs to charge a fee for prioritised access to their networks.

This decision, however, sparked pro Net Neutrality rallies across the US and, by the end of a public consultation period in September 2014, the FCC had received as many as 3.7 million public comments, the vast majority of which were in favour of Net Neutrality rules. The neutrality debate in the US is remarkable for the strength of feeling it has evoked from what might be described as civil society. Among the most vocal supporters of Net Neutrality numbered the leading communications law and policy scholars Lawrence Lessig, Tim Wu, law professor at Stanford University and founder of the Center for Internet and Society, and Robert McChesney, communications professor at the University of Illinois at Urbana-Champaign and co-founder of the media reform group Free Press. Already, in 2006, they had made a public intervention, calling upon Congress in *The Washington Post* to vote in favour of Net

Neutrality to ensure that the Internet 'remain[ed] a free and open technology fostering innovation, economic growth and democratic communication', rather than becoming 'the property of cable and phone companies that can put toll booths at every on-ramp and exit on the information superhighway'. Lessig and McChesney argued that '[w]ithout net neutrality, the Internet would start to look like cable TV' with '[a] handful of massive companies ... control[ling] access and distribution of content, deciding what you can get to see and how much it costs'. They counter-posed the vast sums being dispensed by the telecommunication companies on publicity and lobbying against Net Neutrality with the economically, socially and politically diverse 'grass-roots coalition of more than 700 groups, 5,000 bloggers and 750,000 Americans who ha[d]rallied in support of Net Neutrality at http://www.savetheinternet. com/', remarking in the process that 'coalitions of such breadth, depth and purpose [were] rare in contemporary politics' (Lessig and McChesney 2006).

The response to the public consultation on the new rules, through the above expressions of public support for Net Neutrality mobilised by Free Press and allied groups in the form of public lobbying of congressional offices, public rallies, and public reply comments to the FCC, appeared highly influential. At the very least, it played a significant role in the FCC's subsequent decision to revert to its former position by, on 26 February 2015, ruling in favour of Net Neutrality by taking the highly important decision to re-classify broadband access as a telecommunications service, thereby making Title II (common carrier) provisions of the 1934 Communications Act applicable to ISPs.

As might be expected, all this activity was also accompanied by an intense battle of political lobbying by proponents and opponents of Net Neutrality within the communications industries. The broadband industry (comprised of telecommunications and cable companies), broadly supported by US Republicans, was opposed to Net Neutrality obligations arguing that it amounted to an unwelcome burden on business. Internet libertarian activists, in a classic 'bootlegger/Baptist' alliance with high-tech companies like Google, argued strongly in favour of Net Neutrality.[1] The former viewed it as a basic principle of Internet freedom, the latter argued that it is a vital incentive to technical innovation and new entry to the Internet marketplace. Corporations on either side of the argument have devoted large sums to lobbying Congress. The pro Net Neutrality coalition was supported by Democrats and, possibly crucially, by former President Barak Obama, who, in November 2014, had himself intervened by publicly calling for the FCC to reclassify the Internet as a common carrier utility. The two Republican FCC commissioners, Ajit Pai and

Michael O'Reilly, voted against the FCC's 2015 rules, but were outvoted by the three FCC Democrats. Ironically, FCC chairman, Tom Wheeler, was a former telecommunications lobbyist. The Net Neutrality provisions, importantly covering both cable and mobile broadband, provided the FCC with the authority to challenge unforeseen barriers to Net Neutrality that ISPs might create as the Internet develops (Rushe 2015). However, the story of Net Neutrality in the USA took another dramatic twist in December 2017. Now chaired by arch Net Neutrality opponent, Ajit Pai, the FCC voted to dismantle the 2015 provisions. The change would in theory allow ISPs to discriminate between content carried across their networks, though the extent to which they will do this in practice, when and against whom, is very much an open question. As might be expected, the lead up to the vote excited unprecedented public interest, with as many as 22 million prior comments having been submitted to the FCC. At the time of writing, it has been suggested that the FCC is likely to face legal and Congressional challenges to its decision (Rushe and Gambino 2017). The debate on Net Neutrality in the US is, therefore, likely to remain a highly active and controversial one for the foreseeable future.

NET NEUTRALITY AND THE EUROPEAN UNION

In Europe, by contrast, the Net Neutrality debate has been considerably more low key in nature, though no less important. In essence, it has been framed by the fact that due to the European Union's policies for liberalising telecommunications markets, there has developed much more competition in Internet access, and market failure concerns were assumed to have been addressed by the EU's Regulatory Framework for Electronic Communications (EURFEC).[2] In contrast to the US, where 'policy has emphasised facilities-based competition and largely abandoned efforts to force owners of infrastructure to share with rivals', unbundling policies in the EURFEC have ensured that 'such provisions exist in Europe, so there are more alternatives to network neutrality policies' (Peha, Lehr and Wilkie 2007: 712). As Cave and Crocioni (2007) note, although three quarters of EU households are passed by at most one wire, normally that of the telecommunications incumbent, thanks to the unbundling policy customers have access to a variety of suppliers. European policy makers have thus framed Net Neutrality squarely within the neo-liberal telecommunications project whose underpinning assumption is that the existence of market competition and consumer choice would deliver Net

Neutrality. Quite simply put, in this rather narrow vision of Net Neutrality, if consumers are unhappy with their Internet service it has been assumed that they can and will switch ISPs with ease. By contrast, in Europe at the national level, a number of recent legislative developments have aimed to address Net Neutrality directly. In the Netherlands, the first neutrality law in the EU prohibited ISPs from throttling and filtering the connections of customers and provided strict guidelines on what constituted unacceptable traffic management, where using filtering software as a surveillance tool (including DPI) without the consent of the user or the serving of a valid legal warrant was deemed unacceptable (MacDonald, Cannella and Ben-Avie 2013). The UK, rather differently, opted for a self-regulatory approach through a code of practice, which emphasised transparency, something which has to be regarded as a major leap of faith in the high stakes Internet industry. Norway has adopted co-regulatory provisions[3] through its 'Guidelines for Internet Neutrality', though, like the UK, these do not have formal legal status and lack the teeth of sanctions.

In the EU, as a result of the 2009 iteration of the EUFREC, transparency is mandatory and all EU Member States must also adhere to the European Convention on Human Rights (Brown and Marsden 2013). Accordingly, the EUFREC gives national regulatory authorities (NRAs) the objective and power to monitor telecom operators' traffic management practices and the possibility of imposing a minimum level of service, if necessary. The EURFEC bears directly upon the issue of Net Neutrality in a number of ways. First, the framework covers the regulation of all electronic communications infrastructures across the EU and thus the development and guaranteeing of competitive market behaviour and provision is a key concern of the EU. Article 8 of the Framework Directive charges NRAs with the task of facilitating users to 'access and distribute information or run applications and services of their choice' (European Commission 2009b: Article 8(4)). Regulators must also ensure that the integrity and security of public communications networks are maintained, in particular to allow interoperability and end-to-end connectivity. It is also the obligation of regulators to take a long-term view of the development of communications networks to deliver the most efficacious technical and commercial environments. Article 21 of the EU's Universal Service Directive requires that consumers be informed fully of any restrictions on access to or use of services and any traffic management measures utilised by a service provider and their potential effects on service quality (European Parliament and Council 2009b: Article 21). The directive also makes provision for the right of consumers to switch between providers and allows NRAs to set minimum quality of service parameters for network transmission services. The EU framework also contains key directives on data protection (European Parliament and Council 1995) and privacy (European Parliament and Council 2001a) whose provisions are relevant to any traffic management or blocking activity that might infringe an individual's right to protection of data and privacy. The EU's essential facilities doctrine refers to network infrastructure that could not be reasonably be replicated by a competitor because of economic cost non-viability. Monopoly network operators in these circumstances may not restrict access to competitors and must offer network access to competitors on Fair and Reasonable and Non-Discriminatory (FRAND) terms.

As far back as 2006, the European Parliament threatened to de-rail the process of revision of the EUFREC going on at the time until concessions were offered to it related to Net Neutrality. The European Commission duly published a *Declaration on Net Neutrality* which became an appendix of the 2009 Better Regulation Directive (European Parliament and Council 2009a) which was followed by a consultation in 2010. Brown and Marsden (2013) note that the consultation produced around 300 submissions, which showed a split between the communications industry, which advocated intervention, and users, which were broadly against. Subsequent hearings by the European Parliament and the Commission were, in their view, industry dominated. Marsden (2010) argues that a narrow network economics approach has tended to be adopted by NRAs within the EU.

In April 2011, the European Commission issued a key policy communication on Net Neutrality in the light of the 2010 consultation. It acknowledged that the debate tended to centre on the nature and extent of traffic management by broadband infrastructure providers and network operators, with particular emphasis on the degree to which blocking and degradation of traffic was occurring in any particular instance and the reasoning behind this. As might be expected, the Commission placed particular emphasis on the role which effectively functioning competition would play in delivering a neutral environment for online services. Highlighted here was the provision of full information to consumers, the ability to churn readily between service providers and the availability of an acceptable number of alternative service providers for consumers to choose from. Fundamentally, the Commission argued that 'the significance of the types of problems arising in the Net Neutrality debate is therefore correlated to the degree of competition existing in the market' (European Commission 2011: 4) providing a clear illustration of the policy straitjacket that over-adherence to a neo-liberal approach creates. The Commission placed emphasis on regulatory measures in the

EUFREC to ensure wholesale access for competitors to incumbent networks as well as spectrum allocation using market parameters. Alongside the regulatory framework, EU competition law was available to deal with problems arising from market dominance. The Commission noted with satisfaction the fact that in the EU Internet access was not subject to specific regulation given the breadth and variety of service provision. Revisions to EUFREC delivered light touch regulatory provisions related to Net Neutrality, such as Article 5 of the Access Directive and Article 22 of the Universal Service Directive.

In the EU framework, Member States can act against direct and indirect attempts to discriminate against content, which applies equally to all ISPs regardless of their market position (Brown and Marsden 2013). The European Commission's Declaration on Net Neutrality noted the importance of Net Neutrality as a 'policy objective and regulatory principle' as well as the agreement among Member States to promote transparency and the prevention of traffic slowing and degradation. The Commission committed to monitor Member States' performance in these respects and to report on them in its annual implementation reports on the EUFREC. It also indicated that it would commit to monitor the impact of developments in technology and the market on Net Neutrality in the EU and resolved to use its competition law powers as necessary to deal with anti-competitive practices that might be deemed to be infringing Net Neutrality.

The Commission has also addressed the issue of traffic management and Net Neutrality, acknowledging the existence of a debate on the extent to which this should be allowed to occur, and in what form. It reported that its consultation had provided a broad indication that there was acceptance of the utility – and even the necessity – of some kind of data traffic management in the interests of network and services efficacy. The Commission concluded that across the EU 'there was broad consensus that operators and ISPs should be allowed to determine their own business models and commercial arrangements' (European Commission 2011: 7) as long as they stayed within the law. Giving a flavour of the evolutionary and somewhat tentative nature of much of the debate on Net Neutrality, the Commission indicated that it would essentially maintain a watching brief in respect of traffic management in conjunction with the work of Body of European Regulators in Electronic Communication (BEREC). Arguably, traffic management can be reasonably deployed for tasks such as blocking spam, viruses and denial of service attacks, to minimise problems of congestion by treating the same type of traffic equally (though not different types of traffic). However according to MacDonald, Cannella and Ben-Avie (2013: 50), 'allowing ISPs to offer guaranteed quality of service exclusively to one or more applications within a class of applications ... should be prohibited'. In a similar vein, the Commission made its position clear that the provision of full and accurate information to consumers was a key aspect of Net Neutrality. Here, it specifically referred to the high-profile issue of discrepancy between published and actual download speeds encountered by consumers. It pointed towards the role that regulation at the national level and EU level, the latter through the offices of BEREC, should play in the future assurance of appropriate quality of service provision, all achievable under the aegis of Article 22 of the Universal Service Directive.

This tentative and rather narrow approach taken to Net Neutrality was also, perhaps more understandably, reflected in the work of BEREC. After its creation in 2010, BEREC's initial focus centred on Article 5 of the EUFREC's Access Directive as well as the dispute settlements procedure highlighted in Article 20 of the Framework Directive in the revised EUFREC. Initial work also focused on service provider transparency obligations and traffic management techniques related to Articles 20–21 of the Universal Service Directive, as well as a new power created as a result of revisions to the EUFREC in 2009, expressed in Article 22 of the revised Universal Services Directive (now known as the Citizen's Rights Directive (CRD)). This gave the Commission the power to take necessary action to prevent reductions of service quality to users. In an important policy statement on competition issues in the debate on Net Neutrality, BEREC referred to the idea of the 'best effort' Internet. This is based on a long-standing goal of advocates of Net Neutrality that service providers treat all Internet traffic on the same terms irrespective of its content, application, service, device, sender and receiver (BEREC 2012a: 4). BEREC noted clear trends away from this approach in respect of a number of key practices, such as premium priced access offers, blocking or thwarting the development of new services on the Internet by technical means, collusion between content and applications providers vertically integrated with ISPs to block new applications and services entrants (so-called 'walled garden' approaches), and collusion through bilateral agreements between ISPs and content and applications providers to ensure prioritisation of the latter's content over other content and applications providers (BEREC 2012a).

Very importantly, BEREC noted that whilst a strict definition of Net Neutrality might focus on the degree to which identical treatment of content might be pursued in regulatory terms into the future, it was also the case that deviations from it could 'cause concern for competition and society ... [where] ... NRAs will need to consider a wider set of principles and regulatory objectives' (BEREC 2012a: 4–5). However, more surprisingly, BEREC cited the EU's Framework Directive (recital 5) to point to the connections between Net Neutrality and fundamental matters of communications regulation such as media pluralism, cultural diversity and protection of consumer rights (BEREC 2012a: 5).

In 2011, BEREC adopted a Framework Report and, in 2012, a further set of guidelines on the matter. The core of the 2012 report focused on the effects on users of ISPs employing 'discrimination practices' in markets for networks, content, applications and services. BEREC noted three specific types of practice: Voice Over Internet Protocol blocking in mobile environments; Peer2Peer blocking on fixed broadband networks; and differential practices in the carriage of traffic from content and applications providers in respect of quality and/or price. BEREC made the important point that there is evidence that Internet growth rates and costs per unit of capacity provision are declining, thereby casting doubt on the argument that discrimination must occur between users to ensure the provision of highly bandwidth consumptive applications (BEREC 2012b: 61). A key finding concerned the potential negative consequences of vertical integration for Net Neutrality, particularly in the areas of VoIP services, which might be stifled by ISPs to reduce threats to their traditional fixed or mobile communications services. Where no vertical integration exists, ISPs may still differentiate between content and applications to increase revenue streams or to manage data traffic more effectively. In this case, BEREC argued that restrictions were justifiable if 'done in a non-discriminatory basis [sic]' (BEREC 2012b: 9).

BEREC made some important recommendations in respect of restricting the behaviour of so-called end-user connectivity providers (ECPs) if found to be behaving in a non-neutral fashion. First, BEREC noted the capacity of NRAs to take regulatory action to prevent the growth of significant market power (SMP). Articulating a key baseline principle, it stated unequivocally that 'any measure aimed to forbid an anti-competitive practice would be a second best compared with a scenario where the market develops in an effectively competitive manner' (BEREC 2012b: 9). BEREC noted that in a competitively functioning market where 'competitors identify that such applications are valuable for end-users, there would be an opportunity to gain market share by eliminating all restrictions imposed by the competitors' (BEREC 2012b: 63). This places a great deal of faith in the ability to determine what an effectively functioning market is and to ensure that it is created. It also assumes that competitors would behave differently to secure revenue rather than similarly. Theoretically, firms, in a not especially crowded marketplace, could follow suit, thereby further restricting the market.

In an effort to ensure regulatory balance, BEREC addressed the issue of using network management strategies albeit in a non-discriminatory fashion. It was acknowledged that fair traffic management could be beneficial if the market was competitively ordered, since cost savings generated might be passed on to consumers – this, again, is a significant assumption not least since BEREC acknowledged that congestion 'has some hidden costs that are difficult to measure' (BEREC 2012b: 64).

BEREC also argued, quite optimistically, for the influence of consumer power in preventing problems of Net Neutrality. Here, the importance of having transparent information available to consumers, as well as the facility to switch readily between service providers was emphasised. BEREC did note the problematic nature of enforcing these but it is nevertheless a heroic assumption even to moot the possibility of this kind of consumer sovereignty in as technically complex a market as Internet services provision. It also made reference to the use by regulators of Quality of Service (QoS) guidelines, a set of which it produced for Net Neutrality, in 2012. This followed on from its Framework for Quality of Service in the scope of Net Neutrality (BEREC 2011). The key legal foundations for QoS parameters to be applied to Net Neutrality are found in Article 22(3) of the Universal Service Directive (European Parliament and Council 2002c) and the Citizens' Rights Directive (European Parliament and Council 2004a). The idea of QoS was nevertheless put forward with caution. BEREC urged Member State NRAs to consider the use of such tools only where there was patent failure of 'traditional competition tools, the enhanced transparency requirements and other relevant tools of the regulatory framework' (BEREC 2012b: 3).

BEREC's guidelines also suggested a range of criteria of assessment to allow NRAs to determine what might be a reasonable regulatory practice. It highlighted two kinds of service degradation: first Internet access service as a whole and, second, that related to individual applications using the access service. A key question for NRAs would be the degree to which so-called specialised services were prioritised over access services. The second case would involve analysing cases of traffic differentiation, such as VoIP blocking, P2P throttling and traffic prioritisation from certain content and application providers (BEREC 2012b: 4). In the first case, monitoring could involve actions such as measuring actual versus advertised download and upload speeds; timing parameters (latency, jitter), network congestion, performance compared to specialised services, and quality perceptions of end users. It is important to note that in line with its raison d'être, BEREC advocated the development of a common EU wide approach to the treatment of quality of service and Net Neutrality. In respect of the second category, BEREC advocated focus on activity occurring within the Internet access service provided. This requires consideration of traffic management practices adopted by ISPs. BEREC also argued that focus should be trained on network security (measures to prevent and monitor unauthorised access, misuse, modification, or denial of networks and network accessible resources) and integrity (measures to maintain or restore the level of performance during network failures and mitigation or prevention of network failures). If any EU NRA decided to impose quality of service measures, it was required to inform the European Commission and BEREC (BEREC 2012b: 7).

BEREC (2012b) made what could in the future turn out to be a key touchstone reference allowing more expansive and progressive future regulatory policies for Net Neutrality. Specifically, in the relation to the debate on the degree to which the EUFREC allows regulators to take action in respect of communications content, BEREC quoted the Framework directive to the effect that 'separation between the regulation of transmission and the regulation of content does not prejudice the taking into account of the links existing between them, in particular in order to guarantee media pluralism, cultural diversity and consumer protection' (European Parliament and Council 2002a: recital 6). In the EU, the must carry regime might be usefully applied to the online environment to ensure that essential public services are provided appropriately (i.e. that they are accessible and then receivable at a reasonable speed) (Musiani and Loeblich 2016).

In 2013, the European Commission released an important proposal for a Regulation on the single market in electronic communication, part of which addressed Net Neutrality. However, the content of the proposal was ambiguous, if not contradictory, in nature. Whilst Article 23 prohibited access providers from blocking, slowing down and discriminating against specific services, content or applications, at the same time access providers would be sanctioned to enter agreements with large content providers that could prioritise content. Access providers could impose data caps in contracts and grant priority to their own services, like Deutsche Telekom did with its T-Entertain service (MacDonald, Cannella and Ben-Avie 2013: 53).

The politics of this regulation internally in the Commission, illustrate its controversial nature. A leaked internal document highlighted concerns from European Commission Directorates General Justice, Enterprise and Industry and EU Commissioners as an internal body (EDRi 2013). The European Parliament moved to urge for strengthening of Net Neutrality definitions and provisions in the Regulation's first reading in April 2014. However, in November 2014, leaked proposals by Italy, then holding the

EU presidency, caused concern, reportedly not least on the part of Andrus Ansip, the then European Commission Vice President for the development of the EU digital single market because they were interpreted as being intended to give network providers the ability to offer different speeds to different sites (Hern 2014). Baker (2014) noted that within the Council of Ministers there was support for pursuing a 'principles-based' approach that would not introduce 'obstacles to innovation and investment' and would be 'more future proof' than the definitions laid out by the European Parliament.

Then, on 4 March 2015, by that stage under the aegis of the Latvian presidency, the European Council of telecom ministers published its position on the development of revisions to the EU telecommunications package which were taking place at the time. Whilst the Council claimed the draft regulation set out to ensure that companies providing Internet access treated traffic in a non-discriminatory manner, critics judged that it would open the door to a two-speed Internet. Andrus Ansip expressed strong criticism of the Member States for their (inter alia) watering down of Net Neutrality provisions by declaring: 'We need to make sure that the internet is not splintered apart by different rules … This is why we need common rules for Net Neutrality. Then, we need an open Internet for consumers. No blocking or throttling' (Keating 2015).[4] The telecommunications package subsequently became the subject of a second three-way negotiation between the Council and the European Parliament, with the Commission trying to preserve some of the spirit of its initial proposal, almost certainly with the Parliament's support (Keating 2015). In October 2015, the European Parliament voted in favour of new Net Neutrality regulations (European Parliament and Council 2015). Despite the EU arguing that the Regulation would deliver Net Neutrality across the EU, concern has been expressed that whilst the rules militate against the practices of blocking and throttling, they leave open the possibility of differential access arrangements to the Internet through provision for paid priority (Marsden and Belli 2015).

A core issue is the future regulatory interpretation of the legislation. Building on its earlier work, in 2016, after a consultation which elicited as many as 481,547 responses, BEREC issued a series of guidelines on the Regulation. Those related to Article 3, whose aim is to protect open access to the Internet, illustrate the complexity of the Net Neutrality issue. Particularly controversial are so-called zero rating practices where 'an ISP applies a price of zero to the data traffic associated with a particular application or category of applications' (BEREC 2016: 11). Here, BEREC was clear that providing a 'zero rating offer where all applications are blocked (or slowed down) once the [customer's] data cap is reached except for the zero rated application(s)' would contravene Article 3. However, potentially open to interpretation was its assertion that applying zero rating to certain applications within a category creates an economic incentive for customers to use such applications and is thus 'more likely' to infringe end users rights, either in essence or materially, compared to when zero rating 'is applied to an entire category of applications' (ibid). Elsewhere, BEREC endorsed the permissibility of specialised services (such as higher than normal quality voice services, online health services and machine-to-machine communications). It noted that these 'may be provided for optimisation reasons in order to meet requirements for a specific level of quality' (BEREC 2016: 19) if there is sufficient network capacity and without degradation of the 'general quality of internet access services for end-users' (BEREC 2016: 27).

CONCLUSION: DEVELOPING NET NEUTRALITY IN A CONVERGING MEDIA ENVIRONMENT

Increasingly, IP networks, both fixed and mobile, are the vectors for consumption of audiovisual content. In an era of media convergence, the debate on Net Neutrality provides a gateway to protect – and even extend – a number of public interest regulatory values and practices into the consumption of online services and associated content.

Beyond network structure, ownership and associated economic behaviour Net Neutrality (or a diminished degree or lack thereof) has a range of fundamental ramifications for individual rights and the public interest. Key issues are freedom of expression and the unfettered and undistorted availability and transmission of digital products and services, as well as the ideas and communications which arise from their content and potential engagement with it (Belli 2013). In fact, Belli (2013: 18) argues that 'it seems essential that, in order to prevent violations of the European Convention on Human Rights, blocking and filtering be utilised exclusively to fulfil pressing social needs and be strictly defined by a precise legal or regulatory framework'. The FCC Open Internet Advisory Committee also noted that a specialised service should not inhibit a consumer's ability to access the Internet and has indicated that should such a situation be seen to exist, it would merit investigation and possible regulatory action.

From a perspective of universal service on the Internet, key Net Neutrality issues concern the availability or otherwise of minimum standards of service to all users, as well as access to (in theory all) the communicative resources of the Internet. Fulfilment of these goals would move strongly in the direction of preventing both the blocking of access, restriction – and by contrast prioritisation – of content and the fencing off of communication into so-called 'walled gardens'. It is important to note that free expression enables social, cultural, economic and political rights. Users should have the right in theory to make choices about what legally allowable information to seek, receive and impart and from which sources and through which services (McDiarmid and Shears 2013: 29). Musiani and Loeblich (2013: 36) argue that the 'discussion on Net Neutrality touches fundamental values (public interest, freedom of expression, freedom of the media, and free flow of information) that communications policy authorities in liberal democracies frequently appeal to in order to legitimize their interventions in media systems'. However, as Chapter 8 of this volume argues, these issues have not taken centre stage in media policy considerations of the future of the Internet to this point.

The debate between protagonists and opponents of strong Net Neutrality law has tended to pit a diverse 'bootlegger/Baptist' alliance[5] of 'open Internet' enthusiasts, radical media reform groups like Free Press, critical political economy of communications scholars and new Internet entrepreneurs, including corporate giants like Google, against established policy networks of communication regulators (at least in Europe), telecoms operators, and free market economists, suspicious of the consumer harm inflicted by over-regulation. As with the issue of copyright, most critical scholars, at least in the US, side with the former alliance: it is seen as a mark of 'right thinking'. However, as with the issue of copyright (see Chapter 5 of this volume), there is also room for a more nuanced perspective. Indeed, the Net Neutrality issue shares key dilemmas with the copyright issue. In an important sense, Net Neutrality could be seen as yet another instance of disruption by new technology of the business model of a set of legacy industries, which in an era of media convergence, raises key, often uncomfortable, questions about the future of media content, because it goes far beyond telecom and cable operators. As Clark (2007) has explained:

> The current structure of the television industry is much more vertically integrated and 'closed' than the Internet, and this structure has sustained a well-understood value chain with stable opportunities to profit from content delivery, advertising, and so on. In contrast, the open design of the Internet limits the ability to profit from the delivery of content, and as the Internet more and more becomes the platform to deliver video, the threat to revenues is obvious … Any attempt to intervene in this battle must first take a realistic view of what the options are for the stakeholders and how the

battle might play out, and must not adopt an over-simple or over-constraining view of what it means to be 'open'. (Clark 2007: 701)

Clark (2007: 704) some time ago made the pertinent observation that the 'fear of gorillas' in the US has focused on phone and cable companies and their monopoly or near monopoly provision of Internet access, while rather neglecting the market power of powerful Internet players. The US concern over lack of competition in the Internet access market is, of course, understandable. The relative lack of critical concern about the so-called Internet platform and service giants is, arguably less so. In Europe, by contrast, with a more nuanced, less polarised though regulatory framework dominated, perspective on Net Neutrality, there is far more concern about these players.

Economists Cave and Crocioni (2007: 669–79), have argued some time ago that the EURFEC's provision for *ex ante* regulatory intervention in specified network or service markets where there is dominance or so-called 'significant market power', notably the aforementioned local loop unbundling, combined with European competition law, 'is adequate to deal with actual or prospective abuses of market power, whereas a blanket prohibition of the kind envisaged by proponents of Net Neutrality is likely in some cases to harm consumers' interests'. This argument is clearly predicated on the assumption of a competitive broadband market in Europe, which as seen is not the case in the US, and on effective (though not excessive) regulation and competition policy. It does not, however, address broader media policy issues associated with media convergence, notably content (see Chapter 8 this volume).

Generally, opponents of Net Neutrality legislation favour a market-based approach which they see as being better for both consumers and (at least some) ISPs. First, the exponential growth in online traffic means that web traffic management is likely to become increasingly necessary, and – as noted already – network management techniques are already well implemented by ISPs, if they own networks, not least to deliver a consistent quality of service to consumers. Second, according to a recent Reuters report[6] the chief executives of Europe's two largest telecommunications carriers, Vodafone and Deutsche Telekom, have highlighted the need in the future to give special treatment to data for certain specialised new services like connected cars and smart electricity meters to ensure that they function properly. Industry expects such specialised services to generate billions in new revenue, and any new rules on Net Neutrality should arguably make provision for such services. Third, large telecoms companies are expected to invest in upgrading infrastructure (notably, fixed fibre networks and 5G mobile infrastructure) to next-generation capacities (see Chapter 2 of this volume). In Europe, they have even been specifically tasked with this objective in the EU's *Digital Agenda*. There is an argument that they should be able to finance this investment in part through an element of commercial management of Internet traffic on their networks.

In respect of converging media environments, the debate on Net Neutrality has led some in the telecommunications business and other commentators to focus on potential infringements of neutrality in the broader Internet service context. Here, concern has been expressed about the activities of vendors of mobile phone operating systems. This market is dominated by Apple (with the iPhone operating system), Google (with its Android operating system) and Microsoft (with its Windows operating system). Each of these systems is incompatible by design and allows the players in question to maximise Internet revenues through prioritising their own websites and applications (O'Brien 2013). Through the use of walled gardens, the major players involved 'manifest, more and more frequently their intention to become broad social platforms underpinning the entire spectrum of web services using these strategies' (Musiani and Loeblich 2013: 40). This tendency is underpinned by examples of content providers increasingly drawing on applications controlled by social network providers (McDiarmid and Shears 2013: 41), most notably Facebook. Both in the fixed link and mobile communications environments, the debate on Net Neutrality is set to rage on as media convergence proceeds.

NOTES

1. Baptist/bootlegger alliance is a concept associated with the regulatory economist Bruce Yandle and refers to cases where regulations are supported by groups with very different attitudes to the regulation's goals. 'Baptists' point to the moral high ground and the laudable public benefits promised by a desired regulation, whereas 'Bootleggers' expect to profit from the same regulations. See https://www.perc.org/articles/bootleggers-and-baptists-retrospect (accessed 23 March 2018).
2. For a detailed study of the establishment of the EURFEC see Humphreys and Simpson (2005).
3. Co-regulation refers to a situation where a range of different parties – for example, private sector players, civil society interests, professional bodies, and public regulatory authorities – contribute to the regulatory process, not necessarily in equal measure.
4. He also criticised their weakening of the proposal for phasing out mobile roaming charges. See Keating (2015).
5. See note 1 above.
6. See: http://www.reuters.com/article/2015/03/02/us-telecom-mwc-deutsche-telekom-idUSKBN0LY1UV20150302 (accessed 19 March 2015).

PART III

Governing content in converging media
environments

5. Copyright in an era of media convergence

Another burning issue raised by digital convergence and the Internet is the future of copyright. Some leading scholars have focused on the exploitation of copyright law by powerful corporate copyright holders to maximise their control of the media industries and their profits. They argue that, against its original purpose, copyright law has limited creativity and innovation. They maintain that the digital era, which has brought a new technological freedom to manipulate media content, provides a welcome opportunity to adopt a new 'creative commons' approach that considerably diminishes the alleged excessive control exercised by the corporate copyright holders. While clearly serious consideration has to be given to such a critique, this chapter argues that that perspective risks underestimating the fact that the Internet has encouraged copyright 'piracy' (illegal) and 'free-riding' (legal, see Levine 2011) on a scale that threatens to undermine the business models that underpin the creative industries, from the recorded music business through to traditional newspapers. At stake are not simply the control and profits of corporate media owners, but the livelihoods of those working in the creative industries and, indeed, the very market that sustains the provision of journalism and cultural content conceived of as public goods as well as commodities. This chapter argues that the vulnerability of a functioning market for the provision of cultural public goods is in danger of being overlooked by those who approach copyright in too critical terms. It also reveals a shade of difference in approach between the USA and Europe, certain European countries – notably France and the UK, but also Germany and Spain – seeming more disposed than the USA to defend their culture industries, and the EU considering making technology companies responsible for what their users upload.

The economic rationale for protection of intellectual property rights (IPRs) has always been to safeguard invention and creation by compensating the creator and innovator. IP protection should render it difficult for low-cost imitators to reproduce and distribute reproductions of the creation or innovation, thereby limiting the return on the costly investment of the creator or innovator. The problem surrounding digital convergence, from the perspective of IP rights holders, is quite simply that digitalisation has made it relatively easy and inexpensive to copy.

In some respects, IPR protection has been steadily strengthened. From a historical perspective it has moved from the national, through the international, up to the global level. The 1787 US Constitution stated explicitly that copyright licences could not be permanent and their initial length was limited to 14 years. Thomas Jefferson's reluctance was founded on his view of it as a government-created monopoly that was effectively a tax on knowledge. In the early republic, it had to be specifically applied for. With the development of new media and powerful media corporations in the twentieth century, Congress was persuaded to make copyright automatic, and its length and scope was 'dramatically' extended to many decades and, lately, even over 100 years (McChesney 2013: 79). The 1976 Copyright Act extended copyright terms to the life of the author plus 50 years, or 75 years for a work of corporate authorship, such as movies. The 1998 Copyright Extension Act extended these terms to life of the author plus 70 years and for works of corporate authorship to 95 years.

International accords were first struck in the shape of the 1883 Paris Convention for the Protection of Industrial Property, covering patents, trademarks and industrial designs, and the 1886 Berne Convention for copyright. In 1893 the Bureaux Internationaux Réunis pour la Protection de la Propriété Intellectuelle (BIRPI – in English, the United International Bureaux for the Protection of Intellectual Property) was established to administer the Paris and Berne Conventions. The BIRPI was succeeded in 1967 by the creation of the World Intellectual Property Organization (WIPO), which was formerly established by the 1970 Convention Establishing the World Intellectual Property Organization, which entered into force on 26 April 1970. According to its Article 3 WIPO's purpose was to promote the protection of intellectual property throughout the world. In 1996, WIPO enacted a World Copyright Treaty (WCT) as a special agreement under the Berne Convention dealing with the protection of works and the rights of their authors in the digital environment and requiring countries to enact anti-circumvention measures, such as those introduced in the United States by the 1998 Digital Millennium Copyright Act (see below).

THE ARGUMENT ABOUT COPYRIGHT AND THE CULTURE INDUSTRIES IN THE DIGITAL ERA

Copyright has always been controversial. Leading US communications scholar and media reformer, Robert McChesney, pointing to the corporations' twentieth-century success in having Congress repeatedly extend 'dramatically' the length and scope of copyright in the USA, argues that it has become

> frequently unconnected to the actual persons who created the original work [and become] something entirely different: it protects corporate monopoly rights over culture and provides much of the profit to media conglomerates. *They could not exist without it.* Copyright has become a major policy encouraging the wholesale privatization of our common culture. It is also an enormous annual indirect subsidy for copyright holders, mostly large media corporations, by the public, in the form of severely inflated prices both for consumers and for cultural producers wishing access to material. (McChesney 2013: 80)

McChesney (2013: 92) suggests that the debate over copyright in the US Congress has been 'entirely one-sided'. His explanation is the unequal balance of lobbying power in the US political economy:

> The powerful media corporations and interests that own most copyrights spent $1.3 billion on public relations and lobbying Congress on this issue from 1998 to 2010. The proponents of protecting the public domain and fair use – librarians, educators, and the like – have spent $1 million in the same period. That is a 1,300-to-1 ratio. (McChesney 2013: 92)

McChesney's figures here come from Lawrence Lessig's (2011: 59) book *Republic, Lost: How Money Corrupts Congress*, in which Lessig admits that these are 'rough estimates ... yet even if even ... wrong by a couple of orders of magnitude, the point is still correct ... the anti-reformers outspend the pro-reformers by at least a factor of ten'. Lessig became a leading figure in the US copyright debate with publication of his earlier book *Free Culture: The Nature and Future of Creativity*. In it Lessig, then Professor at Stanford Law School and founder of the Stanford Center for Internet and Society,[1] developed the argument that in the Internet era copyright law's role is 'less and less to support creativity, and more and more to protect certain industries against competition' (Lessig 2004: 19). In this manifesto for the creation of a 'creative commons', in which 'reasonable copyright law' would facilitate rather than obstruct the creative building upon other people's work, the culprits are 'Big Media', the copyright holders (Lessig 2004: 282 ff.).

Against this, another leading US protagonist in the copyright debate, a former editor of *Billboard, Wired* and the *New Yorker*, Robert Levine (2011: 81), argues that while

> [m]ost observers see technology companies as the underdogs in their disputes with major [music] labels and movie studios … In reality, the big money comes from telecom companies: Disney spent about $3.8 million on lobbying in 2010, while Verizon spent $16.8 million, according to the Center for Responsive Politics. Although Google is still a newcomer to Washington, it spent $5.2 million in 2010, compared with $5.5 million from the RIAA[2] and $1.7 million from the MPAA[3].

The argument as it relates to the relationship between the culture industries and the Internet within the developed world is certainly widely seen as a conflict between corporate industries and a new 'digital generation', 'a kind of David and Goliath battle, between a tough, well financed industry and its lawyers versus millions of anonymous individual consumers' (Horten 2012: 28). To a certain extent this is true. The issue that has attracted much popular attention has been controversy over the extensive illegal downloading of copyright material, largely music and films, through peer-to-peer file sharing by young people who do not regard this activity as being at all illegitimate. Peer-to-peer file-sharing, facilitated by websites like Napster in the 1990s and, later, the more decentralised (and therefore less vulnerable to control) operations like Kazaa and The Pirate Bay, quickly became a vehicle for copyright 'piracy' on a massive scale (Goldsmith and Wu 2006). The robust responses of those corporate industries affected and the draconian legal remedies that they sought and often achieved (leading inter alia to Napster's and The Pirate Bay's demise) have led to much concern on the part of civil liberties organisations and freedom of speech activists.

Yet, as Horten (2012) explains, it should not be overlooked that struggles over intellectual property rights have always also been about struggles between rival corporate interests, typically between those whose business models have been threatened by the development of new technologies and those who developed the new technologies and/or sought to exploit the new market opportunities that these technologies provided; until now, the matter has customarily been resolved by the development of new business models. The gramophone, for instance, was once seen by sheet music publishers as a technology that could be used to steal their (and composers') copyright, but of course it soon led to a new industry for distributing music; later, the development of the videocassette recorder was initially viewed by Hollywood studios as a device enabling mass infringement of copyright, leading to an ultimately unsuccessful law suit by Universal and Disney against the electronics company Sony for 'contributory infringement' (the famous Betamax case). Ironically, the VCR and its successor the DVD recorder were to become the source of the film industries' greatest profits, though the studios had failed to anticipate this. The arrival of the Internet has seen vigorous demands for copyright protection from legacy industries, setting them against other corporate interests that have gained from the new scope offered by the Internet for cheaply distributing information (for detail on the role of copyright in the historical struggle for the control of markets, see Horten 2012: 13–27).

The question is: can the copyright industries whose business models are currently adversely affected by Internet piracy confidently be expected to develop new business models? In other words, can the free market be left to take care of the copyright matters? Or is the transformation of the market environment brought about by the Internet so revolutionary that without public policy intervention to reinforce existing or produce appropriate new IPR protections, the copyright industries may well not survive, with dire implications for all who depend upon them for their livelihood and ultimately for all those who enjoy their products?

Aligned on one side are those arguing that IP protection has been strengthened inordinately in the digital era. One interesting line of argument points to the 'copyright wars' that have occurred over an overblown punitive regime that have resulted from 'moral panics' in a context of outdated business models and the failed economic ideology of free market fundamentalism; in these 'copyright wars' opponents have been demonised at the expense of rational policy discussion and all too often poor policy decisions have followed (Patry 2009). Much concern has centred on concerns about surveillance, privacy, civil liberties and censorship surrounding the measures used to implement the new IP protections demanded by copyright industries and mandated by policy makers. A related line of argument holds that 'intellectual property is a method of commodification … enabl[ing] the expansion of capitalism into areas hitherto regarded as a realm outside direct exchange relations', just like the enclosures of common land that occurred in the UK between the fourteenth and eighteenth centuries, and that 'the information society is a new period of enclosure' by commodifying the products of intellectual effort and creation (May 2000: 43). Similarly, in his *Politics of Media Policy* (Freedman 2008), in a chapter on 'The Politics of Digital', Des Freedman provides an interesting perspective on the 'problem' of piracy and the action taken by governments and industry in the US and UK who have sought to tackle it, thus far with rather little evident success. Freedman's stress is not on the damage done by copyright theft, rather it is on dangers of current policies actually increasing corporate control of intellectual property. Thus, Freedman characterises copyright as 'a deliberate strategy to impose market disciplines on cultural goods in order that they may be exchanged for a price' (Freedman 2008: 188). Such a perspective sees the new copyright enforcement measures as an intrusion on the 'digital commons'. The promise of the Internet, to liberate creativity from the realm of property relations, according to the dictum 'information wants to be free',[4] is thus frustrated.

On the other side, a compelling case has been made that since the onset of the online era traditional media have been 'looted', legally, by new digital organisations – the likes of Huffington Post, Google and YouTube – that have pandered to the new consumer expectations that online content should be free. It is important therefore to realise that piracy is far from being the only serious copyright issue. According to Levine (2011: 4), '[t]he real conflict line is between the media companies that fund much of the entertainment we read, see, and hear and the technology firms that want to distribute their content – legally or otherwise'. Levine (2011: 6) explains: 'Most online companies that have built businesses based on giving away information or entertainment aren't funding the content they're distributing ... In economic terms, these businesses are getting a "free ride", profiting from the work of others.' Pointing to the threat posed to the future sustainability of the culture industries, Levine (2011: 8) asks: 'Why would anyone invest in a staff of reporters and editors when it's so much cheaper to aggregate the work of others? How can any company compete with a rival that offers its products but bears none of the expenses?'

In 2009 Rupert Murdoch reportedly called Google and other search engines 'content kleptomaniacs' (*The Economist* 2012). This became a recurrent theme in the press. In September 2015 Robert Thomson, the chief executive of News Corporation, reportedly accused Google in a letter to the European Commission of stifling competition and facilitating piracy (Dean 2015; *The Sunday Times* 2015). With Google the main problem has been seen to be its arguably parasitical impact on the wider media industry. In 2015 a *Times* editorial put the issue of Google's news service thus:

> [it] aggregates stories from news providers and places on its website the headlines and opening sentences ... That is anti-competitive. It damages the organisations that do the task of researching, reporting and providing news by stealing their content. Google claims to be directing consumers to the websites of news organisations but that is an extraordinary defence ... The potential for Google to sell advertising alongside these snippets ... threatens to damage the revenues of the sites on which it preys ... Alongside the

existing charges against Google, the regulator should lay down a simple requirement: if it wants to publish other people's material, it should pay for it. (*The Times* 2015)

This demand has been echoed by other leading figures of the press. In 2017 Ashley Highfield, chief executive of Johnston press, another of the UK's largest newspaper groups, reportedly suggested that Google and Facebook should be required to pay a levy for the news they took from other media outlets unless they agreed to share more of the ad revenue (Frean 2017). Most recently, Tina Brown, former editor of *Vanity Fair* and *The New Yorker*, reportedly echoed these voices: accusing web giants like Facebook and Google, of having 'stolen so much that it's high time they gave some of it back', she suggested in the form of a 'vast philanthropy fund for journalism' (Moore 2017a).

The criticism could be levelled against other online news aggregators, but Google's significance is obviously of a particularly high order. For years large newspaper publishers like the German publishing giant Axel Springer and Rupert Murdoch's global News Corporation have wanted to charge news aggregators like Google for the use of their content. In Germany and in Spain laws have indeed been enacted to cover this 'neighbouring rights', otherwise known as 'ancillary copyright', issue. However, in those two specific cases, the legislation backfired. In the German case, Google News simply reduced its use of such content, which clearly impacted negatively on the newspapers' profile. When publishers took Google to the German competition authority, the latter ruled that the search engine's news aggregator service was under no obligation to reproduce excerpts from the newspapers if it did not wish so to do. Google even shut down Google News in Spain (Meyer 2016). Despite these policy failures, publishers have maintained their pressure, lobbying the EU for action, apparently with some effect as will be seen later in this chapter.

So far, however, copyright protection has focused on tackling illegal piracy rather than legal free-riding. Copyright law has extended generous protection to the technology firms that distribute Internet content. According to 'safe harbour' provisions in both the USA and Europe, ISPs and other Internet intermediaries, like Google and its subsidiary You-Tube, have been treated as platforms rather than as publishers and given only limited responsibility for the content they distribute, as will be explained. Therefore, much of what follows on copyright protection concentrates on approaches to combatting illegal copyright infringement. Legal 'free riding' has been allowed to continue to flourish, though as will be explained there has been some indication of movement towards extending the main burden of copyright enforcement, beyond monitoring by the copyright holders (backed up by the threat of legal action in the courts), to the placing of more direct responsibility on the part of the technology companies. As will be seen, the technology companies themselves have made some voluntary movement in this direction (most likely in response to the pressure), and in Europe there is a debate about making them take more responsibility for material that their users upload and discussion about treating Internet intermediaries as publishers rather than as platforms and conduits of information.

ENFORCEMENT

There are essentially two contrasting perspectives on the impact of the Internet on the ability actually to enforce copyright. On one side, there are those that point to the way the Internet, not least because it is a global medium, is not amenable to easy regulation and that the curtailing of illegal peer-to-peer file-sharing, like many other abuses, is effectively beyond practical policing. On the other side, there are those who draw attention to the way that the Internet is most certainly controllable through such techniques as software controls and network filtering (Goldsmith and Wu 2006). Indeed, it has been argued that network filtering has actually enhanced the ability to enforce copyright and that it has presented to copyright holders new scope to profit from their 'property' (Lessig 2004, 2006).

The customary approach in the modern era to dealing with copyright infringement had always been litigation by the rights holder in the courts. Thus, in the USA between 2003 and 2005 the music recording industry had issued nearly 12,000 law suits seeking punitive damages, mostly not against corporate infringers but against individual file-sharers, many of whom were college students and teenagers (Goldsmith and Wu 2006: 114–15). However, the sheer scale of copyright infringement in the Internet era inevitably led rights holders to demand new measures. In response, policy makers designed a 'strikes' approach, whereby after a series of warnings the broadband provider has a responsibility to suspend offending Internet user accounts. Unsurprisingly, the telecoms industry vigorously opposed this obligation, as did a coalition of citizen rights and Internet freedom campaign groups. Such an approach has been tried in the USA. In Europe, France was the first country to develop such a law; Britain followed suit shortly after. The EU attempted to adopt the same approach in its Telecoms Package, but the issue became embroiled in an inter-institutional conflict between the European Parliament (EP), which was sensitive to the aforementioned citizen rights and Internet freedom lobbies, and the Council of Ministers (CoM), through which France and Britain sought to defend their graduated response laws (Horten 2012). The following explores developments in the USA, EU, France and the UK.

THE USA CASE

In the USA, policy makers readily responded to the complaints about Internet piracy from the film, music and media industries. As Freedman (2008: 189) notes, 'a raft of copyright laws has been proposed since the mid-1990s, some of them falling at the last hurdle but many of them still making it on to the statute books'. The most important was the 1998 Digital Millennium Copyright Act (DMCA) which implemented two 1996 treaties of the WIPO, respectively its Copyright Treaty (WCT) and its Performances and Phonograms Treaty (WPPT). According to Freedman (2008: 189) this Act created a particularly strong legislative frame-work in the USA for rights holders against piracy by 'leverag[ing] existing property rights into the online world', making it illegal to circumvent copy-protection technology, criminalising the use or distribution of technologies designed to circumvent copy-prevention measures (such as encryption), and generally increasing the penalties for copyright infringements on the Internet. The DMCA's anti-circumvention provision was seen by opponents, including many in the academic community and some creative elements, as an affront to free speech and an obstacle to digital copying for fair use and innovation.

In fact, a strong case can be made that the 'Act, a compromise between media conglomerates on the one hand and telecom companies on the other, devastated the first group and helped the second soar' (Levine 2011: 15). This was because, in response to pressure from the second group, the Act also gave 'safe harbour' to ISPs and online companies like YouTube protecting them from secondary liability for acts of copyright infringement on the part of their subscribers.[5] Under these rules, the website management has to be unaware of the infringement, should not be profiting from it, and should remove copyright infringing material once notified about it. YouTube users are shown a message asking them to respect copyright, but copyright is not checked before posting; it is left to copyright holders to issue takedown notices. The Act allows technology companies like YouTube to benefit from uploaded copyrighted material so long as they take it down it when asked to do so. Not only did this allow sites like YouTube to grow on the back of content they did not pay for, it also absolved Internet access providers from responsibility to prevent or discourage copyright infringement by their subscribers. The onus to protect copyright was placed firmly on creators and content providers, who would have to assume the expensive and often impractical burden of monitoring the Internet for unauthorised copies of their work. As will be seen, this state of affairs contrasts somewhat with the thrust of policy – if not the current state of legislation – being developed in the EU and certain Member States, and casts the US legislative framework for protecting rights holders against piracy in a rather weaker light.

Subsequent attempts to tighten up copyright law stalled against substantial opposition. A Combating Online Infringement and Counterfeits Act (COICA), introduced by Vermont Democrat Senator Patrick Leahy, failed to pass in 2010. With hardly any delay, two more ('rewrite') congressional bills were introduced: a Senate bill for a Protect Intellectual Property Act (PIPA), again by Vermont Democrat Senator Patrick Leahy, this time with eleven bi-partisan co-sponsors, in May 2011; and a House of Representatives bill for a Stop Online Piracy Act (SOPA) by Texan Republican Representative Lamar S. Smith in October 2011.

> The bills would not only crack down on websites that give net users a platform to share movies and music illegally, but US-based internet service providers, payment processors and advertisers would be outlawed from doing business with sites that infringe copyright, even if they are based abroad where copyright laws are laxer. (Aaronovitch 2012)

The bills were supported by the corporate copyright holders and groups representing artists and workers in the creative industries. Opponents of the bills claimed that they represented the slippery slope towards censorship of the Net. One novel protest, to raise awareness of Congress's threat to 'the free and open Internet', was a one-day blackout of Wikipedia. On the other side of the argument, this action could be taken as a sign that the 'online world [was]n't serious' about the unscrupulous online theft and 'fencing' (in the case of file sharing sites) of copyrighted material (Aaronovitch 2012). Facing the copyright holders was a loose 'bootlegger/Baptist' coalition co-aligning the free-Internet and fair use activists alongside powerful corporate players like Google (owner of YouTube). McChesney (2013: 92–3) observes how over the 2011–12 debate over SOPA, 'Google joined an avalanche of public opposition to battle the unprecedented extension of government policing power desired by the copyright lobby ... [and in] that rare instance, the pro-copyright forces were unable to get their dream legislation passed.' Given the scale of dissent, the drafting of both bills was postponed in January 2012; thus, the US legislators appeared unable or unwilling to act. A factor undoubtedly working in favour of the new technology companies was politicians' concern not to damage the new technology industry, which was such an American success story. Notably, President Obama was reportedly supportive of Google (Yang and Easton 2009).

Characteristically for the US policy style, the most important development in the USA arose through the combination of a famous lawsuit and market forces. In March 2007, the giant content company Viacom filed a US$1 billion lawsuit against Google and YouTube (acquired by Google for $1.65 billion in 2006) for alleged copyright infringement for allowing users to upload and view copyrighted material owned by Viacom. In 2010 Google won a motion seeking dismissal of the case on the grounds that the DMCA's safe harbour provisions shielded it from the Viacom's claim of copyright infringement. The issue went through a lengthy appeal process, during the course of which the original finding in favour of YouTube was confirmed in 2013, but before the appeals process was finally concluded, the parties settled the original action out of court in 2014, reportedly without any damages. The settlement would appear to have been largely reached by dint of Google's peace-making with the large content companies on the one hand by introducing a 'ContentID' filter system that allowed copyright owners easily to track their material and on the other hand by striking a series of content licensing agreements with content providers. In the words of a Columbia Law School IP specialist: 'Content providers and service providers [w]ere finding it more constructive to work together rather than litigate ... Content providers need a Google to filter material, and Google needs content to attract people to its websites' (Stempel 2014). How positively this legal/market-led settlement between giant corporations' augurs for the likes of independent creators and media companies with less resources at their disposal for negotiating favourable licensing deals and for policing the Internet remains to be seen.

A voluntary 'six strikes' anti-piracy scheme was agreed in 2013 between content bodies such as the Recording Industry Association of America (RIAA) and the Motion Picture Association of America (MPAA) and several of the US's large ISPs. Administered by a collaborative body established by the content community and ISPs, called the Center for Copyright Information,[6] a 'copyright alert system' (Cas) issued warning notices to subscribers whose accounts had been used for copyright infringement. On their fifth or sixth notice, they faced punishment, to be determined by the ISP, which could involve termination of their account. However, after four years the programme was terminated, with little information about how successful it had been being available (BBC 2017).

THE EUROPEAN UNION

In contrast to the USA, from its inception the European Union (EU) lacked a direct legislative competence in the area of copyright. The EU's competence derived solely from European Community Treaty provisions enabling the Community to harmonise its Member State laws with regard to the freedom of movement of goods and services within the internal market (Articles 45, 47[2] and 55). Unless copyright distorted the internal market, it remained an exclusive matter for the Member States. Harmonisation of copyright was further complicated by the different copyright legal traditions in Europe, most notably the difference between on the one hand continental countries' copyright statutes belonging to the realm of civil law *droit d'auteur*, which gave stronger protection to the creator's rights and were distinct from economic rights – so that even if the latter had been conferred on a third party the former still retained 'moral rights' – and on the other hand, the UK's more utilitarian Common Law approach with the emphasis on economic right protection, like the USA. Even among continental civil law countries copyright varied according to their distinct cultural, legal and social differences. Yet the EU's internal market interest in harmonising copyright law becomes obvious given the scale of the European copyright industry, which one estimate based on 2000 data put at more than €1.2 trillion, producing value added of €450 billion, representing more than 5.3 per cent of the total value added of the Member States. In pushing for harmonisation, the European Commission itself stressed the prime imperatives of market liberalisation and catering to technological developments (Montagnini and Borghi 2008: 214–15; Littoz-Monnet 2007: 122–5).

Accordingly, the EU embarked on a series of 'piecemeal' (Hugenholtz et al. 2006: 16 cited in Montagnini and Borghi 2008: 229) harmonisation measures, designed primarily to facilitate the single market, the first batch of which were based on a European Commission Green Paper on Copyright and the Challenge of Technology (European Commission 1988). There followed in quick succession a Council Directive (European Council 1991) on software protection; a Directive (European Council 1992) on rental and lending rights; from a communications policy perspective, there followed a highly significant Directive (European Council 1993a) on satellite and cable retransmission, designed to remove barriers to trans-frontier broadcasting and facilitating the key regulatory (many say 'deregulatory') principle of licensing of satellite broadcasters in the 'country of origin'; then, a Directive (European Council 1993b) harmonising copyright terms (length of protection) on 70 years *post mortem autoris*; followed by a Directive for the copyright protection of databases (European Council 1996); and lastly a Directive designed to eliminate disparities resulting from different national treatment of resale rights (European Council 2001). All of these Directives could be seen as a 'first generation' of instruments addressing issues raised in the EC's 1988 Green Paper largely concerning barriers to liberalising the EU market. However, a number of issues were not addressed, among them the issue of moral rights, viewed differently between common law and civil law jurisdictions, and the issue of piracy (Montagnini and Borghi 2008: 217–19).

There followed a 'second generation' of Directives, both of which were similarly enacted under the EU's single market provisions, that adopted a 'more horizontal' approach (Montagnini and Borghi 2008: 226–7), namely blanket Directives on: (1) copyright protection in the Information Society (European Parliament and Council 2001b), applicable to all copyright subject matters and right holders; and (2) enforcement (European Parliament and Council 2004b), which covered a wide range of intellectual rights and requires the Member States to apply effective, dissuasive and proportionate remedies and penalties against those engaged in counterfeiting and piracy (Article 3 [2]). The 'Copyright Directive' is the EU's equivalent of the USA's DMCA, implementing the WIPO Copyright Treaty (see above). Like the DMCA, the EU Directive established protection for digital rights management (DRM), systems and prohibited activities promoting their circumvention such as the sale of technical devices and services that are designed primarily to facilitate circumvention. The enforcement Directive essentially harmonised rules on standing (*locus standi*), evidence, interlocutory measures, seizure and injunctions, damages and costs, and judicial publication. These twin Directives were designed to increase significantly the level of copyright protection for works in the digital environment which clearly represented a major challenge, given the ease with which copyrighted products could be copied, transformed and otherwise exploited without the knowledge of the copyright holder.

However, the EU's approach to copyright in the Information Society has come in for considerable criticism. First, it has been criticised on the grounds that there are still considerable harmonisation shortfalls, and that fragmentation, and inconsistency of approaches among the Member States endures. Thus, Montagnini and Borghi (2008: 237) conclude that 'territoriality of copyright has only partially been overcome, and there is a long way to go to establish a Community copyright regime'. Unlike the DMCA, the EU Copyright Directive required subsequent transposition into the national laws of its Member States and consequently the latter could exercise considerable discretion in their detailed interpretation of the Directive's requirements.[7] The EU's enforcement Directive provided for a minimum measure of harmonisation of the remedies available in the civil courts, but not criminal offenses, and it allowed Member States considerable scope for varying approaches and measures for dealing with online copyright infringement. A European Commission staff working document documented the extent of this variety (see: European Commission 2010c; also see Foundation for Information Policy Research n.d.).[8]

Another criticism is more normative and relates to the previously discussed arguments about the merits and demerits of copyright in the digital era. It is that the stronger protection afforded to copyright in the Information Society has, to the extent is has occurred in practice, actually been dysfunctional. Montagnini and Borghi (2008: 238) observe that it has, albeit unintentionally, had 'detrimental effects on market competition and cultural diversity'. This reflects, they argue, a 'paradigm shift' towards an economic-utilitarian rationale which has progressively empowered rights holders but failed adequately to embrace the ways that digital technologies might benefit both the economy and culture under a copyright regime that takes relatively less account of the rights holders' interests in maximising their protection and opens up relatively more scope for peer production, distribution and sharing, and for consumers' access to the products of creativity and knowledge. According to Littoz-Monnet (2007), who shares this concern about the arguably deleterious impact on culture, intentionality is not to be disregarded. Rather than represent an albeit only half successful attempt to introduce a harmonised higher level of protection for copyrighted works at risk in the digital environment, in Littoz-Monnet's view this second phase of the EU's harmonisation of copyright legislation should be seen as the political triumph of a coalition of economically liberal actors in achieving a pro-competition free-market scenario, favoured by Northern European Member States and consumer groups, over a more cultural policy sensitive *dirigiste* approach, led by the French and rights holders groups. In this, Littoz-Monnet (2007) focuses her critique on the aforementioned differences of copyright tradition between the French inspired *droit d'auteur* approach to copyright, which she sees as being more sensitive to cultural policy, and the 'Anglo-Saxon' economic utilitarianism approach. Others, however, have regarded this distinction as not being so significant. Thus Horten (2012: 42) observes, 'for the purposes of copyright enforcement, there appears to be little difference in the

practical effect, since both traditions protect an economic right to control
the use of creative works ... and provide for legal sanctions against
unauthorised copying and infringement'. Littoz-Monnet, on the other
hand, stresses the paradigm shift from what she terms a more *dirigiste*
French-favoured approach to the more free-market oriented Anglo-Saxon
approach, with the Commission decisively promoting the latter.

Littoz-Monnet shows how from its 1988 Green Paper on, the Commission used its single market and competition authority powers backed by
judgments of the European Court of Justice to promote *negative integration*, market-making liberalisation, rather than *positive integration*, catering to more positive values like culture. Moreover, she wryly observes,
'[d]eveloping an "economic" approach towards copyright issues was ...
an efficient way to circumvent the absence of EU competence in this
field' (Littoz-Monnet 2007: 124). She notes how cultural interest groups
'reacted with dismay to EU policy developments in the field of copyright' and how '[n]ational governments, and most notably France, where
policy preferences in the cultural sector are the most salient, felt that their
policy traditions were being questioned by the approach developed by
EU institutions' (Littoz-Monnet 2007: 128). Littoz-Monnet paints a
detailed picture of a confrontation of two advocacy coalitions (Sabatier
1998) in a struggle over the emerging EU approach to copyright. On the
one side, were aligned France, southern European countries, Germany,
and cultural interest groups; on the other, the European Court of Justice,
the 'economic' DGs of the European Commission (notably the competition and internal market DGs) and private economic actors. In the
1980s, there were victories for the cultural coalition, which ensured a
significant degree of protection for European *auteurs*; this manifested
itself, for instance, in adoption of a 70-year term of copyright protection
favoured in France and Germany rather than 50 years that most Member
States had allowed. Another victory was the granting to an *auteur* the
exclusive right to authorise or prohibit the broadcasting of his or her
works by satellite and the rejection of compulsory licensing scheme
favoured by the Commission (Littoz-Monnet 2007: 130). However, with
the Information Society agenda 'new policy actors entered the game' and
this created 'a constellation of interests less favourable to *dirigiste*
solutions'. Network operators successfully formed a liberal coalition –
even winning over consumer groups – to promote the cause of market
liberalisation over the concerns of the cultural coalition. Littoz-Monnet
evaluates the resultant 2001 Copyright Directive as formulating 'only
vague guidelines meant to create a "minimal" level of harmonisation'
which promoted market liberalisation but hardly any positive integration
(Littoz-Monnet 2007: 142–9).

Over the enforcement issue, the network operators' interests clearly prevailed over the rights of the rights holder, whether the latter is defined as intellectual creator *(auteur)* according to the civil law *droits d'auteur* model or as simple economic owner according to the Anglo-Saxon common law model. The EU's E-commerce Directive, Article 12 (European Parliament and Council 2000), provided IAPs with a 'safe harbour', immunising them from liability for damages and penalties from acting as a 'mere conduit' for information,[9] which it is claimed has disinclined them from actually taking action against alleged unlawful use of their Internet services for breach of copyright (Barron 2011: 317). The Directive grants a somewhat less substantial 'safe harbour' to ISPs that host or store content, to the extent that in this case hosts are required to take action against unlawful users of their services once they are informed that such activity is occurring. Nonetheless, just like the USA's DMCA, this leaves the burden on copyright holders to identify unlawful usage and inform the ISP. Furthermore, the ISP is only required to remove, or disable access to, the allegedly offending material (Barron 2011: 317–18). Article 15 of the E-commerce Directive prohibits any general obligation on ISPs to monitor the information they transmit or store. These 'safe harbours' have had to be transposed into Member State legislation.

However, the issue of the indirect liability of network operators and ISPs has been kept on the EU policy agenda by energetic lobbying from creative industry organisations and also by national copyright protection initiatives of prominent EU Member States, notably France and the UK. An opportunity presented itself in the form of the EU's review during 2000–2009 of its 2002 Electronic Communications Regulatory Framework (ECRF, for a detailed study of which see Humphreys and Simpson 2005), which sought to create a common set of regulations for the digitally converging electronic communications sector across all 27 EU Member States.[10] The review addressed a package of directives addressing the regulation of service provision, access, interconnection, users' contractual rights and users' privacy, and it included an EC Regulation creating a new European regulatory body, BEREC. The review was needed to address the growth of broadband Internet. Though not direct subjects of the ECRF, copyright and net neutrality (see Chapter 4) quickly became the most controversial issues. A very detailed study by Horten (2012) of the attempt to strengthen copyright enforcement through amendment to the European telecoms regime shows how the creative industries lobbies, which spanned a range of actors from the Motion Picture Association of America (MPAA) through to European film directors' and producers' organisations and the European Grouping of Societies of Authors and Composers (GESAC), sought to have graduated response measures being proposed in France and the UK (see below) included as amendments[11] to the EU regulatory framework for electronic communications. Essentially, this would require network operators and Internet Service Providers to enforce copyright according to a 'three strikes' regime. Horten describes in detail the political conflict over the issue which involved three readings in the European Parliament, and the drafting of a compromise amendment finally acceptable to the three key European institutions, namely the Parliament, Commission and Council. In fact, the 'compromise' Amendment 138 amounted to a defeat for the creative industries lobby to the extent that it stated that any restrictions on the end-users' access to electronic communications services and applications can only be imposed if they are proportionate and respectful of the right to privacy and judicial review was guaranteed.

However, the matter did not rest there. In 2010 the European Commission (2010c) produced a report, reviewing the effectiveness of the EU's 2004 Directive on Intellectual Property Rights. It described the scale of online piracy in Europe as 'alarming' and posited the need for stronger laws, possibly enlisting Internet Service Providers (ISPs) in the service of enforcement (Levine 2011: 194). As will be discussed below, such measures have been contemplated, and to an extent implemented, in certain Member States. In December 2013, the EU opened a public consultation on modernising and reforming EU copyright law,[12] which closed in March 2014. The European Commission's Report on the Responses to the Public Consultation on the Review of the EU Copyright Rules by the EC Directorate General Internal Market and Services Directorate D – Intellectual Property D1 – Copyright, was duly published in July 2014.[13] The consultation covered a wide range of copyright issues, which cannot be explored in this chapter.

As regards the key issue under consideration here, namely the need for measures to improve copyright enforcement (see section VII 'Respect for Rights', pp. 83–89 of the report), it was predictable that end-users (58 per cent of the survey's total respondents) were generally not in favour of the EU strengthening enforcement, including for infringements committed for a commercial purpose, an issue raised by the consultation. Notably, consumers did not favour any requirement for ISPs to monitor content and to police infringement and they were against involvement of ISPs in the detection and enforcement of intellectual property rights through the use of filtering technologies. Many felt that the balance was already tilted too far in favour of rights holders. Equally predictably, many authors and performers (constituting 24.8 per cent of the survey's total respondents), concerned about commercial and non-commercial infringement alike, complained that the existing enforcement regime was failing to provide adequate protection in the modern digital environment. Among publishers, producers and broadcasters (8.6 per cent of respondents), while some considered the existing system satisfactory, others called for stronger enforcement against infringement with commercial purpose, and some even called for criminal remedies. Broadcasters in particular were more concerned about whether infringement was commercially damaging than whether it was committed on a commercial scale. Many publishers expressed concern about the insufficient involvement of ISPs and other intermediaries in preventing copyright infringement, some pointing to the fact that servicing illegal content was actually financially attractive for many intermediaries. ISPs, search engines, social networks and cloud services, it was argued, should bear liability. The argument was made by some respondents that the safe harbour provided for by the EU's E-commerce Directive was no longer justified, there being many means by which ISPs and other intermediaries might be involved more in policing copyright infringement. There were some calls for legislation to force intermediaries to cooperate, rather than relying on industry-driven initiatives. As regards the balance between IPR and fundamental rights (notably, privacy) protection, it was widely felt by this group (publishers, producers and broadcasters) that IPR protection should trump the need to protect to the anonymity of copyright infringers and the protection by ISPs of the privacy of personal data. Of course, most representatives of intermediaries (mainly ISPs) felt that the existing liability regime for intermediaries provided by the EU's E-commerce Directive was adequate and did not see any need for more efficient enforcement of copyright infringement committed with a commercial purpose. Internet intermediaries also felt that the existing framework provided suitable balance between copyright protection and fundamental rights. Member States were divided on the need for revision of the legislative framework, the report not identifying the individual positions of the eleven Member States which responded.[14]

The possibility that Internet intermediaries might be made liable in EU copyright legislation took a step closer with the drafting of a new EU copyright Directive. As usual it was concern about the digital internal market that drove the matter forward. The EU's Digital Single Market Strategy, adopted in May 2015, had identified the need 'to reduce the differences between national copyright regimes and allow for wider online access to works by users across the EU' (COM [2015] 192 final). So, in December 2015, the European Commission issued a Communication *Towards a Modern, More European Copyright Framework* (COM

[2015] 626), which outlined a long-term vision to modernise EU copy-right rules. This was duly followed in September 2016 by a *Proposal for a Directive of the European Parliament and of the Council on Copyright in the Digital Single Market* (COM [2016] 593 final). The reform aimed to facilitate more cross-border access to content online; to open up wider opportunities for the use of copyrighted materials in education, research and cultural heritage; and to improve the functioning of the copyright marketplace.

The two measures which generated most controversy as the draft passed through the committees of the European Parliament at the time of writing (2017) were: (1) the draft's suggestion of a new special copyright for press publishers, an ancillary right, providing them with rights for the digital use of their press publications, effectively enabling them to charge licensing fees for links to their content, a measure long sought for by newspaper publishers like News International (now called News UK) that would affect search engines like Google (Article 11); and (2) a radical shift towards holding Internet intermediaries like Google and its sub-sidiary YouTube responsible for what their users upload, for instance through introducing measures such as the intermediaries' effective, appropriate and proportionate use of content recognition technologies to police copyright infringement (Article 13). However, according to one informed source, '[p]ositions on the new draft European Union Copyright Directive [lay] so far apart in the European Parliament that compromise ... seem[ed] nearly impossible' at least in the near future (Ermert 2017).

The proposed draft directive had been referred to the EP's legal affairs committee and its rapporteur, Therese Comodini Cachia (EPP, Malta), had finalised a report in March 2017 which opposed the creation of a new right for publishers for the digital use of their content, stating the need for an 'open Internet' and proposing instead that publishers should be given more powers to help them legally to enforce their copyright claims more effectively (European Parliament Committee on Legal Affairs 2017, Amendment 18). However, her successor, Axel Voss (EPP) reportedly immediately distanced himself from this position and sup-ported the Commission's proposals, and while the EP's culture commit-tee reportedly supported the Commission's proposal, the internal market and consumer protection committee was divided, as were the EP parties (Reda 2017a). The other EU legislative body that would have to enact the directive, the Council, was reported, on the basis of leaked information, to be similarly divided on the issue (Reda 2017b).

FRANCE

There have been notable attempts at national level to counteract piracy. As noted above, French copyright law is based on the *droit d'auteur*, which dates back to a law enacted in January 1791 following the French Revolution. As the words imply, it ties copyright particularly closely to the author or creator of the work, who is deemed to exercise a moral right (*droit moral*) as well as a property right (*droit patrimonial*), and therefore copyright scholars distinguish it from Anglo-Saxon (UK and US) legal tradition. This might help explain particularly strong concern in France for copyright protection, alongside traditional French protectionism of its culture industries (for a study of this applied to the audiovisual sector see Gibbons and Humphreys 2012). Unsurprisingly, therefore, in the digital era, French governments have sought, with ample determination, to introduce tough anti-Internet-piracy measures, though so far these have all met with little practical success.

The European Union Copyright Directive (EUCD) was implemented in France by the conservative (UMP) government under President Jacques Chirac, in the form of the so-called 'DADVSI law' of June 2006 (*Loi Sur le Droit d'Auteur et les Droits Voisins dans la Société de l'Information*, the law on author's rights and related rights in the information society). The law brought French copyright law in line with the 2001 EU Directive (European Parliament and Council 2001b), which in turn implemented the 1996 WIPO copyright treaty (see above). The DADVSI law criminalised peer-to-peer exchanges of copyrighted works and the circumvention of digital rights management protection measures. It introduced fines of between €38 and €150 per illegal download. The bill provoked a huge amount of popular resistance, backed by a variety of organisations, including Internet user groups and advocates of free software. Parliamentarians were inundated with letters and emails. Some parliamentarians argued that it would effectively criminalise millions of Internet users, especially the young. In July 2006 the Conseil Constitutionel, France's version of a constitutional court, struck down the provision for fining P2P file sharers on the grounds that it would offend against the principle of equality to introduce a copyright penal regime specifically for P2P infractions (Horten 2012: 83; Conseil Constitutionel 2006).

President Nicolas Sarkozy, elected UMP President in May 2007, determined to press on with introducing a strict copyright protection regime. In September 2007 his government established a high-level commission of inquiry on the subject of copyright in the digital era, the 'Mission Olivennes', which duly reported in November 2007 (Mission

Olivennes 2007). The report highlighted the 'massive and diverse' scale of piracy, and citing a number of studies, drew attention to the 'specificity' of the French case. It explored a number of options and made a number of recommendations, among which was to put in place: 'a targeted policy of action, that is to say a warning mechanism and sanctions going as far as the suspension and termination of the subscription contract, this mechanism being applicable to all internet service providers. It may require the establishment of an independent authority' (Mission Olivennes 2007: 25).[15] This recommendation inspired the so-called 'Hadopi law' which was subsequently presented by the government to the French Senate (upper house) on 18 June 2008. In October 2008 the government, eager to see the issue progressed, placed the bill under a 'declaration of urgency' procedure, meaning that it should only require a single reading in each house of parliament, with disagreements between the two houses being quickly resolved by joint committee. The bill was adopted by the Senate in October 2008 and presented to the National Assembly (the Parliament's lower house) in March 2009, which adopted an amended version in April 2009. Accordingly, a joint committee was called into play. While the Senate immediately adopted the revised bill, it had to be presented a second time to the National Assembly because of a controversial mass abstention on the part of the Socialist Party (PS) which vigorously opposed the bill at every stage. Nonetheless, the bill was finally passed by the conservative UMP majorities in the French National Assembly on 12 May 2009 and in the Senate on 13 May 2009.

The law created a new government agency called the HADOPI (*Haute Autorité pour la Diffusion des Oeuvres et la Protection des droits sur Internet*, the High Authority for the Diffusion of Creative Works and Copyright Protection on the Internet), which would report to the French Ministry of Culture. This agency was empowered to apply a graduated response to complaints by rights holders about Internet piracy. The agency would employ a 'three strikes' enforcement procedure. Upon receipt of a complaint from a copyright holder, an email would be sent to the Internet access subscriber, derived from the IP address involved in the claim, specifying the time of the incident but no other detail (the claimant's identity is not revealed). Then, if after six months the copyright holder(s), the ISP or HADOPI suspected that a repeat offense had occurred, a certified letter would be sent to the Internet access subscriber with similar information to the original email. Finally, once an individual had been warned about a third online copyright infringement, he or she would enter a mechanism which would see them reported to a judge. After a hearing the judge would have the power to cut the individual off from the Internet and issue a range of other penalties, including fines. The ISP could be required to suspend Internet access for the Internet connection for a duration of between two months and one year; also, the Internet access subscriber would be blacklisted among other ISPs. However, the Socialists referred the bill to the Conseil Constitutionel,[16] which on 10 June declared that aspects of the Hadopi Law violated the 1789 Declaration of the Rights of Man and of the Citizen with regard to freedom of speech and the presumption of innocence. Finally, on 22 October 2009 the Conseil Constitutionel approved a revised version of the law approved by parliament in September 2009 (Assemblée Nationale 2009), which now contained a provision requiring judicial review before an individual's Internet access could be blocked. Despite the watering down, the measure was designed to be a tough and effective measure. However, this was not to be.

By 2010 the Hadopi had issued more than 100,000 warnings, leading the agency to be dubbed 'Big Brother' by its critics (Crisafis 2010). Unsurprisingly, the law was highly controversial. Opponents attacked it for being a draconian offense against civil liberties. As seen, the Left voted against it consistently during its parliamentary passage and tried to block it through recourse to the Conseil Constitutionel. The European Parliament even suggested that cutting off an individual's Internet access amounted to a breach of a fundamental right. Frozen by the scale of opposition and not least by the uncertainty on the EU front, the Hadopi law only ever disconnected a single individual's Internet access, and for a mere 15 days. In July 2013 a new government – coming into office in June 2012 after a general election the month after the presidential election of Socialist François Hollande – enacted a decree which overturned the disconnection sanction, leaving only in place a system of fines which would start by being relatively low (Ministère de la Culture et de la Communication 2013).

THE UNITED KINGDOM

The economically liberal UK with its economic-utilitarian approach to copyright has also been in the vanguard of European anti-piracy policy; a fact that is doubtless explained by the size and importance of its cultural industries, which are as economically weighty as those of France, considerably more so in the audio-visual production sector (for a comparison see Gibbons and Humphreys 2012). The United Kingdom quickly implemented the 2001 EU Directive on Copyright (European Parliament and Council 2001b) in the shape of its 2002 Copyright and

Trade Marks (Offences and Enforcement) Act, which amended existing provisions in the Copyright, Designs and Patents Act of 1988 and the Trade Marks Act of 1994. Significantly, the new Act increased the penalties for software piracy.

The New Labour governments between 1997 and 2010 displayed a growing awareness of the issue of copyright protection as a necessary ingredient of their globalisation and creative industries agendas. In December 2005 the (then) Chancellor of the Exchequer, Gordon Brown (Labour), commissioned Andrew Gowers, who between 2001 and November 2005 had been editor of the *Financial Times*, to head up an independent review of IP. The Review was published on 6 December 2006. While it contained a number of suggestions for more flexibility, it did stress the growing importance of copyright in the globalising, digital era. It opened its executive summary thus:

> Globalisation and technological advance are changing the shape of the world economy ... The UK's comparative advantage in the changing global economy is increasingly likely to come through high value added, knowledge intensive goods and services. The Intellectual Property (IP) system provides an essential framework both to promote and protect the innovation and creativity of industry and artists ... [However] while global and technical changes have given IP a greater prominence in developed economies, they have also brought challenges. Ideas are expensive to make, but cheap to copy. Ideas are becoming even cheaper to copy and distribute as digital technology and the Internet reduce the marginal cost of reproduction and distribution towards zero. As a result, the UK's music and film industries lose around twenty per cent of their annual turnover through pirated CDs and illegal online file sharing. (Gowers 2006: 3)

In April 2010 the government rushed to process New Labour's Digital Economy Act through Parliament before the upcoming general election, as a result of which it received only limited discussion. Both process and content of the Act were controversial. It placed an obligation on ISPs to notify subscribers of allegations of peer-to-peer file-sharing copyright infringements reported by the copyright holder. This would provide a body of evidence which copyright holders could then deploy in court against infringers. Further, the Act provided for the ISPs' deployment of technical measures against repeat infringers which ranged from limitation of the speed of the broadband connection, through restricting access to particular material online, to complete suspension (disconnection) of the service. The precise implementation details were left to the UK media and communications regulator Ofcom to work out. In June 2012 Ofcom duly produced a draft code which provided for a 'three strikes' policy for

illegal downloaders to come into effect in 2014. Web users would receive
three warning letters from the ISP after which their identity and
file-sharing history could be passed to copyright owners to support legal
action on piracy grounds (Sweeney 2012). However, in 2014 the
Conservative/Liberal Democrat government, elected in May 2010,
announced that it would not proceed any further with work on the Digital
Economy Act regime in favour of a turn towards a lighter touch 'industry
solution', which would be more streamlined, flexible and economical,
and less open to the legal challenge,[17] based on a voluntary agreement
that had meanwhile been reached between rights holders and ISPs.
Accordingly, warning letters would still be sent to alleged infringers on
the basis of evidence collected by the rights holders but this 'Creative
Content UK Alert Programme' was intended to be purely awareness
raising, and it dropped the more stringent legal and technical measures
envisaged in the DEA. ISPs would not be required to pass the details of
suspected infringers on to rights holders to enable them to pursue redress.

However, demand for stronger action has persisted. In 2013, the House
of Commons Culture, Media and Sport Committee 'firmly repudiate[d]
… laissez-faire attitudes towards copyright infringement', aiming this
particular barb at the copyright reform Open Rights Group, and the
committee noted the 'systematic failure to enforce the existing laws
effectively against rife online piracy'. The committee also 'strongly
condemn[ed] the failure of Google, notable among technology companies, to provide an adequate response to creative industry requests to
prevent its search engine directing consumers to copyright-infringing
websites'. The committee pointed out that 'Google co-operates with law
enforcement agencies to block child pornographic content from search
results and it has provided no coherent, responsible answer as to why it
cannot do the same for sites which blatantly, and illegally, offer pirated
content' (House of Commons Culture, Media and Sports Committee
2013: 3–4). By and large the committee did not see need for substantial
copyright reform but it did urge the government promptly to implement
the anti-piracy measures proposed in the 2010 Digital Economy Act and
it also contained the suggestion that the maximum penalty for copyright
theft be increased to ten years in prison (House of Commons Culture,
Media and Sports Committee 2013: 4). The latter suggestion was
subsequently enacted by the Conservative government's own Digital
Economy Act 2017. The most recent development is news that the
current Conservative Culture Secretary, Karen Bradley, 'is considering
changing the status of Google, Facebook and other internet companies
amid growing concerns about copyright infringement and the spread of

extremist material online'. Although she was reportedly 'wary of label-ling Internet companies publishers ... the government wanted to find a balance between harnessing the benefits of the web while making it safe for users and protecting intellectual property' (Ruddick 2017a). This followed closely upon an announcement by the chairperson of the UK media regulator, Patricia Hodgson, that she believed Internet businesses such as Google and Facebook were publishers, Ofcom having discussed Internet regulation at a recent strategy meeting (Ruddick 2017b).

CONCLUSION

Clearly, there remains a very uncomfortable tension between efficient copyright protection and fundamental rights protection in the digital era. This is manifest in the conflicting demands of those who stress the need for stronger enforcement measures, such as restricting Internet access for those guilty of copyright infringement, and those who cite Human Rights legislation in the belief that Internet access is now to be considered a basic human right. It pits those who would see a stronger involvement in policing – and indeed liability – for Internet intermediaries (ISPs, search engines like Google, video-sharing websites like YouTube) and those who, again citing Human Rights legislation, prioritise privacy, even if that means protecting the anonymity of copyright infringers. The out-come of the fierce struggle at EU level and in France over the 'three strikes' graduated response measures, which would make broadband providers cut off alleged copyright infringers' Internet access, bears testament to the strength of the fundamental rights opposition to stricter enforcement.

Public expectations that information should be free in the Internet era combined with the fact that digital technology facilitates extremely easy copying has led to such widespread unidentified infringement that copyright industries have come to focus less on pursuing private indi-vidual acts of piracy through the notice and take-down process and litigation and increasingly on expanding copyright law to recognise indirect commercial infringement by service providers, software provid-ers and websites that facilitate individual acts of copyright infringement. In particular, the European policy debate about reforming copyright law appears to have gained a degree of momentum from persistent demands for holding Internet intermediaries more to account for what their users upload. For their part, important measures have been taken by the likes of Google, YouTube and Microsoft to combat commercial copyright infringement as well as individual acts of piracy. According to Google's copyright section in its 2017 transparency report,[18] 1.11 million websites had been targeted with link removal requests on the grounds of copyright infringement. As noted above, in the USA the Google/YouTube versus Viacom affair culminated in a 'peace settlement' whereby Google introduced a 'ContentID' filter system helping copyright owners to track their material. Similar measures have been taken by Microsoft's Bing.[19] In the UK in 2017, a further landmark development occurred when Google and Microsoft (operator of the Bing search engine) entered into a voluntary agreement with copyright industries and the UK government to reduce the visibility of copyright infringing content (Titcombe 2017). However, according to a report by the *Times* technology correspondent (Bridge 2017a), despite this, Google's search engine continued to make it too easy to find piracy sites. Thus the issue persists.

A wider question is the issue of 'ancillary copyright', which in Europe has found a definite place on the policy agenda. The latest draft EU legislation contains the controversial suggestion of a new special copyright for press publishers, providing them with rights for the digital use of their content, a measure long sought for by newspaper publishers like News International. However, there have already been legislative attempts at this in Germany and Spain, which have failed, and the latest signs are that the European Parliament may only be prepared to go as far as giving publishers the power to sue Internet intermediaries that showcase their work without permission, which is rather less than the Commission was suggesting (Spillane 2017). Here again, part of the solution will likely depend on the willingness of the technology companies themselves voluntarily – albeit under the threat of possible regulation (mandating greater responsibility) or penalties (fines, taxation) – to move towards addressing the concerns of the copyright holders. And here again, Google has displayed a measure of willingness to lead the way. According to a recent report (Moore 2017b), Google has dropped its so-called 'first click free' policy to which many publishers, trying to make their business sustainable in the digital era through adopting paywall strategy, objected because the policy compelled them to offer for free three articles a day in order to feature high on Google's search listings. This, they complained, compelled them to give away too much content and impeded their ability to attract subscribers.

In October 2017, Google announced that it would change its policy by allowing the publishers themselves to determine how many articles they wanted to provide free. This was part of a package of measures that Google said it would introduce to help make life easier for news organisations in the digital era. At the time of concluding this book, Google was reported to have offered to share the advertising revenue it gained from new digital subscription tools which deployed its wealth of personal data, allowing it to target ads and largely explaining its dominance of digital advertising, to help news publishers find new and retain existing subscribers (Murgia 2017).

This chapter does not conclude that there is no case for reforming copyright law so that it operates in the digital era as originally intended, namely to promote creativity and innovation. Indeed, copyright reform might take a more permissive approach to personal, non-commercial file copying. It might significantly expand the parameters of fair use for creative purposes and be considerably more facilitative of the work of librarians, university researchers, and public service institutions like the BBC and the British Film Institute. In the digital era, a new approach might be adopted for content distributed through public-service platforms, towards the establishment of a 'creative commons'. Improvements might be made to the process of licensing and selling rights, particularly for small, low-value transactions, to facilitate the buying and selling of creative content. This might involve the establishment of a new public agency to mediate between those wanting to license music, film and other digital content, and rights owners, in order to 'streamline' the process. Such changes have been suggested by a 2011 report of a review commissioned for the UK government and headed by Ian Hargreaves, a former *Financial Times* journalist and current Professor of Digital Economy at Cardiff University (Hargreaves 2011; also see Hooper and Lynch 2012).

Moreover, the chapter certainly does not advocate the imposition of harsh sanctions on individuals, often young, unlucky to be identified as copyright infringers in a world where unidentified infringement is so widespread and where commercially motivated piracy websites are a far more worthy target of punitive measures. It also has to be taken into account that there exists some confusion about copyright law; many individual infringers may be unclear about the legal status of material posted and downloaded, or the legal status of their manner of usage of the material. Certainly, individuals' privacy and freedom of expression are important human rights that need to be balanced against the copyright holders' claims for more effective enforcement. The academic criticisms of copyright have some purchase. Some of the demand for stricter copyright enforcement may well have the flavour of special pleading by powerful creative industry elements and may not reflect the position of all elements of the industry, some of which have better adapted to the digital challenges. There may be scope for industry itself to do more to adapt to the new technologies. A case can be made for some rebalancing of the relationship between creators and authors on the one side and corporate rights owners on the other. Lastly, as these academic critics argue, it is certainly the case that monopolistic (or oligopolistic) control of rights presents as much a problem for media pluralism and diversity as any other choke point control over access and distribution of content. Dominant media corporations with extensive content rights erect market entry barriers for competitors, distort the market, and command higher prices for consumers (on media concentration see Chapter 6).

While the issue is clearly complex and there are no easy answers, the fact remains that the Internet has encouraged both copyright 'piracy' by individuals and piracy websites (illegal) and 'free-riding' (legal) by giant technology companies on a scale that, in Robert Levine's (2011) words, promises to 'destroy the culture business'. It can be plausibly argued that the 'free-riding' by giant technology companies has not yet been adequately addressed. As it is currently regulated, the Internet permits technology companies to offer substantial content at zero cost to themselves by allowing them to build their businesses with content copyrighted by others. A core argument of this book is that one of the most important media policy issues in the digital future, if not *the* most important, will be the production of sufficient quality content. If the latter becomes unprofitable because of legal free-riding, the amount of cultural content offered by the technology firms – which are intermediaries rather than content creators – will become increasingly impoverished. At stake are not just the profits of the media owners, but the livelihoods of all those working in the creative industries and the very market that sustains the provision of journalism and cultural content conceived of as public goods as well as commodities.

The chapter therefore concludes that those who, albeit from a progressive ideological and a critical intellectual perspective, have focused mainly on seeing copyright as excessively profiting corporate media producers ('Hollywood', 'News Corporation', and so on), should acknowledge at least that they find themselves in an uncomfortable 'Baptist/bootlegger' alliance with the giant technology corporations (Google/YouTube, and the like). However, as the chapter has indicated, the way forward is unclear. Like the Google/Viacom settlement and Google's more recent efforts to placate the publishers, it will almost certainly depend on more than regulation, but further regulatory steps will likely need to be taken to address a problem that threatens to lead to cultural impoverishment in the digital, online future. Without effective copyright protection it is quite simply difficult to see how in the long run the market for quality content will continue to function. One obvious way to address the problem would indeed be to establish some kind of 'philanthropy fund for journalism' (see p. 107 above), which could be funded by an industry levy on the ISPs and Internet intermediaries, a theme which will be taken up in Chapter 7.

NOTES

1. He is currently professor at Harvard Law School.
2. The Recording Industry Association of America.
3. The Motion Picture Association of America.
4. This was coined by the American Internet activist Stewart Brand at the first Hacker convention in 1984.
5. The DMCA did provide for a 'takedown notice', which required ISPs to act 'expeditiously' to take down unauthorised works when requested by copyright holders and it did provide for 'repeat' offenders to be cut off, but these elements of the Act 'were left vague' (Levine 2011: 29).
6. See http://www.copyrightinformation.org/ accessed 5 December 2017.
7. The Commission had to take European Court of Justice proceedings against six Member States for failure to transpose the Directive by the deadline of 22 December 2002 (Belgium, Finland, France, Spain, Sweden, United Kingdom).
8. Some Member States were late in transposing the Directive, and some failed to provide application reports in time for the production of the Commission's report, or else provided information of only a general nature.
9. So long as the ISP has not itself initiated the transmission or had any editorial part in the transmission.
10. The review consisted of a package of directives addressing the regulation of service provision, access, interconnection, users' contractual rights and users' privacy, and an EC regulation creating a new European regulatory body (BEREC).
11. These were amendments to the telecoms package's Authorisation Directive and its Universal Service Directive.
12. See http://ec.europa.eu/internal_market/consultations/2013/copyright-rules/index_en.htm. And for the consultation document http://ec.europa.eu/internal_market/consultations/2013/copyright-rules/docs/consultation-document_en.pdf accessed 21 March 2018.
13. Available at http://ec.europa.eu/internal_market/consultations/2013/copyright-rules/index_en.htm accessed 17 July 2017.
14. Denmark; Estonia; France; Germany; Ireland; Italy; Latvia; the Netherlands; Poland; Slovakia; and the UK.
15. My translation of the French 'une politique ciblée de poursuites, soit un mécanisme d'avertissement et de sanction allant jusqu'à la suspension et la résiliation du contrat d'abonnement, ce mécanisme s'appliquant à tous les fournisseurs d'accès à internet. Il peut nécessiter la mise en place d'une autorité indépendante'.
16. This referral requires 60 parliamentarians, a requirement the Socialist opposition easily met.
17. Although a challenge to force a judicial review of the DEA that had been mounted by BT and Talk Talk had actually been thrown out by the court of appeal in March 2012.
18. See https://transparencyreport.google.com/copyright/overview accessed 25 September 2017.
19. See https://blogs.bing.com/webmaster/april-2017/bing-refines-its-copyright-removals-process accessed 25 September 2017.

6. Regulating media concentration in a converging media environment

Media concentration might at first appear to be a traditionally thorny media policy issue that thankfully no longer applies in the Internet era. Some scholars have echoed industry voices arguing that the abundance of digital media outlets now available should free us from undue concern about concentration of ownership and control of those media outlets which provide us with our sociocultural goods and in particular the news and information content that feed our democracies. This chapter outlines why this is not the case, and why consideration still needs to be given to ways of ensuring media pluralism in the era of digital convergence and the Internet. First, however, the chapter asks why worry about media concentration, before going on to explain why the media are particularly prone to media concentration. The chapter then explores how the issue of media concentration has featured in media policy debates first by looking at the US case, then the European. It shows how the universal trend has been the progressive de-regulation of sector-specific structural rules designed to limit media concentration, the principal argument against them being that they are no longer appropriate in a converging new media environment. Thereafter the chapter provides a discussion of the Internet and media concentration, showing how, contrary to the tempting assumption of its pluralising impact, media concentration remains a serious issue that needs to be addressed through policy and regulation. The chapter concludes by suggesting pointers towards policies that might be adopted, which are further discussed in the book's conclusion. An important conclusion of this chapter is that, given the decreasing purchase of sector-specific anti-concentration regulation, a key approach to promoting media pluralism in the new media and Internet era might be a new approach to subsidy, a theme that is taken up in the next chapter.

WHY WORRY ABOUT MEDIA CONCENTRATION?

It is important, at the outset, to note that not everybody sees concentration as a major problem. Many see media markets as pluralistic and anti-concentration measures as sufficiently effective to maintain pluralism. In his classic work *Media Concentration and Democracy* (2007), C. Edwin Baker considers such arguments in detail in chapters with self-explanatory titles, 'Not a Real Problem: Many Owners, Many Sources' and 'Not a Real Problem: the Market or the Internet will Provide', though his work eruditely and skilfully refutes such arguments and demonstrates that it is indeed a major problem for democracy. In *Media Ownership* (2002: 11–29, 13) Gillian Doyle draws attention to the irrefutable fact that the relationship between media ownership and pluralism is not straightforward. The simple fact of diversity of ownership does not necessarily guarantee a diversity of content. Moreover, higher levels of market domination with fewer competing suppliers might mean more cost-effective use of resources, the availability of more resources for innovation, and increased range of output. Craufurd Smith and Tambini (2012: 38) note that 'empirical research, backed up by economic theory suggests that where there is scope for only a few operators in a market, diversity will be enhanced by greater consolidation, with companies seeking to cover all interests rather than simply compete in the most popular fields'. The size and wealth of the media market is an important variable. In small media markets concentration of indigenous media may even be the price of resisting domination by foreign media conglomerates and maintaining their cultural industries (see Ferrell Lowe and Nissen 2011). The claim that the digital era renders strict media-specific anti-concentration measures unnecessary rests on two further arguments. First, it is suggested that digital technologies and the Internet have dramatically pluralised the media landscape. Second, the economic pressures that the Internet, mainly through the migration of advertising to the Internet and the fragmentation of advertising markets, has placed on the business models of many traditional media businesses means that consolidation in these traditional media sectors is necessary for them to survive in the new media environment.

The undoubted complexity of the issue notwithstanding, this chapter proceeds from the straightforward premise that media pluralism is a fundamental pillar of a healthy democracy and that the latter is threatened if media – whether international, national or local; and whether newspapers and magazines, broadcasters, or online providers – are dominated by a restricted number of powerful players (see, for example, Bagdikian 2004; Baker 2007; Barnett and Townend 2015). In the words of a past UK government White Paper on media ownership (Department of National Heritage 1995: 3), democracy flourishes where media 'provide the multiplicity of voices and opinions that inform the public, influences opinion, and engenders political debate'. This desirable state of affairs is threatened when media are unhealthily concentrated. Another premise of the chapter is that 'external pluralism' – a multiplicity of media outlets and owners – is required; reliance on 'internal pluralism' within media companies, some kind of notionally market-demand-driven diversity of voices, is insufficient. Given that media ownership conveys the potential at least to determine the news agenda and editorial line of media outlets, it is clearly of high importance – on prudential grounds – that policy should aim for diverse ownership of externally pluralistic media. In the words of Lord Justice Bryan Henry Leveson:

> There is no question about the importance of maintaining plural media. The requirement of the broadcasting code for broadcast news to be impartial provides some degree of assurance that the public will have access to unbiased news coverage, but it remains vital to ensure that there are many different sources of news, controlled by many different people, and reaching the public by many different routes. It is only through this plurality, specifically in relation to news and current affairs, that we can ensure that the public is able to be well informed on matters of local, national and international news and policy and able to play their full part in a democratic society. (Leveson 2012, Executive Summary: 29).

Yet to single out news and current affairs provision is too narrow. The media influence society and public opinion through social and cultural content too. But what causes media concentration?

WHY IS THERE MEDIA CONCENTRATION?

In his critical exploration of the thesis about the alleged pluralising impact of new digital media *Digital Disconnect* (2013: 74) Robert McChesney explains, in succinct words, the economic reason why the media are especially prone to concentration:

> It is not simply the standard tendency toward market concentration in capitalism [which *Digital Disconnect* also amply addresses]; it has to do with the nature of entertainment media markets. In such markets, the "first-copy" costs – say, of producing a film – are enormous, long before a penny of revenue is earned. This is a very high-risk industry. On the other hand, the marginal costs of serving additional customers after the first are rock-bottom, so blockbusters can be extremely profitable. Having size and being a conglomerate is the smartest way for firms to manage risk.

Grant and Wood (2004: 42–60) make the same point in their examination of global media markets, *Blockbusters and Trade Wars*, in which they discuss at length the 'curious economics' of the culture industries. Among the ways in which cultural products differ significantly from ordinary commodities, they point to the following. Rather than serve a 'utilitarian purpose', cultural products 'communicate ideas – information or entertainment'. Rather than emerge from an 'assembly line process', with each unit requiring significant resources, they emerge from 'an expensive one-time process' that 'creates intellectual property that can be cheaply stored, duplicated and delivered' (clearly the scale of the costs varies between, for instance, feature films, television, sound or newspaper article, but the same principle applies, especially in the digital era). As noted, unlike for ordinary commodities, the marginal costs of production are 'insignificant'; the costs are incurred by production of the master copy. Moreover, unlike many ordinary commodities which compete with other brands, cultural products enjoy limited substitutability; and 'copyright law protects [a] monopoly on each title'. However, again unlike for ordinary products, it is 'difficult to estimate demand in advance of incurring cost', which helps explain the high-risk nature of the business. Indeed, much cultural production fails in the marketplace (and genres like news and information, and investigative journalism, are more or less guaranteed to do so). The gamble aspect of the cultural product is increased by the fact that, yet again unlike for ordinary commodities, 'demand falls off sharply after introduction of the product', though of course feature films and television series in particular can enjoy an 'afterlife' as repeats and in DVD (Grant and Wood 2004: 44–5).

Doyle (2002: 37–41) explains how concentration is the product of media companies' pursuit of economies of scale and scope. In a business characterised by 'high initial production costs but very low or minimal marginal distribution costs', large media firms that achieve economies of scale, 'can spread production costs across ever-larger audiences' and 'benefit from diminishing per viewer (or per reader) costs as consumption expands'. Moreover, scale economies can be turned to competitive advantage over rivals by freeing more resources for investment and the adoption of new technologies, thereby promoting further cost savings and efficiency gains. The pursuit of economies of scale, according to Doyle, is the principal motive for monomedia (horizontal) concentration. Vertical integration – ownership of different stages of the supply chain – offers 'valuable strategic advantages' through giving 'secure access ... to essential inputs or distribution outlets for output', disadvantaging rivals and promoting the market power of dominant firms. In the media field, cross-media (diagonal) concentration offers several efficiency gains. Specialist expertise, such as journalistic skills, can be shared across media. So too can media content. Moreover, firms that have diversified across media gain the advantage of 'spreading the risk of innovating media products across a variety of formats or delivery methods'. All this provides economies of scope. The market power of concentrated media – whether horizontal, vertical, or diagonal – obviously bestows competitive advantage and creates barriers to market entry.

TRENDS IN CONCENTRATION AND REGULATORY POLICY IN THE UNITED STATES

In the first, 1983 edition of his much-cited book *The Media Monopoly*, former journalist and renowned media scholar Ben Bagdikian[1] suggested that 50 corporations controlled the vast majority of all news media in the US. By the fourth edition, published in 1992, the number had fallen to two dozen, and by publication in 2004 of a revised and expanded version, renamed *The New Media Monopoly*, the number had fallen to a mere six: Time Warner, Disney, Rupert Murdoch's News Corporation, Bertelsmann, Viacom (formerly CBS) and General Electric (NBC) (Bagdikian 1983, 2004). Bagdikian's claim stimulated scepticism at each stage, yet it can be corroborated. In a posting of *Business Insider* Lutz (2012) confirmed that just six corporations controlled 90 per cent of the US media, these being: General Electric (whose best known companies were Comcast, NBC), News Corporation (Fox, *Wall Street Journal*, *New York Post*), Disney (ABC), Viacom (MTV), Time Warner (CNN, HBO, *Time*), and CBS, though in this survey reflecting Viacom's takeover of CBS the family-owned German/US Bertlesmann global corporation assumes sixth place.

McChesney (2004: 182) posits three main tiers of media firms. Those identified by Bagdikian (McChesney includes Sony as well) constitute the first tier, these being:

> vertically integrated powerhouses – indeed vast conglomerates – with various combinations of film studios, TV networks, cable TV channels, book publishing, newspapers, radio stations, music companies, TV channels, and the like. Their annual revenues tend to run in the $15–40 billion range, placing them squarely among the few hundred largest firms in the world. Cable giant Comcast certainly is large enough to be first-tier firm, though not especially vertically integrated. (McChesney 2004: 182)

Despite the multiplication of cable and satellite TV channels in recent decades that has challenged the dominance of the established 'Big Three' networks, McChesney notes, five first-tier companies own 20 of the 25 largest cable channels and 'still reach around 90 percent of the total television audience' (McChesney 2004: 183). In the second tier are another 20 firms that are 'major players in a single or two related areas' with annual sales in the $3–10 billion range. This tier includes the likes of Gannett (newspapers and local TV) and Clear Channel (dominant in radio following the 1996 Telecommunications Act – on which see later in this chapter). The third tier is composed of 'thousands of much smaller companies that fill the nooks and crannies of the media system'. These operate in areas regarded as risky or unprofitable by the larger firms, often are dependent on these firms and, if successful, are often targets for merger and acquisition (McChesney 2004: 183).

According to the Pew Research Center's *Project for Excellence in Journalism* annual report for 2012 (PEW 2012), in US national TV, apart from PBS, three network companies had national news divisions, and their combined viewer-ships totally eclipsed that of PBS (by an order of 32 to one!). These were CBS, Comcast (NBC) and Walt Disney (ABC). The CBS Corporation also had very significant interests in local television and radio, as well as other media including CBS Records. Comcast Corporation was the US's largest cable operator, home Internet service provider, and third largest home telephone service provider. In 2011, it gained 51 per cent control of NBC, together with it its broadcast, cable and online news brands, for a cost of $14 billion, making it one of the largest media mergers in recent history (leaving the other 49 per cent in the hands of General Electric). The Walt Disney Company, one of the world's largest media conglomerates, owned the ABC television network and ESPN cable channel as well as a number of local television stations; it also owned Walt Disney Internet Group. The Pew report did not count the highly successful News Corporation-owned Fox network among national network news providers, because, unlike ABC, CBS and NBC, the Fox network did not air national news programmes. However, the Fox network certainly did carry political reporting, including election coverage, it provided breaking news reports, and its magazine programming could also reflect political content. Further, the Fox News Channel, technically a separate entity which launched in 1996, could be found on virtually all pay television providers in the US and was highly influential. News Corporation was the global media company founded in 1980 by Rupert Murdoch, incorporated in the United States 2004, with operations in numerous media markets including film, television, newspapers and book publishing. Its US holdings included Dow Jones & Company, the *Wall Street Journal*, 20th Century Fox, the Fox Broadcasting Company, Harper Collins Publishers, and MySpace.

In US cable television, the Pew report noted, four companies owned all the news channels: Time Warner, News Corporation, Comcast and

Bloomberg. Of these, three were media giants. Comcast and News Corporation have already been mentioned. Time Warner Inc., the product of a 1989 merger between Time Inc. and Warner Communications, was a giant in film (Warner Bros.), cable networks (Turner Broadcasting and HBO) and publishing (Time Inc.) and a major provider of news through its ownership of CNN, *Time* magazine and celebrity news website TMZ.[2] The Pew report on news media ownership showed more diversity in local TV stations, but those with by far the most significant reach were owned by CBS, Comcast, News Corporation and Walt Disney, already mentioned, and additionally Gannett, one of the United States' largest newspaper publishers, Tribune, another important newspaper publisher (owner of the *Chicago Tribune* and *LA Times*), and the leading Hispanic American TV and radio company Univision (PEW 2012).

The Pew Research Center's state of the news media report for 2016 (Pew 2016) showed little change in the above noted ownership patterns of the traditional media, with further consolidation in the newspaper industry (and newspaper closures) and radio markets, and substantial merger and acquisition activity in the local television market. The main development by then was the depth of the financial crisis in the newspaper sector (though the television sector was still faring rather better it too faced the problem of changing audience habits) and the market impact of digital media and Internet platforms like Facebook and Google, a handful of such companies dominating the digital advertising market (on the Internet see later in this chapter).

Media policy has contributed to this state of affairs. The 1920s and 1930s can be seen as a critical juncture for the development of broadcasting (then purely radio), resulting in the triumph of commercial over non-profit forces, itself a reflection of the corporate domination of the media policy process. This established a policy path dependency such that with the arrival of television in the mid twentieth century, commercial interests dominated, in marked contrast to Europe where public service monopolies were the rule (McChesney 1993; Streeter 1996). The immediate post-war years saw a debate in the USA, possibly a second critical juncture, which might have led to reform and the introduction of European style public service broadcasting, but due to its influence in Washington corporate libertarianism again triumphed (Pickard 2014). Nonetheless, the USA retained a commitment to ownership regulation to ensure media plurality. In a commercial system, it was widely assumed both politically and popularly, to be very necessary in order to maintain the diverse and local media system that Americans prized (Gibbons and Humphreys 2012: 26–32).

However, as a number of studies show (McChesney 2004; Freedman 2008; Klinenberg 2007; Gibbons and Humphreys 2012: 26–32), since the Reagan era policy turn to neo-liberalism, which can be seen as a third critical juncture in US media policy, these media ownership rules have been whittled away (though rules against foreign ownership in conventional broadcasting remain in place, nominally on national security grounds). The Reaganite FCC chairman, Mark Fowler, once described television as nothing more than 'a toaster with pictures', thereby revealing the prevailing deregulatory philosophy he would apply to his regulatory mandate. Ironically, though, the single most far-reaching act of deregulation occurred under the Democrat presidency of Bill Clinton, in the shape of the 1996 Telecommunications Act. McChesney sees the neo-liberal period as by far the greatest 'upheaval in U.S. media regulation since the critical juncture of the 1920s and 1930s' and goes on to observe that '... the main story of the final two decades of the twentieth century has been the decisive increase in the business domination of media policy making' (McChesney 2004: 21, 48; also see Streeter 1996; Klinenberg 2007; Freedman 2008; Pickard 2014). Exactly how did this state of affairs come about?

In the cause of broadcasting pluralism, regulation of accumulations of interests in domestic ownership in the USA commenced in the 1940s, justified as part of the Federal Communication Commission's (FCC) power to license under its public interest mandate. In 1953 duopolies (common ownership of more than one station of same type of service in a given community) were prohibited. Common control of AM and FM radio was limited to seven stations, and common control of television to five, which was increased to seven with UHF in 1954. Early concern over networking arose over the quickly established market domination by CBC and NBC and led to FCC measures to regulate network access and exclusivity. Notably, NBC was compelled to divest itself of one of its networks, which became the third major network ABC. Early in the Reagan presidency (1981–1989), in 1983, the national ownership caps were raised from seven to twelve stations, so long as they reached no more than 25 per cent of the national audience. President Clinton's deregulatory 1996 Telecommunications Act removed the ownership caps entirely so long as the stations reached less than 35 per cent of the national audience; in 2004, this was raised to 39 per cent of the national audience. Cross media restrictions, introduced in the 1970s, were relaxed from 1989 onwards, receiving special impetus from the deregulation introduced by the 1996 Telecommunications Act (for a fuller account see Gibbons and Humphreys 2012: 27–9).

The stated objective of the 1996 Telecommunications Act of 1996 was to open up markets to competition by removing regulatory entry barriers, but its execution was technocratic and its effect deregulatory (Aufderheide 1999). It led to a surge in mergers, acquisitions and joint ventures, and many local, independent media were quickly gobbled up by big companies with little interest in local content, which had invested huge amounts in a lobbying campaign against media ownership caps (Klinenberg 2007). Its immediate effect was on the radio sector, which prior to the Act had been impressively diverse and local. The radio industry experienced a tidal wave of concentration, leaving the sector dominated by a few giant companies, most notably Clear Channel. This was at the cost of the localism, hitherto a prized attribute of US media, and diversity, not least political pluralism (Prindle 2003; Klinenberg 2007). According to McChesney (2004: 117) 'as radio ownership concentrated due to the 1996 Telecommunications Act, editorial power concentrated in the hands of companies like Clear Channel, which have long histories of supporting right-wing politicians'. In television the changes were slower (Gibbons and Humphreys 2012: 29). Nonetheless, the Pew Center's *Project for Excellence in Journalism* annual reports on *The State of the News* chart a significant impact. As with radio, large media conglomerates ate up smaller, local station owners. Between 1995 and 2002 the ten largest local television companies, which included the four major networks (ABC, CBS, NBC and Fox), had doubled their revenue and trebled the number of stations they owned (cited in Klinenberg 2007: 94). According to Klinenberg, the impact on journalism was similar to radio (2007: 92):

> In the past decade, the concentration of ownership among a small number of large station owners that are particularly driven by bottom-line concerns has shifted editorial resources and programming control from the local to the national level [resulting in] a decline in primary television news reporting, the rise of fake local news broadcasts, and an increase of canned content such as infomercials and video news releases promoting commercial products or political propaganda. (Klinenberg 2007: 92)

The 1996 Telecommunications Act mandated the FCC to evaluate and adjust as necessary its media ownership rules every two years; in 2004 this was raised to four years. These reviews saw an apparent increased commitment to evidence-based evaluation of US media ownership policies, though the objectiveness of the research has been questioned by one scholar with knowledge and experience of the workings of the system, who points to concerns about 'biases in favour of pre-determined policy positions' (Napoli 2015: 102). The scholar was led to conclude that the state of affairs 'for now and the foreseeable future' seemed to be

> one in in which research conducted and submitted by those parties with a stake in the policy outcomes, and with the resources to conduct the most convincing research in support of their preferred outcomes, will increasingly influence the FCC's decision making and/or be used to justify decision outcomes ... a scenario, in which policy research is essentially nothing but a tool of policy advocacy. (Napoli 2015: 111)

Studies such as those by McChesney (2004), Klinenberg (2007) and Freedman (2008) show how the deregulation of media ownership was driven by intense corporate lobbying, though the pathway was not always smooth. The deregulatory march of the FCC's approach to regulation and media policy continued in the new century, with the appointment in 2001 of Michael Powell to its chair shortly after the election of George W. Bush to the presidency the preceding year. Powell soon demonstrated his intention of further deregulating media ownership, repeating the neo-liberal mantra that had governed policy since the Reagan era that the competitive nature of the converging media markets no longer justified restrictive ownership rules. However, the public's attachment to diverse local media in a system which relied so strongly on market-based provision of pluralism and diversity was illustrated by a remarkable 'public uprising of 2003' uniting elements on both the Left and Right of US politics against further deregulation of media ownership, graphically described by McChesney (2004: 252–97). However, the horses had – mostly – already bolted.

As for the press sector, highly localised, it had never been seriously regulated in the USA and single town monopoly newspapers and newspaper chains soon became the rule. If anything, legislation and regulation served to promote concentration as a means to save struggling newspapers from collapse. Thus, the 1970 Newspaper Preservation Act (NPA), whose nominal purpose was to maintain some diversity in local markets, did so by allowing newspapers to cooperate, notably by letting them operate as monopolies vis-à-vis advertisers. McChesney (2004: 229–30) suggests that the law was introduced after heavy industry lobbying, it failed to save many newspapers, and it benefitted 'a handful of ... publishers'. Although it required the newspapers to maintain complete editorial independence, C. Edwin Baker (2007: 180) points out economics explains its failure to work effectively, since '[o]nce one of the papers becomes dominant in circulation, both companies in a combined operation often would benefit by eliminating the cost of operating the weaker paper, closing it, and then dividing between them the subsequent monopoly profits of the surviving paper'.

TRENDS IN CONCENTRATION AND REGULATORY POLICY IN EUROPE

What have the trends in Europe been? Historically, the concentration in the press sector had never been effectively limited, and concentration was marked. Humphreys (1996) points to a long-standing regulatory deficit, with a number of countries having no specific provisions for the press, some countries having only weak regulation (on Germany, also see Humphreys 1994), and other countries either failing to introduce strict controls (on France see Humphreys 1996: 96–9), or failing to implement regulation effectively. Thus, in the UK where ministerial consent had been required for any merger leading to a combined circulation of over half a million to be referred to the competition authority, Rupert Murdoch's News International, already owner of the mass circulation tabloid, *The Sun*, was permitted to acquire not only *The Times* but also *The Sunday Times* without any such referral. The argument deployed at the time, that the newspapers were failing (tenuous in the case of *The Sunday Times*), is that the acquisitions saved them from collapse which would have actually increased concentration (Humphreys 1996: 100–1). Later, as will be seen, because of News International's strong market position in the newspaper sector, special exceptions to the deregulation of the ownership rules for broadcasting were made for cross-media ownership.

Broadcasting and cross-media ownership have historically been more strictly regulated, but a number of detailed studies have pointed to increasing concentration across Europe in media markets which have been left by the EU largely to the control of national politicians and regulators. Well over a decade ago, Ward (2004) produced a path-breaking *Mapping Study of Media Concentration in Ten European Countries*,[3] for the Dutch media regulator, showing that – while concentration levels varied between countries and media markets – the general trend over the preceding decade had been increased media concentration in nearly all countries and markets. Around the same time, Alison Harcourt (2005) also provided detailed data on a number of national media markets,[4] showing increased media concentration, the growth of a number of European media groups but their overshadowing by giant US-based corporations, and access to digital broadcasting controlled by a handful of national gateway operators. Since then a similar picture has been painted by detailed work done by concerned journalists' organisations, media regulators, and bodies such as the European Parliament and Commission, the Council of Europe, and the Open Society Foundations.

Research conducted at Manchester University (reported in Gibbons and Humphreys 2012) shows that a degree of (de)regulatory competition was an important driver of the deregulation of structural media ownership rules in European media markets, with media policy being conducted along the lines of trade and industry policy, and (de)regulatory competitive strategies between regulatory jurisdictions being pursued in order to promote local media investment and companies, thereby encouraging a deregulatory 'race to the bottom' (on deregulatory competition see Carey 1974; Scharpf 1997, 1999). In the UK case, a drawn-out period of incremental deregulation of media ownership rules dating back to the 1990s saw the progressive whittling away of restrictions on accumulations of interest in broadcasting companies. This culminated in New Labour's Communications Act 2003 which removed the remaining rules preventing the accumulation of broadcasting licences, leaving only prohibitions on local cross-media concentration and between the press and the holder of the ITV television licence at the national level (the latter aimed at Rupert Murdoch). In pursuing such a policy, New Labour was very explicit about its keenness to attract investment in the UK media industry and to promote internationally competitive domestic media companies. Converging market conditions were also cited as a reason for deregulation (Gibbons and Humphreys 2012: 103–5; see also Doyle 2002: 118, 122–3). In the French case, conservative and socialist governments alike were no less explicit in justifying deregulation of media ownership rules, which saw the loosening of restrictions on shareholdings and accumulations of interest in media, particularly in the field of satellite television, by pointing to the need for the French media sector to remain internationally competitive (Gibbons and Humphreys 2012: 81–2). The German case similarly saw a deregulation of restrictions on shareholdings and accumulations of broadcasting licences and the adoption in their place of a very liberal audience share model (with a 30 per cent limit), which effectively legitimised the already highly concentrated television market in the country that had been allowed to develop during the late 1980s and early 1990s. In Germany, the competitive-deregulatory dynamic was more of one of inter-*Land* competition for media investment within a federal system (Humphreys and Lang 1998; Gibbons and Humphreys 2012: 127–8).

In 2005 the European Federation of Journalists (EFJ) produced a major report, *Media Power in Europe: The Big Picture of Ownership* (EFJ

2005). The study reported the situation in no fewer than 33 European countries. In its preface, Aidan White, the EFJ's General Secretary, observed that

> new information technologies [were] now giv[ing] people the opportunity to get their journalism and information from a kaleidoscope of sources – the telephone, the computer, their iPod or Walkman, as well as satellite television, digital radio and the traditional range of newspapers and broadcasting outlets. (EFJ 2005: 4)

White asked:

> [W]e are overwhelmed by information, but is it of good plurality? Is it our democratic values? Is it creating genuine pluralism? Is concentration bad news for Europe, or is it opening the door to real choice for consumers and citizens. (EFJ 2005: 4)

He concluded on the basis of the report's evidence that

> pluralism [wa]s under pressure ... The global media [we]re dominated by American media interests ... T[he] survey [wa]s a wake up call to the European Union ... [that] it [wa]s a European issue that require[d] a European response. (EFJ 2005: 4)

Against the expectation of some that the media market had never been more diversified, the report found overwhelming evidence of ongoing media concentration which was posing two dangers, first the economic and market-related one of the impediment to competition and ultimately consumer welfare posed by the creation of significant market power and, second, pertaining to fundamental democratic values, the threat of curtailment of media plurality, diversity and freedom of information.

> The argument that the choice of media has never been so broad [wa]s true ... But this [wa]s a simplified picture of reality, since a small number of companies often control[led] both distribution channels and the content distributed. The increase in the absolute number of offers did not lead to more diversity, i.e. different offers, instead it leaded [sic] simply to 'more of the same'. (EFJ 2005: 5)

The report showed how large internationally operating media companies were the best placed to invest in new and multiple channels and meet the voracious demand for content, thereby establishing a dominant market position and barriers to market entry for smaller-scale competitors. Further, new media were creating new bottlenecks – cable and satellite systems, digital platforms, and if written a little more recently the report would have included Internet intermediaries – giving those who controlled them new powers over what was distributed. In sum, the report found that media concentration was increasing in all parts of Europe, media ownership was increasingly transnational and as a result, national media regulations were no longer so applicable and enforceable, media companies were more mobile in their search for markets and economies of scale, and there were more and more vertically integrated companies (combining different levels of production) and diagonally (cross-media) integrated companies. In Eastern Europe foreign investment – including very high levels from Western European media groups – was highly significant, rendering more difficult the development of independent nationally based media groups in those countries. The whole situation was exacerbated by a lack of transparency about media ownership, the obligations regarding which varied widely, rendering it difficult to study the exact nature of the threat to pluralism.

The Council of Europe, too, has long been concerned by media concentration. As far back as 1996 it published an academic study commissioned by its Committee of Experts on Media Concentrations and Pluralism. Entitled 'The Impact of New Communications Technologies on Media Concentrations and Pluralism' (Prosser, Goldberg and Verhulst 1996) the report is one of a number of studies at around that time already exploring the media convergence that was accompanying the then new technologies of digitalisation, optical fibre (cable) and the early Internet. It drew attention to converging media markets, increasing interactivity in media usage, and presciently saw emerging bottleneck issues as the main danger to pluralism. In 2000 The Council of Europe established an Advisory Panel on Media Diversity – AP-MD – as a working group to monitor developments in the field of media diversity and pluralism. In 2004 the AP-MD presented the Council of Europe's Steering Committee on the Mass Media (CDMM) with a report *Transnational Media Concentrations in Europe* (Council of Europe 2004) which highlighted the same concerns as the European Journalists Federation, notably that large, transnational conglomerates, operating in many countries directly or through subsidiaries, joint ventures or shareholdings, were exerting market power to the disadvantage of weaker national media publishers or broadcasters, with central and eastern Europe being particularly affected. Significantly, the report commented upon the increasing difficulty of applying national media regulations and remedies to these transnational media undertakings. Noting the increasingly commercial orientation of media and the weakening of public service broadcasters, the report expressed concern about the diminishing diversity of content production and its impact on the media's contribution to the public sphere:

> The new media environment at the European and global level has led to a wider choice for the viewers and consumers in the number of channels and other media products available, but has not so far led to the same diversity regarding content ... With digitisation, actions by gatekeepers who control the bottlenecks can actually lead to a reduction of pluralism and diversity ... Unchallenged, content in a media environment dominated by transnational media owners will most likely become less local, less controversial, less investigative and less informative. (Council of Europe 2004: 5)

The report made a number of recommendations, which included the need for monitoring and annual reporting; support for public service broadcasting as specific providers of diverse content and content producers on new technological platforms; development of community media; public policy measures to strengthen the editorial pluralism of the media through legislation and other means; and industry initiatives to develop functioning self-regulatory mechanisms to safeguard editorial independence.[5]

As regards the European Union, the European Parliament has long drawn attention to the negative effects that media concentration, and especially transnational media concentration, has had on media pluralism and cultural and linguistic diversity in Europe. However, notwithstanding the aim of cultural diversity and pluralism being one of the key objectives of the EU as set out in the Lisbon Treaty, culture falls within the areas where the Union only has a power of supporting, coordinating or complementary action. Primarily the media remain a Member State competence. An attempt to develop an EU level regulatory regime for media concentration was made in the 1990s when a proposal for a Directive (European Commission 1996 and 1997b) was produced by the European Commission, following a Green Paper on *Pluralism and Media Concentration in the Internal Market* (European Commission 1992) and a subsequent Commission Communication (European Commission 1994b). However, it has been well documented how the draft Directive was unsuccessful, blocked by opposition of key Member States and hard lobbying by some major private media companies. Harcourt (2005) explores in detail the failures of EU policy in this field, despite the EU's potential for problem-solving (for an overview, see Gibbons and Humphreys 2012: 151–4).

Since then, the EU appears to have adopted transparency (monitoring, reporting) as its principal policy for addressing media concentration, albeit adding an additional dimension, namely risk assessment. Despite failure to produce any harmonised EU approach to media-specific regulation of the issue, both the European Commission and the European Parliament continued to be concerned about the issue. In 2007 the

European Commission published a staff working document (European Commission 2007) which looked at the issue of media concentration and provided country studies of all 27 Member States. Thereupon, the European Commission contracted a team of academics and a consultancy firm to elaborate concrete and objective indicators for assessing media pluralism, a report being duly produced in 2009 (Katholieke Universiteit Leuven et al. 2009) which produced these indicators together with a monitoring tool, the Media Pluralism Monitor (MPM), which following two pilot test operations has been fully operational since 2016. The operating institution, the Centre for Media Pluralism and Media Freedom (CMPF), established in 2011 in the European University Institute at Florence, works through a network of national expert teams, which provide the data to assess the levels of risk at country level and draft the country reports, with the CMPF supervising, ensuring consistency of the data collection, and assessing the levels of risk. Interestingly, the MPM takes into account a wider range of variables than simply media concentration, also reporting on such criteria as journalist professionalism, independence and effectiveness of the media regulators, protections for media freedom and rights to information, media reach and Internet access, political independence and editorial autonomy, and the independence and funding of public service media (Katholieke Universiteit Leuven ICRI et al. 2009).[6] Similarly noteworthy is the Council of Europe's *European Audiovisual Observatory* which operates the MAVISE database[7] providing very detailed profiles of 42 national markets, based on data collected by its team of national experts and helped by the European Platform of Regulatory Authorities.

Despite the undoubtedly important contribution that transparency, monitoring, and risk assessment can make, EU policy regarding media concentration, which as seen is clearly a problem transcending Member State borders, has nonetheless been notably weak. Rules about plurality and diversity of the media have been left to the Member States which are constrained only by the Commission's role as protector of competition and the four freedoms (of movement of capital, goods, services, people) of the Internal Market. As seen, at the national level, the trend has been deregulatory, policy makers displaying a concern to make national (or in Germany's case, regional) markets attractive for media investment and bolster national (or regional) media industries. In the case of Europe's smaller countries, and Canada, concentration has been a way some countries have retained national players in markets vulnerable to foreign penetration by giant neighbours (Gibbons and Humphreys 2012; also see Ferrell Lowe and Nissen 2011). It is certainly true that the EU has intervened through competition law on a number of occasions to keep markets open, including the development of rules for conditional access regulation (conditional access systems being a classic bottleneck) that has ensured a degree of non-discriminatory access for programme services to pay-TV systems owned by media concerns with significant market power. The European competition authority has also blocked the occasional high-profile merger. However, by and large the European competition authority has tended to wave large, transnational media mergers through, the reasoning appearing to be that the expansion of large companies in other Member States does not establish a dominant position at EU level and that Europe needs more globally competitive media companies. Moreover, a major weakness of reliance on competition law to protect media pluralism – and an argument for a media-specific approach – is that economic competition law does not recognise a firm's dominance, in itself, to be a problem, provided that markets are deemed contestable. As Gibbons (2004: 63) has pointed out, this fails to take into account the impact of such firms on diversity of content.

THE INTERNET AND MEDIA CONCENTRATION

Celebrating the 'Pluralising' Impact of the Internet

Robert McChesney commenced his important 2013 book *Digital Disconnect* with a reference to the seemingly prophetic work of the neo-liberal economist George Gilder *Life After Television*,[8] published in 1990, which predicted that 'telecomputers, connected to a nationwide fiberoptic network', in other words the Internet, would render broadcast television obsolete, banish the problem of media concentration, and remove the need for media policy (Gilder 1990 cited in McChesney 2013: xii). McChesney himself observes that writers on the Internet have tended to fall into two camps: celebrants and sceptics. A considerable number of scholars have greeted the Internet with considerable enthusiasm and optimism, perhaps most famously of all Manuel Castells, who in *Communication Power* defined it as a new means of 'mass self-communication' with the potential for the global sharing of information (Castells 2009: 55). By 'self-communication' Castells was pointing to the fact that the receiver of information is self-directed and the retrieval of information, self-selected. Thus, the Internet appeared to constitute a non-hierarchical medium par excellence (however, at the same time Castells pointed to the dominance by major corporations of the Internet business – see next section). Another prominent 'celebrant', Harvard law professor Yochai Benkler (2006) made a similar argument in his *Wealth of Networks*, pointing to the emergence of the 'networked information economy' (NIE) that challenges the nineteenth and twentieth century 'industrial information economy', the former enabling the emergence of non-hierarchical 'commons-based' peer production that escapes the centralised control of the latter. Compaine and Gomery (2000: 439) observe that 'unlike older media models based on proprietary systems and tangible assets, the Internet is a collection of technologies, hardware, software and systems that does not lend itself to concentrated control'. Compaine (2005) rejects the concept of a media monopoly as mythical and points to how competition is actually expanding sources of information in the USA. Negroponte's work *Being Digital* (1995), which generally applauds the decentralising, globalising, and empowering potential of digital technologies, is similarly optimistic, arguing that 'industrial-age cross-ownership laws' will become obsolete (Negroponte 1995: 57–8, cited in Curran 2012a: 42). Highly noteworthy too are Clay Shirky's journalism and books (2008, 2010) which have done much to propagate optimism about the revolutionary potential of the Internet to end hierarchical dominance of communications and the mass media (and society at large).

Chris Anderson (2004, 2006, 2009a, 2009b) is perhaps the best-known theorist of the 'new economics of abundance' in the entertainment and media industries (and, indeed, beyond) of the Internet era; he has presented an optimistic vision of new media facilitating endless choice and unlimited demand, and enriching culture and democracy. When his theory of the 'long tail' was first published in *Wired* in 2004 it quickly became the most cited article the magazine had ever run; subsequently, he further popularised his theory in two widely acclaimed books (Andersen 2004 and 2006). His core idea was that the businesses of the future, like Amazon (books – originally), Netflix (DVDs) and Rhapsody (music tracks), could exploit the Internet's access to almost unlimited choice. Benefiting from negligible inventory and distribution costs they could serve a highly profitable market of 'non-hit items' – the 'long tail' – in addition to selling large quantities of popular items which marked the limits of traditional providers. This new 'economics of abundance', Anderson argued, would create a new cultural richness and diversity. In his words: 'If the twentieth-century entertainment industry was about hits, the twenty-first will be equally about niches' (Anderson 2009b: 16). Indeed, in Anderson's theory, the new economics of abundance liberates true consumer sovereignty from the constraints of the poor supply-and-demand matching that characterised the commercial mass media era

> Bringing niches within reach reveals latent demand for non-commercial content. Then, as demand shifts towards the niches, the economics of providing them improve further, and so on, creating a positive feedback loop that will transform entire industries – and the culture – for decades to come. (Anderson 2009b: 26)

Further, according to Anderson, there is a democratising impact. Long tail production is 'democratised' by the mass availability of digital video-cameras, desktop music and video-editing software, and blogging tools which leads to a huge increase in the numbers of producers, both commercial and non-commercial; long tail aggregators like Amazon, iTunes and Netflix 'democratise' distribution, making all items – not just the popular ones – easily available; and long tail filters like Google (ranking pages), reviews posted by the likes of Amazon and Netflix, blogs, sophisticated recommendation engines (such as Amazon's and Netflix's) and simple individual recommendations, all directly tap consumer sentiment to connect supply and demand, thereby democratising taste-making and overcoming the constraints of traditional mass media's lowest common denominator offerings (Anderson 2009b: 57ff.).

It has often been suggested in the media that the Internet might be 'ringing the death bell' for the dominance in the USA of the Hollywood entertainment model, whose leading entertainment companies relied for the success in large part on their stranglehold on distribution. Now, however, 'video downloaded on the internet has cracked the cartel ... The tightly controlled, top-down distribution business for films and television has been displaced by a more open, bottom-up system.' The question is whether today's media incumbents 'have absorbed the lessons' of earlier waves of technological change 'and are willing to use the technology of internet television to help cannibalise their long-standing businesses' (McCourt 2007: 15). It has also been claimed that social media, blogs and the like have had a pluralising impact on politics. For instance, in discussing the 'media politics of dissent', Cottle points to the 'political opportunities for protest organisations, activists and their supporters to communicate independently of the mainstream news media' (Cottle 2008: 854). Deibert (2000) shows how the Internet greatly facilitated the activities of the opposition movement against the Multilateral Agreement on Investments. In his introduction to the second edition of *Communication Power* Castells (2013) similarly reflects on the impact of the Internet and the 'networked society' on the Arab Spring, social movements against austerity, and Wikileaks, among other things. From a journalist's perspective, Gowing (2011), has pointed to how new digital media (notably, the capacity of mobile phones to film events) have empowered the citizenry and transformed the reporting of international crises and conflicts, challenging official media frames of these events. Certainly, the Internet is a platform where non-corporate media, critical perspectives and support for social change have all flourished. A key question, of course, is the extent to which such developments have challenged the mainstream. Ofcom's studies show that the BBC is still the UK's most popular news website. Other very popular online sources are the *Guardian* and *Daily Mail*'s websites. Undoubtedly, though, established media face increasing competition from non-traditional sources. Increasingly consumers are obtaining their news from social media sites such as Facebook, which by 2010 was accounting for one in every six-page visits in the UK according to Experian Hitwise (Robinson 2010).

Reasons to be Sceptical about Internet's Pluralising Impact

In his highly regarded work *Media Concentration and Democracy*, C. Edwin Baker (2007: 97–123) maintained that new media do not weaken the case for policy action against media concentration and dismissed those that argue that this is the case as 'faddish' and 'intellectually sloppy'. Whilst acknowledging that the Internet brings significant gains to communication, he argued that these 'are different from – are complementary to, and may even be in part dependent on – the more traditional performance of the mass media ... These particular developments have no bearing on any debate about the dangers or objections to media ownership concentration' (Baker 2007: 99). There are key economic reasons why, despite facilitating near zero marginal costs, the Internet might actually promote media concentration, rather than pluralism and diversity. First, significant resources are still required for the production and marketing of high-quality content (Freedman 2010a: 88; Grant and Wood 2004: 46–7). Second, as C. Edwin Baker (2007: 105) has explained, whilst virtually zero distribution costs might promote a tendency towards diversity,

> these reduced 'marginal costs' generate an incentive to make greater first copy expenditures that attract larger audiences, concentrating attention and thereby reducing the likelihood that small-audience content creators will succeed commercially. This second tendency, to increase concentration, might be called the 'Hollywood effect'. It corresponds to how Hollywood's capacity to spend huge amounts on the first copy long allowed it to dominate the world's movie industry.

Critical political economy scholars of the media are highly sceptical. In his 2004 work, *The Problem of the Media: US Communication Politics in the Twenty First Century*, McChesney already dismissed as technological determinism the notion that the Internet was developing as a key factor for undermining the position of the powerful. Indeed, he argued that 'the oligopolistic market [was] trump[ing] the subversive potential of the technology' (McChesney 2004: 221). In his more recent work *Digital Disconnect* (McChesney 2013: 97), he observes that

> What seemed to be an increasingly open public sphere, removed from the world of commodity exchange, seems to be morphing into a private sphere of increasingly closed, proprietary, even monopolistic markets. The extent of this capitalist colonization of the Internet has not been as obtrusive as it might have been, because the vast reaches of cyberspace have continued to permit non-commercial utilization, although increasingly on the margins.

In this later work, McChesney provides a detailed political economy analysis of how 'capitalism [by which he is referring to the 'real existing capitalism of large corporations'] conquered the Internet – an institution that was singularly non-commercial, even anticommercial, for its first two decades'. He identifies the monopolistic developments marked by the rise of new 'digital corporate giants' (McChesney 2013: 97–8).

From a radical critical political economic perspective, Herman and Chomsky (2002: xvi), have argued that their 'propaganda model' critique of the corporate domination of US media still applies in the Internet era. In the preface to a new edition of their well-known book *Manufacturing Consent* they observe that despite providing a

> valuable addition to the communications arsenal of dissidents and protestors ... the internet is not an instrument of mass communication for those lacking brand names ... [and] only sizeable commercial organisations have been able to make large numbers aware of their internet offerings. The privatization of the Internet's hardware, the rapid commercialization and concentration of Internet portals and servers and their integration into non-Internet conglomerates ... and the private and concentrated control of the new broadband technology, together threaten to limit any future prospects of the Internet as a democratic media vehicle. (Herman and Chomsky 2002: xvi)

Des Freedman, too, has provided a critique of the hype surrounding the new digital economy in two chapters of a co-authored volume *Misunderstanding the Internet* (Curran, Fenton and Freedman 2012). In one chapter, he exposes the false foundations of 'economy of abundance' optimism, instead showing the extent of concentration and arguing 'the pipes may be increasingly digital, but the piper is still being paid and looking to make a profit (Freedman 2012a: 70). In his second chapter, Freedman argues that Internet regulation has been 'outsourced', by which he means largely left to self-regulation by the private sector and machinations by special interests. Significantly, he notes inter alia the exemption of ISPs and other Internet intermediaries from any liability for content 'where they can establish their status as mere conduits' (Freedman 2012b: 101), a theme we have already explored in relation to copyright but which is clearly also relevant for the theme of media concentration. The overall thrust of this second chapter is the need for 'robust regulation for the public good ... [and] a commitment to forms of regulation that are *not* subservient to corporate pressure, government priorities or elite control ... regulatory actions that are required precisely to fend off the distortions to the public good by special interests' (Freedman 2012b: 116–17).

A number of leading scholars who in their overall analytical approach are not to be aligned with the aforementioned critical political economists and radical sceptics note that the Internet has been accompanied by significant concentration. Thus, Eli Noam's (2009) wide-ranging and highly empirical study of the US information sector, too, found that:

> Generally, the more electronic and 'digital' a media subsector is, the more highly it seems to be concentrated ... Strong economies of scale, network effects, distance-insensitivity, and high complexity have led to a consolidation for the Internet itself as well as for many of its major applications. This pours cold water over the hope that the Internet will solve the media concentration problem. Key parts of this sector exhibit the same dynamics leading to concentration. If anything, its greater rate of change drives it there faster. (Noam 2009: 5)

Network effects, also referred to as demand-side economies of scale, make for concentrated markets, and even monopolies, because the more users join the network the more attractive it becomes for others, creating a kind of bandwagon effect. Search engines like Google and social networks like Facebook owe their market dominance in large part to the value they have in terms of the number of users/members they have attracted (though clearly this is partly based too on the quality of their service), the amount of data the latter provide, and because of this, their attractiveness to advertisers.

Tim Wu's (2010) *The Master Switch*[9] qualifies the optimism surrounding the Internet through a masterful historical survey of US communications developments, showing that each major new medium from the telephone, through radio and television, to satellite TV has demonstrated a cyclical pattern of idealistic optimism followed by the reality of corporate domination, suggesting a similar trajectory for the Internet as corporate giants struggle to control 'the master switch'. Moreover Castells, despite his overall optimism about the Internet's potential for 'mass self-communication', in his renowned analysis of the transformation of the global media industry by the Internet and mobile communication, acknowledges the concentration trend and points to the dominance of Internet business by major corporations. Castells (2009: 75) observed that as many media mergers occurred between 1990 and 1995 as occurred between 1960 and 1990. He noted how the trend continued, with some truly 'mega mergers' occurring in the new century, symptomatic of the increasing concentration of ownership and control of both traditional and new media firms in the hands of a select number of transnational corporate giants. In 2000, the Internet company American acquired Time Warner for $164 billion. In 2005, News Corporation acquired the social networking platform MySpace and its parent company Intermix for $560 million. In 2007, Google acquired YouTube for $1.6 billion (Castells 2009: 79).

It is not just concentration of ownership and control of the companies themselves that is the cause of concern, it is the concentration of users on a number of popular websites. Dahlberg (2005: 160) points to the 'colonization of attention' around a few popular sites, usually connected to traditional media giants. In *Misunderstanding the Internet*, Curran (2012b: 19), too, notes that the most read websites are online versions of the pre-Internet mass media outlets. In his celebrated work *The Myth of Digital Democracy*, Matthew Hindman (2009) explains how the big media players dominate the supposedly open and pluralistic Internet platform. He observes that, though it is certainly true that the Internet has greatly lowered the barriers to entry, promoting the appearance of a vast array of alternative voices, there is a huge difference between having a voice and being taken into account online. Hindman argues that Internet gatekeepers effectively limit people's ability to be heard online and instead they favour commercial mainstream web entities both through the hyperlink structure by which the Internet operates and through the search engines which are themselves dependent on the same hyperlink structure (Hindman 2009: 13–15). Hindman shows how, accordingly, the traditional media giants receive the lion's share of Internet traffic and, among the few newcomers, hyperlinking has promoted the rise of a select number of new giant gatekeepers like Google and Facebook. Indeed, he has referred to 'Googlearchy' (see also Hindman et al. 2003).

Hindman explains how '[d]ata follow a power law distribution when the size of an observation is inversely and exponentially proportional to its frequency' (Hindman 2009: 41). Applying this to hyperlinks, which are the foundational part of the Internet and feature prominently in most search engine algorithms, he explains that:

> A few popular sites (such as Yahoo! or AOL or Google) receive a large portion of the total links; less successful sites (such as personal Web pages) receive hardly any links at all. Traffic, like link structure, follows a power-law distribution with roughly the same parameters (Huberman et al. 1998; Adamic and Huberman 2000). There is thus a small set of sites that receive most of the links, and a small set of sites that receive most online visitors. (Hindman 2009: 42).[10]

Hindman's findings about the continued dominance in the Internet era of traditional media giants is confirmed by other research. In 2011, the Pew Center published a report *Navigating News Online* (Olmstead, Mitchell and Rosenstiel 2011) which identified the top 25 news providers for US online traffic in 2010. The Pew Center researchers explored data from three e-market research organisations: Nielsen, comScore and Hitwise. Strikingly, all three organisations found that legacy organisations[11] constituted around two thirds of the top 25 most popular news websites. Typically they were those of leading US newspapers and network TV news providers, though interestingly the UK BBC and *Guardian*, *Telegraph* and *Daily Mail* websites also featured. The other third, online only ventures, included the pure aggregators *Google News* (news.google.com), *The Examiner* (examiner.com), *Topix* (topix.com) and *Bing News* (news. bing.com) which relied mainly or heavily on popular legacy news providers. Only a small number of hybrid online-only sites, notably *Yahoo News* (news.yahoo.com), *AOL News* (news.aol.com) and *Huffington Post* (huffingtonpost.com) mixed original reporting with aggregation.

According to a 2015 Pew Center research report eight out of the ten most visited news websites were still the digitised versions of 'legacy' (that is, existing before the Net) mass media outlets. These were, in rank order, with the new entrants italicised: Yahoo–ABC News Network; CNN Network; NBC News Digital; Huffington Post.Com; CBS News; USA Today; Buzzfeed.Com; *New York Times*; Fox News Digital Network; and the UK's *Daily Mail* (PEW 2015). Interestingly, among the next ranked ten, were two more highly popular UK sites, namely the BBC in fifteenth place and the *Guardian*, in seventeenth. Similarly, a survey by the e-business research organisation eBizMBA (2015) found all but three of the most popular Internet news websites, averaging out global and US traffic rankings, to be news websites of leading US network TV news providers (CNN, Fox News, NBC News, ABC News), the UK BBC News, leading US newspapers (*New York Times, Washington Post, Wall Street Journal, USA Today*, and *LA Times*), and the UK *Guardian* and

Daily Mail newspapers. It did find, though, that the top three (most popular) websites were Yahoo News, Google News and *Huffington Post*. These were all news aggregators, therefore not news providers in the traditional sense but largely purveyors of news from the most popular mainstream media.

CONCLUSION: IMPLICATIONS FOR POLICY

To conclude, how might media policy in the digital era help ensure that there should be a sufficient range of independent media voices with extensive reach and accessibility and that media consumption should not be too highly concentrated, ideally with citizens being exposed to and consuming news, information and sociocultural content from a range of sources? There are a number of ways in which policy makers might address the issue. One important demarche will be to adapt structural measures (those that remain post-deregulation) to the digital era. Traditional remedies for limiting concentration involving structural measures in clearly defined 'relevant media markets' (press, broadcasting, cross-media), such as limits on shareholding and accumulations of interest have, as seen, been largely dispensed with. However, this occurred following a neo-liberal policy turn in the 1980s with the development of new media and digital convergence being held up as the rationale, and with other rationales, notably competitive deregulation to attract media investment, also being apparent. However, it can be maintained that there is a case, notwithstanding the neo-liberal deregulation that has occurred, for retaining such measures in markets that still remain clearly defined. As the UK Media Reform Coalition (2014) has argued in a detailed report, steady deregulation of media ownership rules has been accompanied by 'concentration within some news and information markets [having] reached endemic levels' (p. 26), while 'appropriate methods for measuring and monitoring plurality exist for all of the key sectors'.

Clearly, though, in the long run sector-specific controls are unlikely to be so practical in the digital future, given the convergence of media markets where the same product can be distributed over a number of platforms and where media markets are fluid, making it difficult if not impossible to determine the 'relevant market' that is crucial for regulatory intervention. Therefore, for the converged future a new innovative approach to structural regulation clearly needs to be developed. A formula will be required for measuring *media power* in a converged media environment so that when media corporations reach a certain threshold of media power there can be regulatory intervention. As in the past, media power might be identified through a metric that is still related to market data even in this complex converging media environment. There are difficulties in achieving this. One mooted difficulty is that different media sectors have had their own industry-specific metrics. However, reformers (Media Reform Coalition 2014) have pointed out that there are reliable measurements of audience share, which have in the past been employed as a useful metric of market power in distinct sectors, covering all the main sectors for news and information: radio, television, newspapers, and online; moreover, they point to two useful cross-media measures that are discussed below, one developed by Ofcom and the other by Enders Analysis. The trick will be to calculate a market share measurement that combines the data to measure media power in a converged media environment, particularly given that different media have been held by many analysts to exert different levels of influence.

Crauford Smith and Tambini (2012: 47) discuss how this might be achieved by weighting different media. They point to Germany, where regulators have employed a weighting approach (otherwise referred to as an 'exchange rate') in reviewing a case of cross-media ownership that assumes a greater media effect of television on public opinion than that of newspapers. In Germany, broadcasting companies whose channels command more than a 30 per cent share of the total audience are held to have too great an influence on public opinion, and at a 25 per cent share other cross-media interests can be taken into account by the regulator. In the one major case that has arisen, when in 2006 Germany's largest newspaper concern, the Axel Springer publishing group, made a bid to take over one of the country's two leading private television companies, Pro7/Sat 1 Media AG, the country's Media Concentration Commission (the *Kommission zur Ermittlung der Konzentration im Medienbereich*) applied a 2/3 weighting to determine that the Springer group's 26 per cent share of the daily print market equated to a 17 per cent share of television audience, which together with Pro7/Sat 1 Media's share brought the merged company over the limit. In the event, the decision was negated by a court ruling that the television company's share was actually under the 25 per cent threshold that triggered regulatory intervention, though in the event Springer pulled out when the takeover was queried by the country's competition authority as well as the Media Concentration Commission (Gibbons and Humphreys 2012: 127–8).

However, as Crauford Smith and Tambini (2012: 47) note,

> weighting is ... controversial, not least because products *within* media sectors are more or less influential, and *specific individuals* attach very different weights to particular print and audiovisual services. Without further research

into how individuals receive and process information from the various media sectors, attempts to weight different media sectors potentially add to, rather than resolve, the existing methodological problems.

Crauford Smith and Tambini (2012: 48–9) go on to discuss how Ofcom (2010), in reporting a merger case it had been required to scrutinise, namely the controversial bid announced in 2010 by News International to fully take over Sky (which was withdrawn in wake of the News International phone hacking scandal), developed a 'share of reference' approach to address these problems, where 'share of reference' is calculated by survey, the respondents being asked to indicate from a list which news sources, from across a wide range of platforms and including an 'other' category catering for international sources, search engines and websites that they used regularly and which they considered to be their main source of news. This approach allowed the regulator to determine for each news provider both its overall influence by calculating its share of total references and also its reach by calculating what proportion of those surveyed accessed it on a weekly basis. Ofcom's review of the data found the BBC having the largest share of reference (37 per cent), followed by a group of four other significant providers of news, ITN (providing news for ITV and Channel 4), News Corporation and Sky, each with a share of reference of around 10 per cent, followed by a third group with reference shares of between 1 and 5 per cent, and finally a large tail totalling a reference share of 11 per cent.[12] This data led the regulator to conclude that the proposed combination of News Corporation and Sky could be 'expected to operate against the public interest' (Ofcom 2010, paras 1.28 and 1.57). Crauford Smith and Tambini (2012) note that thus Ofcom had developed a method for cross-platform analysis that was both based on firm evidence for individuals' news consumption rather than any artificial weighting and that would be flexible enough to 'accommodate new and evolving forms of media use'. They note too, however, that the withdrawal of the aforementioned takeover bid meant that Ofcom's proposed share of reference model did not receive further consideration.

Another interesting approach for developing new cross-media controls, outlined in a submission by Enders Analysis (2012) to the Leveson Inquiry (which was established to look at the culture, practice and ethics of the newspaper sector in the wake of the News International phone hacking scandal), suggests the use of revenue to measure cross-media share and a cap on the total revenues of the UK's media industries that can be held by one company to prevent it wielding too much control. This approach can justifiably claim to have the benefit of not focusing, like Ofcom's, solely on the plurality of news and current affairs, which Enders Analysis deemed (and this chapter agrees is) too narrow to ensure true diversity and to prevent deleterious significant market power in the creative industries. The Enders Analysis submission's rationale is as follows:

> The media industries act as the gatekeepers between the creative professions and citizen. We suggest that the core purpose of plurality obligations is to ensure that no gatekeeper can exert too much power. Since such power is generally exerted through financial dominance, it may make sense to restrict the percentage of the flow of money controlled by a single company. (Enders Analysis 2012: 2)

The Enders Analysis submission continues:

> A company or individual with very large financial firepower could easily control output in a certain media – through paying more for popular journalists, scoops, successful TV shows or the rights to televise popular sports such as Formula 1 motor racing. One consequence would be that this company would probably gain viewers and revenues, creating a greater concentration of media power that would force less successful players out of the market. (Enders Analysis 2012: 2–3)

The Enders Analysis submission adopted a wide-ranging definition of the total media market, covering 'advertising and subscription revenues, ticket sales, newsstand payments and physical media such as DVDs'. The submission suggests that a cap of 15 per cent would ensure that 'at least seven companies will always be participants'. This would constitute 'as media converge ... a better – and much clearer – regulatory intervention than other forms of control' (Enders Analysis 2012: 3). Enders Analysis's detailed analysis of the UK media markets in 2010 found that News Corporation, were it to be allowed to have a 100 per cent stake in BSkyB, would have been the only main market participant to exceed that proposed cap, at 20 per cent of the market. However, with its existing stake of 39 per cent of the broadcaster, its market share fell below the proposed cap, at 11 per cent, and BSkyB's share was just below the cap, at 14 per cent. The particular merits of this revenue-based approach are first that it takes social and cultural influence into account, not just dominance over news and information, and second, as it claims itself, its essential clarity.

Both of these UK proposals provide indicators of media power that could be developed in the context of media convergence to allow identification of a potential threat to pluralism and diversity. Then if such a potential threat were to be identified, a public interest test might be triggered whereby an independent regulatory authority would decide whether or not a particular concentration of media power presents a danger to the public interest. Such a test is indeed provided for in the UK, though it is not adapted to digitally convergent markets and the minister has the ultimate discretion, not being bound by the advice of the regulators. A number of public interest criteria are set out in the Enterprise Act 2002 for the triggering of an 'intervention notice' from the minister on the basis of media pluralism concerns relating to merges involving newspapers or newspapers and broadcasters. The key calculation is whether a media merger endangers 'sufficient plurality' of views and owners or controllers of media in media markets. The Office of Fair Trading refers a merger to the Competition Commission where the turnover of the company being taken over exceeds £70 million or where one of the companies has at least 25 per cent of a newspaper or broadcasting market share. In media mergers, the minister has both the discretion to decide whether to proceed with a Public Interest Test, and the test having been conducted and advice received from the regulators (the Competition Commission and Ofcom), the minister also has the discretion to decide the ultimate outcome. The communications regulator Ofcom (2010) made clear its discontent with this mechanism, notably that it only related to media merger transactions, that it did not take account of the new media technologies, and that it did not cater to concentration arising from the organic changes in the market shares of key players (Gibbons and Humphreys 2012: 105–6; for more detailed analysis see Crauford Smith and Tambini 2012). These criticisms are of course all valid, as is that of the political discretion involved (on which see Humphreys 2015), but that does not mean that the model could not be adapted to address these issues.

A number of recommendations for policy reform have been produced following a series of media plurality seminars led by Professor Steven Barnett at the University of Westminster, London, which took place at the end of 2013 and involved a number of academics and leading figures in media policy, law and regulation.[13] These include: periodic plurality reviews, which would not be tied to old technologies; parliamentary guidance on what constitutes 'sufficiency' (of plurality of views, of persons with control of media enterprises); consideration of a sliding scale of market concentration, with (soft rather than hard caps) and discretion to impose behavioural remedies on companies with the largest market share; and decision-making discretion to be invested in an independent body rather than the Secretary of State. That body might be, for example, a statutory Board of Ofcom, the communications regulator, equivalent in status to its existing Content Board. To be sure, implementing these recommendations would require addressing a number of complex considerations. Crauford Smith and Tambini (2012) provide a detailed discussion of the nature of the task. In view of convergence, 'delimiting the market for information' would not be a simple undertaking, nor would deciding on the weighting or exchange rate for calculating the varying levels of influence represented by different media, nor determining the geographical delimitation. Another thorny issue is the question of choice between fixed limits, thresholds and wide-ranging 'holistic' plurality impact assessments by the regulator. Each have their merits and demerits. 'Fixed limits create the greatest certainty, while multi-factor investigations, though time-consuming and costly, may result in more sophisticated and better targeted intervention' (Crauford Smith and Tambini 2012: 55). 'Soft caps' or thresholds triggering a public interest test would allow more flexibility, but also involve more discretion, which might lead to concerns of political motivation or, in the case of the regulator, agency capture (for detail, see Crauford Smith and Tambini 2012).

Should the public interest be found to be in jeopardy by the market power of a media entity then blocking a merger or acquisition, or even divestment, might be required. Alternatively, rather than risk adverse effects, for instance when divestment or preventing a merger might result in a media company going under, a number of behavioural remedies to regulate the future conduct of the company might be implemented. The regulator might require that entity to adopt internal measures to ensure the independence and integrity of its journalists, for instance by mandating editorial codes and committees free from proprietorial intervention, and by requiring the involvement of the journalists in the election and removal of editors-in-chief. Another obvious behavioural remedy would see the regulator laying a number of specific public interest obligations on the media entity in question. This might, for instance, involve the mandating of an internal pluralism requirement (slots for independent, third-party journalism). Journalists and possibly external societal representatives might oversee its implementation, as is the practice in German broadcasting regulation. Certain amounts of funding might be required to be put towards particular journalistic functions, such as independent investigative journalism.

In order to facilitate regulation, increasing transparency will clearly be vital; currently patterns of media power are often very opaque. So a monitoring authority will need to conduct regular investigations of media markets to ascertain the scale of concentration and threat to media pluralism. As seen, such a body has been developed at EU level, though it lacks any regulatory teeth. Again, Germany could provide a model. In 1996 a Media Concentration Commission (*Kommission zur Ermittlung der Konzentration im Medienbereich* – KEK) was established to monitor media concentration in the TV sector and also cross-media concentration (though research by Gibbons and Humphreys cited earlier in this chapter found the concentration horse had already bolted the regulatory stable!). Composed of six experts in media and economic law, nominated by the prime ministers of the German Länder (broadcasting being a competence of the states in the German federal system), the KEK provides an annual list of TV-services and their shareholders and every three years a very detailed report on the state of media concentration and measures taken to ensure diversity of opinion, taking into account horizontal, cross-media (diagonal) and international concentration. This could provide the model (Humphreys 2015: 163–4).

In assessing media power, there is clearly a need to address ownership or control of media bottlenecks (or gateways) such as digital cable, satellite and terrestrial systems, electronic programme guides (EPGs), and market-dominant Internet intermediaries (ISPs, Google, YouTube). The answer might appear to be to rely on competition law combined with what is called 'conditional access regulation', whereby bottleneck controllers are required to provide access to both content providers and end-users on fair and non-discriminatory terms, and this has indeed been the general thrust of media policy at national and EU levels. An EU TV standards Directive regulates the conditional access systems for pay-TV systems (the 'set-top box'), though as Levy (1999) has shown the ways this directive has been transposed into national law and implemented has varied. The navigation bottleneck can be regulated for linear services; thus, Ofcom's code of practice requires platforms operate to give 'appropriate prominence' to the main public service channels (BBC, ITV, Channels 4 and 5 and S4C) and prescribes a fair, open and non-discriminatory method of allocating listings. It is, however, unclear how such a system might work for non-linear EPGs and Internet search engines.

Digital convergence means that media bottlenecks will continue to become increasingly the focus of attention since those who control entry to or movement along the value chain for media content wield considerable – and potentially overweening media power – over the news, information and sociocultural material that citizens consume and by extension therefore over public opinion. Potentially at least, awesome new media power is being acquired over content by new bottleneck-controllers of the means to access content. Much debate has surrounded the bottleneck power of Internet platforms like Google and Facebook.

While there are absolutely no grounds for suspecting that Google uses its search algorithms for any editorial purposes that may impinge on public opinion and democratic pluralism, there remains the potential. Moreover, there can be little doubt that there can be political effect, even without intentionality. In the case of the social media, Facebook and Twitter, there has been considerable recent alarm about their negative impact on the quality of political debate, and demands for greater regulation of these 'social media giants', possibly recasting them as publishers rather than platforms, and for prosecution and the imposition of sanctions, notably large fines or taxes (Coates 2017; Bridge 2017b). This connects with questions discussed in Chapters 5 and 7. Should Internet intermediaries be treated as platforms (simply conduits for content) and left to self-regulate, or should they, given their tremendous potential media power, be treated more as publishers and subjected to greater external supervision and regulation? Should powerful communication companies, whose main or sole function is the *distribution* (through cable, satellite, or the Internet) of other people's content, not be obliged to pay a small levy to fund the *production* of quality content?

In order to provide a counterbalance to the large commercial communication giants, there continues to be a crucial role for strong, well-resourced public-service broadcasters (PSBs) which have an extensive – rather than minimal – and internally pluralistic programme remit. Further, these PSBs should be given the political encouragement and financial means to develop into public service media (PSMs), adapted to the Internet era. The flagship role of key PSBs like the BBC is crucial, but the UK's commitment to the principle of public service plurality is also merit-worthy, and the means should be found to maintain commitment to other PSBs, like Channel 4, and their developments as PSMs. Yet, policy might also involve giving greater encouragement to a diversity of other media ownership forms: such as trusts like the one that owns the *Guardian* newspaper, foundations like the Knight Foundation in the USA,[14] charities, community groups, and other non-profit organisations. An obvious means to do this would be to deploy new subsidies to support media plurality. This is very much the thrust of the following chapter which surveys existing subsidy policy and suggests that this might be extended, imaginatively, towards granting direct support to certain media functions, such as investigative journalism and other public service journalism. Subsidies might be directed to the creation of a funding mechanism to support new start online journalistic initiatives, community media, the practical training of journalists, and student media in universities and other colleges. Consideration might be given to encouraging partnerships with and between publicly funded bodies, such as public service broadcasters, universities, and museums. The aforementioned recommendations from the University of Westminster seminars on media plurality included financial support for plurality, mooting the possibility of a 'consolidated fund, subject to contestable funding bids for media start-ups in local, regional areas'. The following chapter discusses how this kind of subsidy approach would be highly appropriate to the converged, digital, online media environment, but not just to support local media. The University of Westminster recommendations also called for consideration of new ideas for revenue-raising, 'based on media subsidies and transfer of resources (within reason) from new technology companies which have benefited from the creativity/journalism of others'.[15] That particular idea connects with the previous chapter too.

NOTES

1. Dean emeritus of the University of California, Berkeley, Graduate School of Journalism.
2. Time Warner merged with Internet giant AOL in January 2001, to create AOL Time Warner, but disappointing performance led to the spin-off of AOL at the end of 2009.
3. Belgium, France, Germany, Italy, Luxembourg, the Netherlands, Spain, Sweden, Switzerland, and the UK.
4. France, Germany, Italy, the Netherlands, Spain, and the UK.
5. The report included statistical appendices on the largest media companies in Europe; media companies with broadcasting activities in more than one European country; and an overview of national legislation concerning media concentration.
6. The MPM can be accessed at: http://cmpf.eui.eu/media-pluralism-monitor/.
7. http://mavise.obs.coe.int/, last accessed 27 July 2017.
8. Gilder was an economist, Republican Party activist, and co-founder of the Discovery Institute. His 1981 international bestseller Wealth and Poverty advocated the supply-side economics promoted in the Reagan era.
9. This work won the Spear's Business Book of the Year award in 2011 and featured among the best books of the year in a number of publications, including the *New Yorker* and *Fortune*. Tim Wu is professor at Columbia Law School, whose academic expertise includes antitrust, copyright and communications law. He has advised the US government. In 2006 he was recognised as one of 50 leaders in science and technology by *Scientific American*.
10. Hindman (2009: 43) describes how the 'importance' of a website is decided by an algorithm called PageRank on the basis of the number of hyperlinks directed to that particular website. Also the more pages on a specific topic a website has, the more likely it is to have a higher number of hyperlinks directed to it.
11. Those linked to a news operation of a pre-Internet platform, notably TV, press or wire service.
12. The model built in a distinction between retail and wholesale provision of news, namely the distinction between the news outlet that people accessed and the company that actually provided that news. Notably, this allowed it to take account of ITN's wholesale provision of news to ITV and Channel 4.
13. The seminars were organised by Steven Barnett, Professor of Communications at the University of Westminster and by Judith Townend, Research Associate at that university. Peter Humphreys was one of the academics involved. For other participants and more detail on the discussions and proposals see: https://mediaplurality.com/2013/12/23/

recommendations-on-plurality-to-the-house-of-lords-select-committee-on-communications/, last accessed 22 March 2018.

14. This is a non-non-profit foundation dedicated to fostering 'informed and engaged communities which [the foundation believes] are essential for a healthy democracy'. The foundation invests in quality journalism and the arts. See https://knightfoundation.org/, last accessed 24 October 2017.

15. The recommendations included seeking 'ways of harnessing BBC expertise ... without top-slicing the licence fee'.

7. Subsidies: sustaining public service communication in a converging media environment

This chapter's core theme is how policy should confront the challenge facing journalism as a public service. Convergence, new media, lifestyle changes and generational change combine to present a powerful challenge to traditional quality journalism and news media. First, the chapter examines the challenge to journalism and traditional media organisations represented by the changing technological and market environment they function in. The chapter goes on to examine the case for public subsidy, showing that in Europe where subsidies have been deployed in both the press and broadcasting sectors the case for continuing to subsidise has been challenged on the grounds that convergence, the new media and the Internet in particular have rendered unnecessary public support, certainly on the scale of the past. The chapter refutes this perspective, but points to the need to rethink public support for journalism in the Internet era. It suggests that media convergence has rendered increasingly anomalous the imbalance between public support mechanisms for specific media (press, broadcasting, online) and explores how public policy might instead support in a technology neutral manner deserving media outlets that provide public service journalism. While arguing that public service broadcasters (PSBs) should continue to be generously supported to become public service media (PSM), the chapter also suggests that interventionist support will be required to ensure the continued fulfilment of important public service journalistic functions in a technology neutral way across a range of electronic, digital delivery systems and media companies. While established public service media institutions should most certainly continue to play a crucial role in guaranteeing the fulfilment of communication needs in the Internet era, the chapter argues the need also to explore complementary new ways of developing and funding digital public service journalism. To be precise, it suggests that there is a need to resurrect the concept of the 'Public Service Publisher', mooted by UK regulator Ofcom (as a policy to support plurality of public service broadcasting in the digital era), in order to guarantee the survival of public service journalism in the Internet era. It suggests how this might be funded without damaging established PSB/PSM institutions. Hence the chapter concentrates on the UK case, showing how the UK has always been a generous subsidiser of public service media and how the policy debate continues to produce highly interesting ideas for innovation, even if they have so far not been implemented.

THE CHALLENGE FACING JOURNALISM AS A PUBLIC SERVICE

Despite the continuing dominance of certain legacy media companies in the Internet era which the preceding chapter has described, there can be little doubt that the business model underpinning quality journalism is being dramatically undermined by the new technologies. Chris Anderson, editor-in-chief of *Wired* magazine, has written two path-breaking works on the subject of the way that the online revolution has undermined the traditional business models in the culture industries at large. In *The Long Tail* (Anderson 2006) and its revised version *The Longer Long Tail: How Endless Choice is Creating Unlimited Demand* (Anderson 2009b) he pointed to the revolutionary significance of the 'infinite shelf space' offered by the Internet, which is transforming the market for cultural products like books and music through online selling, thereby undermining the traditional retail outlets' business models. In *Free* (Anderson 2009a), subtitled *How Today's Smartest Businesses Profit by Giving Something for Free*, he pointed to how traditional business models are being undermined by the growing flood of free digital goods which can be produced and distributed at virtually no marginal cost, so that the default price of the online economy is zero. He points to how 'today's smartest businesses' profit by giving digital product away rather than charging for it. A taste of the problem that this has created has already been seen in relation to copyright. For news journalism and cultural production more generally, it is of course problematic simply because quality journalism is so expensive to produce.

Traditionally, the business model of non-publicly funded media has relied on advertising revenue; sales of newspapers in particular has never been enough to sustain the industry. Advertising follows audiences and readerships. The problem is that audiences and readers are increasingly going online for news, information, entertainment and cultural fare because it is free and easy to access. In the online world the competition for advertising has become extremely fierce as audiences and therefore advertising markets have fragmented, and digital advertising has become dominated by technology companies, notably Google and Facebook. Correspondingly legacy media business's advertising revenues have shrunk. Combined with the expectation that web content should be free, this has impacted negatively on newspapers in particular, despite the fact that many have embraced the new media. According to the American Pew Research Centre, in the ten years 2006–2016, annual advertising revenues of US newspapers shrunk by 63 per cent leading them to shed a corresponding nearly 40 per cent of their reporters and editors (*The Economist* 2017a; for detailed data see PEW 2016). While digital revenue as a proportion of newspaper's income showed signs of significant increase during this period, from five per cent to around 25 per cent, this has not compensated for the decline in print revenue. As Kaye and Quinn (2010: 9) explain:

> Newspapers, in many cases, have been attracting huge numbers of readers to their online sites – far greater numbers than they have ever attracted in print. But with the content mainly given away for free, and the online advertising rates far lower than print, the revenue earned online has not been enough to make up for the drop in earnings on the print side.

Kaye and Quinn (2010: 12) go on to point out that:

> [J]ournalism is a rare type of business in the sense that its product [they specify news, but they could also have mentioned other quality journalistic fare] provides a public good or service ... When a huge drop in advertising threatens the financial viability of the news business, the media's public good role is threatened.

What we might term traditional 'public service journalism' is under mounting pressure, attaining crisis proportions in the US media environment. A 2009 report in the *Columbia Journalism Review*, opens thus:

> American journalism is at a transformational moment, in which the era of dominant newspapers and influential network news divisions is rapidly giving way to one in which the gathering and distribution of news is more widely dispersed. As almost everyone knows, the economic foundation of the nation's newspapers, long supported by advertising, is collapsing, and newspapers themselves, which have been the country's chief source of independent reporting, are shrinking – literally ... Commercial television news, which was long the chief rival of printed newspapers, has also been losing its audience, its advertising revenue, and its reporting resources. (Downie and Schudson 2009: 1)[1]

The authors acknowledge that the Internet has certainly facilitated interesting new ways of gathering and distributing the news, which

> is being done not only by surviving newspapers and commercial television, but by startup online news organizations, nonprofit investigative projects, public broadcasting stations, university-run news services, community news sites with citizen participation, and bloggers ... Together they are creating not only a variety of independent reporting missions but different definitions of news. (Downie and Schudson 2009: 1–2)

Downie and Schudson (2009: 2) suggest that 'reporting is becoming more participatory and collaborative', that the range of news gatherers has expanded beyond the traditional newsroom to include 'freelancers, university faculty members, students and citizens', and that the 'Internet's easily accessible free information and low-cost advertising have loosened the hold of large, near-monopoly news organizations on audiences and advertisers' (though our chapter on media concentration has cast some doubt on the extent of this loosening). However, the main thrust of Downie and Schudson's piece is their concern that the Internet has 'also undermined the traditional marketplace support for American journalism', by which they mean the traditional, professionalised, social responsibility and public interest kind of reporting that the old media sustained. They point out that 'a serious commitment to accountability journalism' depended upon the abundant advertising revenues of large urban newspapers, and observe that 'independent reporting which provides information, investigation, analysis, and community knowledge' and which fulfils the all-important democratic 'watchdog function' that holds government to account, is now under threat (Downie and Schudson 2009: 3). They note that newspapers are developing new ways to finance themselves, including digital subscriptions, micropayments for reading individual news items, and single click mechanisms for readers to make voluntary contributions. They note too that 'a growing number of newspapers are supplementing their reduced resources for news reporting by collaborating with other newspapers, new kinds of news organisations, and their own readers' (Downie and Schudson 2009: 9). Their article points to a range of new local news start-ups around the country and also ventures like *ProPublica*, the largest start-up non-profit news organisation, which are experimenting with 'pro-am' journalism, with professionals and amateurs collaborating over the Internet. However, they conclude that in the Internet era it is unlikely that traditional and new forms of news journalism alike will able to flourish without new levels of support from society (philanthropists, foundations, universities, and so on) and also from government. While commercial news organisations search for new ways of replacing their lost advertising revenues, non-profits 'struggle to stay afloat', dependent as they are on the time-consuming and energy-taxing pursuit of support from foundations and other donors and sponsors. Downie and Schudson (2009: 23–33) devote the latter third of their article to a discussion of what needs to be done to support the news media. Their call for public intervention by both federal and state governments includes granting tax exempt status to a wider range of news providers, increased congressional funding for the public broadcasting system which they note is served far worse than other countries with comparable economies (on which see below) and establishment of a national fund for local news funded by levies on telecom users, television and radio broadcast licensees or Internet service providers.

Other leading voices in the US media scholarship and journalism communities have called for public intervention to combat the crisis. Robert W. McChesney and John Nichols[2] drew attention to the scale of the crisis of American journalism in an article in *The Nation* (Nichols and McChesney 2009), developing the theme at length in a book pointedly entitled *The Death and Life of American Journalism* (McChesney and Nichols 2010). They paint a picture of an industry in serious trouble, marked by the bankruptcy of great regional dailies like the *Chicago Tribune*, the *Minneapolis Star Tribune*, and the *Philadelphia Inquirer* and the near-bankruptcy of others. They allude to the 'death by small cuts' of surviving newspapers, which were laying off reporters and closing bureaus, leaving 'precious few resources for doing journalism' (Nichols and McChesney 2009: 1; McChesney and Nichols 2010: 29). In their book, they paint a very detailed picture of a 'dying industry', whose problems they argue are deeply rooted in a long-standing tension between commerce and journalism, but brought to a head by the Internet:

> Mired in debt and rattled by revenue shortfalls as advertisers cut back and young readers show no interest, the managers of corporate newspaper firms seek to 'right the sinking ship' by cutting costs, leading remaining newspaper readers to ask why they're bothering to pay for publications that are pale shadows of their former selves. Older readers are giving upon papers they had once relied upon. Advertisers have gone elsewhere. (McChesney and Nichols 2010: 13)

Nor is the crisis confined to newspapers; the broadcasting sector, too, has been scarred by large-scale redundancies in TV newsrooms and increasing lay-offs of foreign correspondents (see also McChesney 2004). The Internet, they suggest, has both dealt the final blow to the business model of traditional media and also offered 'false hope':

As exciting and promising as many of the new online journalism ventures are, we believe that the only honest conclusion available to us is that the overall resources are woefully insufficient to fund a new generation of journalistic institutions and practices that might satisfactorily meet the needs of the American people. (McChesney and Nichols 2010: 99–100)

In pointing to the need for public subsidy, they suggest that the American obsession with the profit motivation and freedom from the perceived threat of 'regulatory interference' and 'direct censorship' are the 'false premises' that stand in the way of the required public intervention (McChesney and Nichols 2010: 100). For them, the crisis of journalism poses a real threat to democracy and therefore subsidising the media means 'subsidising democracy', a theme to which they devote an entire chapter (McChesney and Nichols 2010: 157–212), and one to which we return later in our chapter.

In Europe the picture of a newspaper sector in crisis is familiar. In the UK, a country with a historically strong newspaper market, industry data shows a marked decline in newspaper circulations, except among the national Sunday newspapers. According to a major industry report (Keynote 2010) the sales of regional newspapers fell by around 20 to 30 per cent in the five years between 2005 and 2010, while sales of the national daily papers declined by around 10 per cent since 2007, with a very marked decline in 2009. Since then, according to Ofcom data, the downward trend has continued; overall print circulation for national dailies declined from 9.2 million in 2010 to just 6 million in 2016, with the tabloid *Sun* and the *Daily Mail* being the most-read UK-wide newspapers; the Ofcom data showed circulation of Sunday newspapers circulation dropped from 9.2 million to 5.4 million (Ofcom 2017: 26). While these figures do not account for a marked increase in online newspaper reading, that did not have compensatory impact on advertising revenues. According to a 2016 *Guardian* online report, drawing on advertising industry data, the UK advertising market grew at its fastest rate in five years in 2015, yet 'national newspapers bucked the trend as more than £150 million in print ads disappeared and digital revenues slowed to a trickle' (Sweeney 2016). A worrying trend was that for much of this period the market for quality newspapers appeared to be dropping much faster than the market for popular papers. The case of the *Guardian* newspaper highlights the severity of the economic problems of the press sector in the Internet era. The *Guardian* has been a world leader in providing high quality online journalism. It has repeatedly won Webby awards, the leading international awards honouring excellence on the Internet, yet its digital strategy has not off-set its commercial viability problem. Like its competitor quality newspapers, it has seen advertising migrate to dominant online companies like Google and Facebook. In 2016 it was compelled to lay off 250 staff and more job cuts appeared to be in prospect (Sherman 2017). In 2017, the *Guardian Media Group*, which also publishes the *Observer*, announced that it had made losses of £44.7 million in the year to 2 April 2017 (Ralph 2017). In Germany, another country with historically strong press markets, the picture is similar: shrinking circulations and diminishing advertising revenues. In 2010, only 22.7 million copies of daily newspapers were sold, down from 28.5 million in 2000. Less than half of 14–19-year-olds read a daily paper (Weberling 2011: 6).

In the UK, and in other European countries with strong public broadcasting, television is a rather different case. Predictions about the imminent demise of television have certainly featured a lot in the debate about the future of the media, and there can be no doubting the daunting nature of the challenge, particularly to television companies dependent on commercial funding through subscription and advertising. The top-down linear distribution technologies that the traditional broadcasters deployed are being challenged by the open, many-to-many, interactive, networked medium of the Internet. In America and in Europe, the TV market has certainly fragmented under the impact of digital and online technologies. In America, viewing of traditional pay-TV has been falling since 2010 and younger viewers in particular are now viewing primarily via Internet-based streaming services (*The Economist* 2017b). The scale of the challenge, even to the biggest established media companies, has been underlined most recently by the decision by Rupert Murdoch's 21st Century Fox to sell its entertainment businesses, including its highly successful European satellite broadcaster Sky (though not its news and sport services) to Walt Disney in a mega $66 billion deal (which remained subject to regulatory approval at the time of writing). The deal showed two things especially: first, concerning Rupert Murdoch, 'a recognition that an industry he once dominated has been irrevocably changed by digital streaming and a new generation of competitors from Netflix to Apple' (Garrahan 2017: 1); and, second as regards Disney, it demonstrated 'just how strong the scale imperative had become' in traditional media companies' future fight to retain their position vis-à-vis Amazon, Netflix, Facebook and YouTube (*Financial Times* 2017: 10; Dean 2017). In the UK, too, Ofcom's periodic communication market reports,[3] reveal in detail how new platforms and technology have been changing viewing habits. New digital channels have proliferated and the ease of access to online and mobile platforms has meant that audiences and therefore advertising revenues have fragmented and migrated to the

Internet in a similar way to the press sector, posing an essentially similar challenge to the business models of commercial operators as that confronted by the press.

Yet, for a number of reasons, not least their ability to adapt as well as their popularity and trustworthiness ratings with audiences, some European broadcasters have proved less crisis-prone than the press, at least so far. According to an important 2012 academic study for the Leverhulme Trust on the UK case, 'both television itself and television news are proving remarkably resilient in the face of these enormous economic and technological challenges' (Barnett, Ramsay and Gaber 2012). As regards television news in the UK, mainstream television news providers remain central news providers, despite the rise of 24-hour news channels, and 'there is little evidence to suggest that the plethora of news aggregators and online sources are likely to make any serious inroads into television's attraction as a news disseminator, both in terms of its ease of use and the trust invested in the television medium', television being 'by far the most trusted and frequented source of national and international news' in the UK. The authors of this report concluded that a key factor was that

> the regulatory structure mandates high quality national and international news on the commercial broadcasters in peak-time hours, while the BBC is bound by its public purposes, in particular its role in 'sustaining citizenship and civil society'. All are subject to rules of due impartiality, laid down by successive statutes. (Barnett, Ramsay and Gaber 2012: 33–34)

A recent report by the UK communications regulator Ofcom into UK TV news consumption by adults, found that use of TV for news registered a fall from 78 per cent of adults in 2013 to 69 per cent in 2016, while news use via the Internet or iPhone and computer/tablet apps similarly increased from 32 per cent to 48 per cent.[4] Confirming the crisis of the printed press, usage of newspapers to access news fell from 40 per cent to 29 per cent (Ofcom 2017: 8), though online readership of newspapers added considerably to overall newspaper consumption figures (Ofcom 2017: 26). Yet, among all adults BBC One remained by far the most important news source, followed by ITV, then the BBC website or app (Ofcom 2017: 49, 70). This was true even among the young (16–24-year-olds), though significantly without counting the BBC website or app, Facebook would have been slightly more popular (Ofcom 2017: 70). Of course, television in the UK, and certain other countries in Europe with strong public service broadcasters, has differed considerably both from the crisis-ridden newspaper sector and from the crisis besetting US television news principally because both the quantity and the standard of quality journalism have been provided by heavily subsidised public service broadcasting institutions. The BBC has adapted remarkably well to the digital era. Nonetheless, as will be discussed later in this chapter, from the early 2000s Ofcom became very concerned about a shortfall in funding for public service content as a result of the competitive environment in which the UK's commercial public service broadcasters (ITV, C5 and especially C4) found themselves in the Internet era.

THE CASE FOR MEDIA SUBSIDY IN THE DIGITAL ERA

McChesney and Nichols are sceptical about the common society-based and market-led proposals to deal with the problem that they identify as a crisis of journalism by relying on consolidation of news gathering, donations from citizens, and support from philanthropists and foundations. As for charging access to online content, they hold that the 'last thing we should do is erect electronic walls that block the openness and democratic genius of the Internet' (Nichols and McChesney 2009: 2). At the same time, they suggest that there is no returning to the old model, which was already 'heading due south' before the Internet, due to corporate strategies of ownership consolidation and short-term profit-seeking. For Nichols and McChesney 'only government can implement policies and subsidies to provide an institutional framework for quality journalism.' They are aware of the danger of politicisation, but observe that 'the rude calculus that says government intervention equals government control is inaccurate and does not reflect our past or present, or what enlightened policies and subsidies could entail (Nichols and McChesney 2009: 3).

In their above-cited book *The Death and Life of American Journalism*, McChesney and Nichols (2010) elaborate on the kind of subsidies that should be introduced to combat the crisis and they suggest too how these might be funded. For dealing with the immediate crisis they suggest four measures: first, postal subsidies ('dramatic reduction of the price of postage'), which they emphasise were deployed effectively in the early days of the American republic to support the development of the free press in order to promote democracy; second, the establishment of a journalism division of Americorps, the federal programme that places young people with non-profit organisations to be trained and do public service work; third, a dramatic expansion of funding for student media; and fourth, investment in media literacy classes stressing the civic role of journalism. These educational measures could draw on the expertise of professional journalists and thereby 'put an immediate dent in the surging numbers of unemployed reporters' (McChesney and Nichols 2010: 168–72). For aiding newspapers to 'transition to a post-corporate digital era', they suggest that government should establish an office, funded adequately to be able to purchase collapsing newspapers and to manage their rapid transition from 'failing corporate newspapers that have dysfunctional ownership structures – and, in most cases, the crushing debts that go with them – into post-corporate newspapers', that is independent entities, owned by local consortiums, community groups, non-profits, trusts like the UK Scott Trust which owns the Guardian Media Group, and 'civically and democratically minded publishers' (McChesney and Nichols 2010: 172–82). They suggest the granting of tax credits for newspapers to cover employment of journalists, this being preferable to tax deduction because it does not depend on a newspaper's profitability and could be deployed to support low-profit limited liability corporations (the L3C model), non-profits and cooperatives (McChesney and Nichols 2010: 182–90). They advocate a substantial increase in the funding of public (service) broadcasting, now conceived of as public (service) media in the digital age. Among other things, this would sustain news media, revive localism in the media, engage diverse communities such as minorities and the young, and offer employment to unemployed reporters (McChesney and Nichols 2010: 190–200). As for measures to 'unleash the Internet', they propose the enactment of network neutrality legislation, to ensure that ISPs treat all websites equally; the creation of 'a funding mechanism to spawn viable independent Internet journalism'; and introduction of a 'Citizenship News Voucher', which would be provided to every adult US citizen, who would indicate on their tax return the non-profit news medium to which it should be donated (McChesney and Nichols 2010: 200–6).

They point out that the rough cost of this range of subsidies – which they estimated at around $35 billion annually – is 'close to what the much smaller nations of Finland and Denmark spend in the form of media subsidies on a per capita basis', these being nations with notably healthy democracies and 'vibrant' commercial media sectors. To bolster their argument, they suggest that 'had the federal government devoted the same percentage of the Gross Domestic Product to press subsidies as the federal government did in the early 1840s, it would have spent some $30 billion to spawn journalism'. The money might be found, they suggest, by taxing broadcast spectrum, which has hitherto functioned as a 'massive public subsidy of commercial broadcasting'; taxing consumer electronics; a tax on the spectrum that government 'has been auctioning off … to commercial communication firms for many years'; a tax on advertising; and a tax on ISP-cell phones (phones that access digital services and the Internet). They estimate that these measures would have raised at the time of writing as much as $25 billion towards the aforementioned $35 billion cost of the subsidies they proposed (McChesney and Nichols 2010: 206–11). Other notable US voices favouring subsidy are those of Clark and Aufterheide (2009), directors of Washington University's Center for Social Media, who have suggested that 'taxpayer funds are crucial both to sustain coordination and to fund media production, curation and archiving' in order to fulfil the new participatory opportunities for 'Public Media 2:0' provided by the new more open, many-to-many networked media environment. However, calls for public subsidy will likely fall on deaf ears given the generally neo-liberal and conservative drift of US politics since Reagan (on which see, for example, Micklethwait and Wooldridge 2004, though this stops at George W. Bush).

Europe, however, has been far from averse to public intervention, with its strong public service broadcasting tradition and a number of countries having introduced more modest amounts of press subsidy as well.[5] From the 1960s onwards a notable number of European countries distributed press subsidies in an attempt to mitigate increasing concentration and maintain media pluralism. These varied in form, between general indirect subsidies such as tax breaks which typically were industry-wide and tended to benefit publishers which were already strong, and direct subsidies which more controversially took the form of selectively allocated direct transfers from the state to particular publications, usually in order to prop up weaker publications and ensure a diversity of opinion. Critics pointed to the danger of politicisation this might involve, though safeguards can be introduced (for a full discussion see Humphreys 2006, 2015). Direct press subsidies were embraced enthusiastically by countries with an interventionist state tradition, like France and Italy, both countries with weak press markets, and also by countries with a strong social democratic political culture and a democratic corporatist approach to industry, notably the Scandinavian countries and Austria (Humphreys 2006, 2015). Indirect subsidy, too, could be considerable. Both the UK and Germany, where legislators were averse to direct subsidies on the grounds that they carried the danger of politicisation, granted VAT exemption for their large press sectors amounting to a very sizeable subsidy indeed (Nielsen and Linnebank 2011).

By the digital era, however, these subsidies were being questioned. Critics argued that they had failed to address the underlying economic problems of the print media industries and create more sustainable businesses. They had even failed to prevent the number of titles declining. Instead they had encouraged dependence, sustained inefficiencies and dis-incentivised modernisation and restructuring. Further, it was argued, in the digital era the proliferation of media outlets has rendered them no longer necessary, the convergence of media sectors has rendered them inappropriate. Such arguments were particularly welcome to governments struggling to contain public expenditure (see Humphreys 1996, 2006, 2015). It is also the case that newspapers have sought to adapt to the digital era, some very energetically, by launching their own online sites, and iPad and mobile (smartphone) offerings. After a number of years of doubt about their economic viability, by the time of writing this book a few publications, such as *The New York Times* and *The Washington Post* were achieving some success through 'soft' paywall strategies which 'funnel' subscribers in through offering flexible (for example, metered) payment options (*The Economist* 2017a: 65–6). However, it is by no means clear that this strategy would work for less iconic publications, the sector at large and in particular the ailing regional and local press. This chapter argues, therefore, that in the digital era, particularly in view of the Internet's damaging impact on the main lifeblood of the newspaper industry, namely advertising, the case for press subsidy has actually strengthened, not weakened. In the UK, the former editor-in-chief of *The Guardian* newspaper, a leading quality newspaper struggling against unprofitability (see above), has suggested that consideration be given to imaginative new press subsidies to be introduced beyond the existing VAT exemption, such as the disbursement of contestable funds to support local news reporting and the establishment of a public service subsidy organisation, possibly based on the UK Press Association (Rusbridger 2009: 15–16). Certain countries have indeed responded to the newspaper crisis not simply with increased subsidy, but also with a degree of originality. For instance, in 2009 the (then) French president Nicolas Sarkozy pledged €600 million (£565 million) in emergency aid to his country's ailing newspaper industry and announced that every 18-year-old in France would be given a year's free subscription to a newspaper of their choice (Crisafis 2009).

As noted, European countries have subsidised public service broadcasting far more heavily than the press. This reflects the fact that, in contrast to the USA, broadcasting developed in Europe as a public service monopoly (or in the UK's case duopoly) and a path-dependent policy commitment to PSB ensured its survival through an era of commercialisation into the digital age. Notably, the UK has featured among the very highest spenders in per capita subsidy of public service broadcasting (and that is purely in financial terms, not counting the subsidy of discounted spectrum costs for the commercial public service broadcasters), making the UK one of the highest-ranking media subsidising countries in Europe and challenging Hallin and Mancini's (2004) widely cited classification of the UK media system alongside the USA in their North Atlantic/Liberal model (Humphreys 2011). Data abounds to confirm a subsidy 'league table' with the UK, Germany and a handful of generally north European countries as the high subsidisers, France and other west European countries as middle ranking subsidisers, most east European countries as comparatively low subsidisers, and the US and Canada right at the bottom of the league table (Humphreys 2015: 155–6; Gibbons and Humphreys 2012; Nielsen with Linnebank 2011; Edelvold Berg 2011; Nordicity 2011: 4).

However, public service broadcasters in Europe, hitherto generally conceived as providers of an important and comprehensive broadcast service, are facing a set of existential challenges in the age of digital convergence and global media markets (on the media policy implications of which see Iosifidis 2011). As Gibbons and Humphreys (2012) have described, given the expansion of new media outlets brought by technological advance, most notably digital and online, they face questions about the extent and future basis of their funding, about whether there should be a narrowing of their public service mission, and about restrictions on their scope for expansion into new media. In the digital and Internet age, the case for awarding generous 'subsidy' to an institution that was the product of an era of scarcity of frequencies, has encountered probing and sustained questioning. At a time when the new media environment is placing tight new financial constraints and fierce competitive pressures on private media companies, the latter are increasingly vocal in protesting the BBC's protected and, as they see it, highly privileged status, which is viewed as a significant barrier to entry for new services that could be provided by the market. At the same time, pressure on the funding of public service broadcasting has risen as politicians have become increasingly concerned with public sector cost containment, particularly in the years following the 2008 financial crisis. The future sustainability of the TV licence fee, which has provided the core funding for much public service broadcasting in Europe, has also been questioned since it is essentially a tax levied on ownership of a TV set when increasingly viewing is done online via home computers, tablets, and mobile phones.[6]

So far, European public service broadcasters themselves have responded to the multi-channel, digital media environment by developing a range of new digital and online media services; the extent to which they have met the online challenge has varied according to their own institutional cultures and perceived self-interest, and above all the policy and funding environment in which they find themselves. Until recently, the BBC benefited from a particularly strong political encouragement to develop digital TV and online services. It has developed a range of digital channels, played a leading role in the development of digital terrestrial television through its *Freeview* platform, together with ITV helped make digital switchover a success through extending free TV to satellite through *Freesat*, and developed a major online presence (Gibbons and Humphreys 2012: 98–100; for a detailed comparative study of Denmark, France, Spain, Italy and the UK, see Brevini 2013; for a comparison of the digital strategies of PSBs in UK, France, Spain, Ireland, Sweden and Greece see Iosifidis 2007; for a wider-ranging comparative sweep covering US, Canada, Australia and New Zealand, as well as many European countries, see the edited collection by Iosifidis 2010). Apart from providing an extensive online offer, seen as an appropriate extension of its offline remit and allowing the BBC to serve as a trusted resource for a wide range of online content, the BBC has been characteristically innovative in offering new personalised, interactive services, and encouraging grassroots participation in public debate though online interactive discussion forums and inviting the public to share with BBC news ('have your say@bbc.co.uk'). This engagement was seen by the BBC and government alike as fulfilling a key objective of the Corporation's online engagement, namely to strengthen its relationship with and accountability to its public. However, the role for PSB organisations in becoming public service media (PSM) providers – and even in providing a comprehensive programme service – in an age of communications abundance has been questioned (see, for example, Elstein et al. 2004; Elstein 2008; Armstrong and Weeds 2007). Private media and communication groups have argued strongly against any significant engagement of PSBs in new media activities, seen as a harmful distortion of the market (see, for example, ACT et al. 2009). In Germany, legislators responded to the newspaper publishers' concerns about PSBs' 'electronic press' services, by stipulating that the PSBs should only publish online material related to specific TV programme services; 'press-type offers unrelated to the programme shall not be permitted' (The 12th Interstate Treaty on Broadcasting and Telemedia, Section 11d, cited in Weberling 2011: 15).

Yet the case for maintaining a strong public service broadcasting sector in the digital and Internet era is compelling. The classic economic argument for public service provision is about market failure. In their major work arguing the case for 'a cultural toolkit' for the creative

industries, Grant and Wood (2004: 58–9) highlight the 'curious economics' of the media and observe that 'economists examining ... [media]
markets would describe them as inherently prone to market failure', in
that the 'market as a whole [fails] to do what markets are presumed to do
best, that is, lead to the best possible outcome for the greatest number of
participants', in economists' jargon 'maximise social welfare'. One of the
most obvious market failures is the lack of incentive to produce unprofitable 'merit goods', where in an economist's terms the 'externalities'
(the social benefit) are 'indeterminate' (unmeasurable, or at least hard to
quantify). The social benefits of production of news programmes, investigative journalism, or arts programmes, for example, are not measurable
in terms of their market value, which is almost certain to fall below their
production costs. This argument remains in the digital era as valid as
ever.

Moreover, it can be argued that in the digital/Internet era public-service
broadcasting should be funded and tasked to provide a service of both
scale and scope, that is, continuing to provide 'high quality, challenging,
original, innovative and engaging' content (as required by the BBC
Agreement). This service should be delivered across all genres including
entertainment ('something for everyone'), and by means of close involvement in the development and use of the new media technologies. It can
be argued that this will be even more necessary in the digital/Internet age
in order to fulfil a number of crucially important functions: (1) to
mitigate the declining scope for traditional broadcasting law and regulation to ensure that all society's communication needs are met in the
new media and especially on the Internet, a global medium hardly
amenable to traditional mechanisms of regulating for pluralism; (2) to
help assure (along with a commitment to universal high-speed broadband) a universal service in the digital era; (3) to continue, in the new
media and Internet era, to fulfil the key democratic functions of providing
high quality, reliable news and information, making a responsible contribution to the formation of public opinion and societal debate, and
representing the myriad viewpoints and meeting the cultural needs of a
pluralistic society; (4) to maintain quality journalistic standards in the
context of widespread commercialisation, burgeoning non-professional
citizen journalism, social media, blogs, 'fake news', and so on; (5) to
serve as a trusted source and guide to the Internet (this was highlighted as
a key function for its online engagement by John Birt, the BBC Director
General who instigated its digital and online drive in the late 1990s);
(6) to act as an internally pluralistic counterweight to media concentration in the supposedly 'externally pluralistic' private sector, which has –
as explained in the preceding chapter – even in the Internet era seen the

dominance of a handful of powerful private media companies; and (7) to continue to be a pillar (in the UK's case for example, the main pillar, the BBC and the commercial public service, broadcasters funding around 90 per cent of UK TV production) of national and regional production and, relatedly, to promote national and societal cultural identities in the face of globalisation. According to a 2014 Reuters Institute study, if there were no BBC television and no licence fee, 'investment in first-run UK content would be 25–50% lower', representing 'a severe blow to UK production companies' as well as a 'reduction in both choice and value for money' for the UK viewer (Barwise and Picard 2014: 3).

THE NEED TO RETHINK MEDIA SUBSIDIES

There is an argument, of course, that public service broadcasters like the BBC should not be allowed to become too dominant. In recent years, Conservative ministers – for instance, former Conservative Culture Secretary John Whittingdale[7] and former chancellor, George Osborne[8] – have made very clear that the BBC should curb any 'imperial' ambitions, suggesting that some services on its website could provide unfair competition for the struggling newspaper sector. But the concern does not only exercise conservatives and the BBC's traditional rivals in the media sector. In 2006 *The Guardian* newspaper, which has tended to support the BBC as a standard setter of excellent journalism, was questioning the BBC's (at that time ambitious) online expansion of the Corporation 'into areas where its remit does not run so clearly' and, given the problems of the local press in particular, pointing to the 'pressing danger' of the 'unwitting creation' of BBC 'regional monopolies' where the BBS could become 'within a few years' the sole news provider (*Guardian* editorial 2015: 32). In 2007 the BBC itself came up with its Public Value Test, which has on occasion limited its launch of new services where the public value of the proposed service was not deemed to outweigh its adverse impact on the media market. Moreover, during the charter renewal process which concluded at the end of 2016, the Corporation agreed to drop some online services which had a tenuous claim to being part of any public service remit. In order to address private sector complaints about PSB expansion and comply with European competition law, public value tests have been adopted by other European countries, though their character and implementation have varied according to different political and cultural contexts and media policy path dependencies. Academic evaluations, too, have varied, some seeing them as legitimising PSB evolution into PSM providers by holding them to account for their use of public funds and their market impact, as this chapter agrees in principle (also see Humphreys 2009; Moe 2010), and others regarding them as burdens and limitations on public service actors, which indeed they can be if poorly implemented or taken out of the PSBs' own hands and employed as a neo-liberal tool (for a critical perspective see Freedman 2008: 154–7).[9]

Debates about the extent to which PSB should be allowed to expand in the online world aside, the 'elephant in the room', however, is the need to re-think public subsidies to the media sector at large in the Internet era. As long ago as 1997 the Norwegian scholar Skogerbø (1997: 115) pointed to the problem of media sector specific subsidies. In an article on press subsidies (in Norway) he suggested that their character 'as a technology-dependent regulation [wa]s an obstacle to their survival in the long run'. To subsidise one type of medium using one particular technology (in that case print) and not others (online text) would 'over time create a legitimacy crisis because the issue eventually boils down to the question of supporting the printed word but not digitised text, or in other words, subsidizing paper but not bytes'. How much more sensitive, then, the question of the generosity of broadcast subsidies relative to those directed at the ailing press sector! The media and their markets are converging, the Internet is posing a major challenge to the business model of the press sector, local newspapers are in crisis, quality national newspapers are dependent on cross-subsidies from parent organisations (for example, the News UK owned *The Times*; and the Trust-owned *Guardian*), yet the print and audiovisual sectors remain subject to different media subsidy systems that have remained essentially unchanged over decades. The press remains rooted in a hands-off-state regime inherited from the battles for a free press in the nineteenth century, with only distinctly limited public support having been extended in the second half of the twentieth. Despite deregulation, liberalisation and commercialisation in the late twentieth century, through a path-dependent policy commitment to public service broadcasting the audio-visual media have remained subject to a much more interventionist regime, inherited from the rise of the public corporation and the welfare state in the twentieth century, enjoying far more generous public subsidy. Online-only media organisations and would-be online journalistic pro-viders, by contrast, have not been deemed deserving of any substantial public support. In the UK, where the VAT exemption granted to printed newspapers was not extended to their digital editions; a legal challenge launched by the publisher of *The Times* and a number of other UK newspapers was even rejected by a tribunal in 2018 on the grounds that according to the letter of the law the VAT exemption referred to goods not services although the tribunal recognised that the print and digital editions were essentially the same in content (*The Times* 2018). According to a Reuters Institute report (Nielsen and Linnebank 2011: 4), France was the only country in which support was given, amounting to 'little more than 1/10,000th of all public support in 2008'.

It can be argued, as this chapter does, that it is vital that the public service remit be defined comprehensively rather than confined to some public service 'reservation' (as in the USA) and that PSBs be allowed to evolve extensively as PSMs and continue to be generously subsidised. However, this hardly addresses the 'elephant in the room'. Much newspaper journalism as well as broadcast journalism fulfils a key public-service function. Yet, as seen, the press is struggling in the Internet era, with relatively little public support compared to public broadcasters. And what about the new online-only providers of 'public service' journalistic content? (Humphreys 2015: 157). Media convergence poses the inevitable question of a clash of regulatory regimes, which increasingly demands an answer, as old media experience various degrees of challenge, even crisis, and as popular media usage, particularly by the digital generation, migrates to new platforms. As the aforementioned Reuters Institute report concludes:

> Those who favour public support for the media will therefore have to rethink the role of public policy and in particular how governments can support those private sector companies that provide public goods like the kinds of accessible accountability journalism and diverse public debate that democracies benefit from. (Nielsen and Linnebank 2011: 5)

This chapter contends that this re-think should accept the need for continued generous media subsidy, but with a future emphasis away from technology-specific media subsidy (press, broadcasting, online), towards the technology-neutral distribution of subsidy according to media *function*, these being those that constitute 'public-service journalism' (investigative journalism, high quality and objective news and information, balanced and diverse opinion, diverse social and cultural content, and so on). As far as the institutional framework for future subsidy is concerned, established public service broadcasting institutions should be given ample means to evolve into public service media (PSM) institutions playing a key role in the digital, Internet environment, but there is also a need to explore innovative institutional constructs for developing and funding public service journalism at large in that environment (Humphreys 2008, 2015: 156–8).

A PUBLIC SERVICE PUBLISHER? A 'CHANNEL 4' FOR THE INTERNET ERA

The solution to ensuring the supply of public service content in the online era can be provided by a model that has already been proposed, albeit originally conceived to address a narrower issue, namely a feared shortfall in plurality of public service *broadcasting* in the digital era. UK broadcasting policy has long been sensitive to the need for 'plurality' of public service output beyond the BBC (for a discussion of the history and centrality of the plurality of PSB in UK broadcasting, see Gibbons and Humphreys 2012: 90–4). During the first of its regular statutory public service reviews,[10] in a report published in November 2004, the UK communications regulator Ofcom identified an emerging public service funding gap and deficit in the provision of public service broadcasting in the digital era. The regulator observed that 'the historical compact' in which the public service broadcasting provided by the commercial broadcasters (notably ITV, C5 and C4[11]) in return for discounted access to the analogue spectrum would come under pressure as the audience using the analogue spectrum declined and eventually disappeared with the completion of digital switchover in 2012 (Ofcom 2004: 6). Among its proposals for remedies was the idea of establishing a Public Service Publisher (PSP) with an annual budget of up to £300 million, delivering quality content via broadband and providing local and community services (Ofcom 2004: 81–4). The concept was enthusiastically pushed and developed by Ed Richards, who became Ofcom chief in 2006. Richards stressed that the PSP should be 'very new media focused'. Observing that some of the most innovative ideas were online, he declared Ofcom's shift in focus from public service broadcasting to *public service content* (Gibson and Wray 2006). As the PSP idea evolved, it became clear that the PSP would – like Channel 4 – be a body that would commission material from the UK's independent media sector and this material would then be distributed on a whole range of new digital platforms. Unlike advertising-funded Channel 4, it would be publicly funded, rather than by advertising, sponsorship or subscription. The material it promoted would be chosen on the basis of competitive tender (Ofcom 2005: 68–9).

An Ofcom consultation on a subsequent PSP discussion paper (Ofcom 2007) revealed that the PSP idea received a very mixed reception in the media sector. The independent producer lobby, the Producers Alliance for Cinema and Television (PACT 2007: 4), was highly positive, noting that the 'PSP could represent a potential "Channel 4 moment" for the UK's creative economy ... and help unlock the creative and economic potential of new media producers'. Channel 4 had been a major stimulus for the UK independent television production sector and PACT envisaged that a PSP could play a similar role in the digital online era. Channel 4 itself was 'strongly supportive of the PSP, which [it said] could help deliver public value in new ways and on new platforms'. It pointed to the 'benefits that would accrue from a close relationship between Channel 4 and the PSP' (Channel Four 2007: iii), envisaging itself as the vehicle for providing much of the infrastructure for the PSP and 'welcome[ing] the opportunity to play a leading role in the development of the PSP' (Channel Four 2007: vi). The Campaign for Press and Broadcasting Freedom saw the PSP as 'a welcome and innovative idea', pointing out that 'historically a new provider with a different source of funding (ITV; Channel 4; S4C) has stimulated and invigorated existing broadcasters', but adding the provisos that the PSP's funding 'should not in any way be associated with the BBC licence income' and that the PSP 'should not be used as an alternative to supporting ... the existing commercially funded public service broadcasters' (CPBF 2007: 8). The broadcasting union (BECTU 2007) tentatively endorsed the concept so long as it accompanied 'continuing support for traditional, linear PSB beyond digital switchover'. BECTU was a strong advocate of extra funding for existing commercial public service broadcasters (specifically ITV and Channel 4) through an industry levy on non PSB broadcasters like BSkyB.

However, scepticism came from respondents who questioned whether a new public service institution was necessary and whether there was a lack of plurality in the provision of quality UK content of public value on new media. ITV (2007: 3):

> welcome[d] the debate that Ofcom's discussion paper on the future of PSB and the PSP proposal [wa]s helping to generate [but opined that it was] crucially important to support those areas of traditional PSB delivery that may be under threat as a priority and before examining options to introduce new forms of public intervention through a new model (ITV 2007: 3).

The UK Film Council (2007) accepted much of Ofcom's analysis of the digital challenge but argued that so long as Channel 4 remained a public service broadcaster there was no need for the PSP. The BBC (2007) clearly feared that the PSP would most likely be funded at its expense through 'top-slicing' the TV licence fee revenue, an option that was viewed in policy circles as the most likely option for funding the PSP. A leading UK media scholar even opined that the PSP could be seen as part of Ofcom's and the government's agenda of 'disciplining' the BBC and promoting a more competitive and liberalised media environment (Freedman 2008: 152; Freedman 2009: 109–10). The Guardian Media Group (2007) observed that

> there may be a case for public intervention to ensure that there is a stream of digital content and services that satisfy a public service remit and are high quality (being well funded and produced), UK originated, innovative, challenging, engaging and widely available ... [but also noted] If poorly executed a PSP might stifle innovation and entrepreneurial activity, replicate activities of those in the private sector, and simply compete with existing sources of funding for investment in digital activity in the public, cultural and heritage sectors. (Guardian Media Group 2007: 3–4)

Predictably, the commercial television lobby, the Satellite and Cable Broadcasters' Group (SCBG), expressed a 'natural bias against unnecessary public intervention' and concern that 'a publicly funded competitor inevitably affects investment decisions and commercial strategy' and that 'such a proposal could serve to disincentivise commercial companies from investing in new media ventures' (SCBG 2007: 7). BSkyB told the House of Commons Media, Culture and Sport Committee inquiry on the subject of Public Service Content (2007: 43) that the PSP concept was a 'fairly slippery concept' that had evolved from a 'tool to tackle market failure' to a 'commissioning arm which would create public service content on the Net, of which there [wa]s no shortage whatsoever'. The House of Commons committee itself concluded that:

> [G]iven the huge amount of public service content currently available on new media, we believe that the creation of a new public service publisher, as currently envisaged by Ofcom, is unnecessary. The creation of a new public service content institution for new media would run the risk of distorting the market and impeding innovation. (House of Commons Media, Culture and Sport Committee 2007: 47)

In this political context, it was hardly surprising that the idea of a PSP dropped off the media policy agenda, with the subsequent policy discussion re-focusing on other institutional solutions to the narrower problem that Ofcom had first identified of ways of supporting Channel 4 (the idea of a possible merger with BBC Worldwide was mooted) and other market failure issues raised by digitalisation, notably the provision of local and regional news services that ITV could no longer sustain and the roll-out of high-speed broadband (for detail see Gibbons and Humphreys 2012: 90–4).

FUNDING SUBSIDIES

In floating the concept of a PSP Ofcom was, arguably, somewhat blinkered in the consideration given to how such a service might be funded other than through top-slicing the BBC. This shortfall probably contributed to the shelving of the idea. In relation to the issue of funding public service plurality, in the context of its later 2009 PSB Review, Ofcom acknowledged that 'funds could be raised through a new industry levy, as used in some other countries' (Ofcom 2009: 12). In fact, Ofcom's research had found that 'consumers found an industry levy to be the most acceptable of ... alternative potential new sources of funding', but also that 'in [its] consultation responses, support for an industry levy was more mixed' (Ofcom 2009: 52). Ofcom noted that some respondents 'highlighted that industry levies were already widely used in other countries, particularly Europe, to fund particular content of cultural benefit'. It also noted that:

> [m]any stakeholders were concerned that a levy on new forms of distribution would firstly be difficult to identify and define, and secondly jeopardise development and emerging commercial relationships within these markets. Additionally, respondents thought it unlikely that any levy could be introduced without a negative market distortion or impact, and as such would only re-distribute existing value within the industry rather than grow funding overall. (Ofcom 2009: 52)

In summing up, Ofcom accepted the weight of the latter argument and came down against the idea, observing that there were 'other potential uses for industry funding – for example, individual or joint funding of R&D or infrastructure (Ofcom 2009: 52).

However, the concept of contestable funding for public service content, funded by means other than top-slicing the BBC, continued to receive consideration in the UK policy community at large. In 2009, a consultancy report for the BBC (Foster and Meek 2009) set out how the authors thought Ofcom's existing plans for spectrum pricing for broadcasting could be adapted to support contestable funding for public service content beyond the BBC. They proposed using the proceeds of the post digital switchover pricing of spectrum, destined to go to the Exchequer, instead to finance a public service content fund, 'which would support the provision of news and other public service content by providers other than the BBC ... Funding could be allocated via a contestable process, which would be open to existing commercial broadcasters and to new players' (Foster and Meek 2009: 2).[12] This report's suggestion about using spectrum pricing to this end was subsequently picked up by a

House of Lords committee report the following year (House of Lords 2010: para. 233). The idea of using regulatory assets, notably the post-switchover digital dividend, to fund future public service content was also embraced by a report (Withers 2009) produced by the Centre-Left policy think tank, the Institute of Public Policy Research (IPPR), for the media unions, the Broadcasting, Entertainment, Cinematograph and Theatre Union (BECTU) and the National Union of Journalists (NUJ). Most of this report, however, was devoted to consideration of all kinds of industry levy to achieve this aim. The report estimated that a

> 1% levy on pay television (subscription-based TV services) in the UK, would yield an estimated *£70 million per annum*, based on assessments from the UK's two major pay TV broadcasters, Virgin and Sky. A 1% levy on the five major mobile phone operators in the UK (02, Orange, T-Mobile, 3 and Vodafone) would yield an estimated *£ 208 million per annum*. (Withers 2009: 4)

The report noted that the UK was one of the very few countries in Europe not to have a tax on blank media or recording equipment such as VCRs, Personal Video Recorders, and DVD players (Withers 2009: 26). It also noted that 30 countries raised levies on the retransmission of audiovisual works by cable and satellite platforms that broadcast copyright material for which no direct fee was paid to the original content provider. The report calculated that a

> UK equivalent would be Sky or Virgin Media, which broadcast material created by the BBC, Channel 4 or ITV but do not pay for the content. According to the latest available data [from Sky and Virgin on their subscriptions in 2008] an annual £5 flat-rate levy per subscriber would raise around £45 million from Sky and around £18 million from Virgin – a total of £63 million. (Withers 2009: 30)

The report also made reference to media levies charged on revenue from broadcasters, cinemas and video labels in France and broadcasters in Canada (further on which theme, see below). In a presentation to a BECTU conference the same year, which registered considerable impact at the time, Patrick Barwise, Professor Emeritus of the London Business School,[13] made a compelling case for industry levies to bridge the PSB funding gap. Barwise noted that

> the total revenue of consumer telecoms and technology industries – including fixed and mobile telephony and broadband, internet advertising and hardware sales – [wa]s hugely bigger than the whole of broadcasting' yet 'the growth of

all these industries relie[d] on the continuing supply of high-quality PSB content. (Barwise 2009: 2)

Drawing on more detailed studies, Barwise observed that a simple 1 per cent levy on the combined revenue of £50 billion of UK consumer telecoms, technology and pay TV would generate about £500 million per annum (Barwise 2009: 4).

Such voices did not go unheeded in Parliament. A House of Lords committee report the following year (House of Lords 2010) contained a whole chapter (Chapter 4, paragraphs 208–80) on promoting British television, discussing a number of specific suggestions for supporting UK content production. These included levies on a range of different commercial providers – hardware, software, equipment manufacturers, and search engines. It pointed out that it was widespread practice in the European Union to impose reuse fees, namely a tax on recording devices that are used for recording copyright material.

> The system of reuse fees that already exists in Europe (across the 22 EU states) generated €568m in 2004, with most of the income being recycled back to copyright holders ... Ofcom told us ... that they have not done any work on the amount that reuse fees might raise in the UK, but one study ... estimates that that they could generate around £175m per annum by 2012 in the UK. (House of Lords 2010: para. 257)

The House of Lords report also considered retransmission fees, namely fees paid to copyright owners by those who own channel distribution systems or platforms in return for the right to replay programmes on their systems. Citing Steve Morrison, CEO of the UK independent All3Media and a prominent advocate of industry levies, and Luke Crawley, Assistant General Secretary of the media union BECTU, the report noted that this measure was used in 30 countries in Europe and could bring in as much as £63 million a year. Of particular note, given the issues raised for copyright in the digital era (Chapter 5), the House of Lords committee observed, too, that

> another possible funding mechanism would be a fee on search engines such as Google and Yahoo! which routinely use copyright material from other organisations and content creators to drive their own page impressions and thus generate significant advertising revenue. A recent proposal along these lines in France estimated that such a levy would raise €10–20 million a year.[14] (House of Lords 2010: para. 264)

The House of Lords report suggested that broadband fees might be 'derived from ISPs and mobile phone operators which increasingly benefit from the use of third party creative content but pay nothing towards it'. It observed that such a mechanism had been introduced in France and Spain (House of Lords 2010: para. 265). However, the report noted that government was cool on all these proposals. Powerful industry players like BSkyB and lobbies like the Satellite and Cable Broadcasters group were unsurprisingly averse to the idea of an industry levy, arguing that it would actually restrict their ability to invest. The House of Lords committee itself expressed the view that:

> Although we do not favour the introduction of industry fees in the current economic climate, we believe that the Government should ask Ofcom to assess research already done on possible use of fees in the UK, and commission them to conduct further research to reach firm conclusions on the likely costs and benefits of such fees. This would provide a firm basis on which Parliament might make any future decisions. (House of Lords 2010: para. 268)

At the time of writing, none of these ideas had been taken up by government, which confined itself to a modest extension of the existing film tax exemption to high-end TV drama and animation production and urging commercial broadcasters like ITV and Sky to invest more in UK-originated audiovisual content.[15] That can hardly be surprising given the predominantly neo-liberal ideological complexion of UK governments since the Thatcher era and in view of the post-2008 economic climate, though this does not detract from the promising nature of the proposals themselves. Meanwhile, the call for industry levies on the advertising revenues of commercial broadcasters and Internet players like Google and Facebook and the establishment of a new funding institution – a 'Public Media Trust' (echoing strongly the PSP concept) – has been kept alive by the media reform campaigning group, the Media Reform Coalition (formerly the Coordinating Committee for Media Reform), founded in 2011 during the Leveson judicial public inquiry into the culture, practices and ethics of the British press.[16]

The ideas are hardly revolutionary. Indeed, as argued elsewhere (notably Humphreys 2015), the long-established French audiovisual subsidy system could serve as an interesting model for funding a new digital era public service subsidy distributing institution. The subsidies and running costs of that institution could be covered by raising a levy on major communication companies like BSkyB, Virgin, and Google, which make a profit from distributing content which they largely do not generate themselves (Morrison 2008).[17] In France, a major production subsidy-distributing body, the *Compte de Soutien à l'Industrie de Programmes* (COSIP) which was established originally (in 1946) to bolster the French national film industry and later (during the 1980s) extended to television production, has long been financed by just such a levy on the cinema, broadcasting and communication electronics industries. The obligation to pay a levy based on their profits into the COSIP fund was extended, by a forward-looking 'Television of the Future' law enacted in 2007, to all distributors of audiovisual content, including those doing so via new media like broadband and mobile TV (for detail see Gibbons and Humphreys 2012: 75–9). Though designed to promote French national audiovisual production, not specifically 'public service journalism', this approach to funding public support might serve as a useful model for policy transfer to fund a technology-neutral subsidy distributing institution to support 'public service content' in the digital, online era (Humphreys 2015). In doing so, it would also promote national cultural production. A similar model is the Canada Media Fund (formerly Canadian TV Fund), a public–private partnership between satellite services, cable TV companies and the Canadian government, which funds high quality content from a mix of state grants and levies on distributors of TV content (Gibbons and Humphreys 2012: 49–50).

CONCLUSION

The Internet era has certainly brought an abundance of media content. However, this has featured a torrent of commercialism and unprocessed information, much of it highly subjective and misleading ('fake news'). In this environment, the need for public service journalism will be greater than ever. Yet, as this chapter has detailed, there are grounds to seriously question claims that there will be no shortage of public service content on new media. As explained, the Internet has presented a major challenge to traditional media, especially the newspaper sector. The revenue base of the press has been endangered by declining readerships, particularly among the young, and the loss of advertising revenues, leading to corresponding shrinkage of journalistic and editorial employment in the sector. According to a 2017 Reuters Institute digital news project report (Newman 2017), a survey of 143 leading editors, CEOs and digital leaders found that '33% of respondents from a newspaper background [we]re more worried about their company's financial sustainability than last year; just 85 [we]re less worried'. The report predicted 'further job cuts and losses across the news industry' with more papers in the US and Europe go[ing] out of business, slim[ing] down or becom[ing] online only'. While the evidence suggests so far that broadcast television is faring rather better in the digital era, just as cinema survived the advent of home video, there can be no questioning that television too faces major challenges, as online video streaming services like Amazon and Netflix and on-demand apps like Chromecast, Apple TV and Amazon Fire eat into traditional viewing and as social media eat into TV news viewing, as with newspapers particularly among younger generations. This chapter has argued that it is therefore vital that policy makers encourage and adequately resource established public service broadcasting (PSB) institutions to become public service media (PSM) providers, engaging with all the new technological possibilities for maintaining their audience reach. In this regard, the BBC has been allowed to lead the way, in comparison to other European PSBs (Brevini 2013) and should be given the resources and opportunity to continue to do so as long as the public value test is met. Given the scale of the challenges facing traditional media, rather than rendering existing media subsidies inappropriate in an era of apparent content abundance, as some have argued, the chapter has demonstrated that maintaining and indeed innovating new subsidies to help traditional media meet the new technological challenges will be more than ever necessary in order to maintain support for 'public service journalism'. American media reform advocates McChesney and Nichols have produced some innovative pointers for digital era media subsidies, to tackle the crisis of journalism in the United States, which might also be embraced in Europe, where a similar crisis is impending and where as seen media subsidy has been more accepted and has supported remarkably strong public broadcasting in cases like the UK and Germany. However, in Europe the 'elephant in the room' is the imbalance in the era of digitally converging media between the *unconverged* subsidy systems currently pertaining for broadcasting, press and online media. The chapter has argued that innovating a public service institution along the lines of Ofcom's concept of Public Service Publisher, tasked to adopt a technology-neutral approach to distributing subsidies to deserving journalism and content production on a contestable basis, would address this pressing issue and help solve the question already raised in Chapter 5 on copyright, namely the challenge of producing sufficient quality media content in the Internet era.

NOTES

1. Leonard Downie was formerly *Washington Post* executive editor and Professor Michael Schudson, of Columbia University, is an American academic sociologist of journalism.
2. McChesney and Nichols (2010). McChesney, Professor of Communications at the University of Illinois, and Nichols, *The Nation*'s Washington correspondent, were jointly founders (with Josh Silver) in 2002 of Free Press, a campaigning media reform organisation. On its

website, Free Press describes itself as 'a national, nonpartisan, nonprofit organization working to reform the media. Through education, organizing and advocacy, we promote diverse and independent media ownership, strong public media, quality journalism, and universal access to communications'. See http://www.freepress.net/about_us.

3. These are available at https://www.ofcom.org.uk/research-and-data/multi-sector-research/cmr.
4. The question asked was: 'Which of the following do you use for news nowadays'. The survey also covered radio whose usage remained more or less stable, dropping very marginally from 35 per cent in 2013 to 33 per cent in 2016 (Ofcom 2017: 8).
5. Aside from VAT exemption.
6. The latter issue, however, can be easily settled, given the political will. In 2010 German legislators made the TV licence a household tax to support PSB rather than a levy on ownership of a TV (and radio). Moreover, an independent body was established to determine the appropriate level of the licence fee, for fulfilment of their remit, in terms of the PSBs' own projections of their funding needs (see Humphreys 2015: 162).
7. See Nersssession (2015).
8. See Sam Coates, Deputy Political Editor of *The Times* (2015).
9. In the case of both the BBC and the German ARD corporations and the ZDF the public value tests are in the hands of the broadcasters themselves, though in the UK case the regulator Ofcom assesses the market impact, which is not the case in Germany. For detail see Humphreys (2009).
10. The Communications Act 2003 requires Ofcom regularly to report on the effectiveness of the existing public service broadcasters – BBC, ITV, Channel 4, S4C, Five and Teletext – in the delivery of their public service broadcasting obligations; and to make recommendations for the continuation of public service broadcasting. The first review, conducted in three phases, led to reports published in 2004 and 2005. Two other reviews have followed, with reports published in 2008 and 2009 (a summary of consultation responses and a final report) and in 2015. https://www.ofcom.org.uk/tv-radio-and-on-demand/information-for-industry/public-service-broadcasting.
11. Channel 4 is funded by commercial advertising, though state owned.
12. Significantly, one of its co-authors Robin Foster, had played a key role in the review of PSB in his capacity between 2003 and 2005 as Ofcom partner responsible for strategy and market developments and its other co-author Kip Meek was an executive board member of Ofcom between 2003 and 2007.
13. Between 2011 and 2014, Professor Barwise was a Visiting Fellow at the Reuters Institute for the Study of Journalism, Oxford.
14. This was according to a *Guardian* report: 8 January 2010, http://www.guardian.co.uk/technology/2010/jan/08/google-tax-ad-revenue-france.
15. Just as this book's manuscript was about to be submitted to the publisher, a report in *The Times* newspaper of 30 December 2017 suggested that Karen Bradley, the Conservative Secretary for Digital Culture, Media and Sport had announced that in order to tackle a crisis in the provision of children's programmes, the country's commercial public service broadcasters (ITV, Channel 4 and Channel 5) would be supported by a contestable fund financed by licence fee revenue that had been left over from the previous licence fee settlement, which had been earmarked for the expansion of broadband. The report noted that 'the three-year pilot scheme could provide a model for those who argue that the BBC's rivals deserve subsidies for airing public service content', officials having said that the government would work with the British Film Institute, designated to run the fund, to decide whether to include other genres in the scheme. See Moore (2017c).
16. See www.mediareform.org.uk.
17. Steve Morrison has identified as a 'real elephant in the room' the fact that: 'highly profitable pay platforms don't contribute much to original British programmes although they benefit from the audiences that watch them … The billions that customers pay to these platforms do not usually find their way into high-quality British productions. In the main they go to sport or movie rights holders (Morrison 2008: 93).

PART IV

Challenging the impediments to media convergence

8. Conclusion: governance, policy and the development of media convergence

INTRODUCTION

As Part I of the volume has explained, in a chapter laying out the context and state-of-play of media convergence (Chapter 1), despite an evolution spanning many decades media convergence is still a far from complete process. Through its range of chapter case studies, this volume has shown it to be often, and in many ways, a contradictory and problematic process. Thus viewed, media convergence as a grand commercial and societal project might be considered a failure. However, the central argument of this concluding chapter is that convergence is still very much in development and, as such, presents considerable opportunities. After drawing together and rehearsing briefly the main challenges of media convergence that this volume has elucidated across its preceding chapters, it is to these possibilities for creating a more effective, deeper media convergence that this last chapter turns. Its premise is that media governance and policy can set the context for a more inclusive and progressive process of convergence to unfold. In so doing, the chapter presents a series of key media policy solutions to the current impediments to convergence in its core areas of concern: high-speed broadband infrastructure; Net Neutrality, spectrum; copyright; media concentration and media subsidies. It also explores the connections between each of these fields and posits an agenda for future work that can lead to a richer understanding of the significance and capacity of digital convergence. At the centre of the chapter is the argument that in order to broaden and accelerate the delivery of the undoubted benefits of convergence, the straitjacket of neo-liberally underpinned media governance perspectives and media policy solutions needs to be loosened considerably. An environment as complex as that being created by converging media provides an opportunity to adopt media policies which incorporate, where appropriate – but also move well beyond the boundaries of – predominantly market-based rationality.

MEDIA GOVERNANCE AND THE IMPEDIMENTS TO DEEPER MEDIA CONVERGENCE

Part II of the volume has explored a number of key infrastructural matters: those relating to network development (Chapter 2), re-allocation of spectrum, and the 'digital dividend' (Chapter 3), and the issue of 'Network Neutrality' (Chapter 4). At the core of the development of converging environments for the consumption of media services sit the infrastructures through which they are delivered. So-called Next Generation Networks epitomise the drive towards creating network space within which the former distinctions which demarcated the service worlds of broadcasting, the Internet, publishing and telecommunication can blur and dissolve, ultimately. However, as Chapter 2 has shown, the progressive, even radically transformative, connotations of the NGN term have to be contextualised in a more mundane reality. Put simply, the idea of network upgrade is nothing new in the field of electronic communication, having been pursued in one form or another for the best part of 100 years. Whilst this in no way diminishes the importance of pursuing the creation of high-speed broadband networks of the kind entailed in the concept of NGN, their realisation is usually long term, phased and subject to the cyclical vagaries of the macro-economy. There has been much industry and governmental hype around the transformative capacity of securing network upgrade, though the practical reality has been more modest. Nevertheless, of all the areas covered in this volume, infrastructural improvement appears the one where the strictures of neo-liberalism appear to have been loosened the most. This can be explained in part by the historically well-established economics of fixed link communication network investment, the upfront costs of which are high compared to the short to medium term returns realisable. It is also the case that devoting strategic attention to broadband network upgrade can enhance a state's international reputation, bolster its economy and, not least, generate increased social welfare. The long-established realisation that a pure market logic will not result in the adequate servicing of uneconomic rural and/or socio-economically deprived environments has ensured an enduring level of public sector intervention, even in jurisdictions such as the US. The global economic downturn of the end of the last decade appeared to add urgency to the task, embellished by the idea that investment in the network economy could provide new wealth creating opportunities. However, the level of state investment in NGN is hardly a paradigm shift in proportion, compared to that witnessed in the late 1980s to 1990s neo-liberal transformation of the communications landscape.

In another key aspect of the electronic communication infrastructure, airwave spectrum, the road to media convergence has raised questions over the future allocation and use of a scarce public resource. Here, the desire of the burgeoning mobile communications business to have access to more airwave capacity to deliver services with a digital convergence character is, however, matched by a countervailing goal of players from terrestrial broadcasting – both public service and commercial – to resist such an acquisition at their expense. The spectrum debate is something of a microcosm of the multiple controversies over media convergence more broadly which are explained in this volume. Chapter 1 showed how a key feature of the emerging digital convergence user experience was the possibility of mobility, though it may well be argued that this is now considered an indispensable feature of such service environments. The clash between broadcasters and mobile broadband players over the 700 MHz band of spectrum highlights the kind of commercial dogfights that can arise in the race to exploit the opportunities which convergence can enable. Other chapters have described clashes between established industrial and commercial interests and new technology challengers. They have also highlighted tensions between interests calling for – and benefitting from – non-intervention ('free markets') and voices regarding intervention as vital to safeguard the efficient operation of media markets, but also to promote valued democratic and cultural goals. The clash described in Chapter 3 between broadcasters and mobile broadband players over the 700 MHz spectrum band brings very sharply into focus the cultural difference in approach to communication infrastructure held by players from different quarters of the communication sector. Broad-casters – commercial and public service alike – have emphasised the public service dimension of the activities associated with their use of spectrum. The idea of spectrum as a scarce public infrastructural resource to be utilised strategically sits in contrast to that which views it as a means to deliver on a commercial basis individually tailored customer services. It is interesting that parties from both broadcasting and mobile telecommunications argue that, through different means and from differ-ent perspectives, they can deliver the benefits of convergence in the interests of the public.

The highly contentious matter of Net Neutrality also brings to the fore a number of core problems at the heart of digital convergence. Viewed narrowly, Net Neutrality is about mundane management of network traffic to ensure realistic and fair network access and minimum quality of service. As shown in Chapter 4, Net Neutrality highlights a clash between the original communication culture of the Internet where traffic was treated equally in terms of access and carriage and, by contrast, liberalised market ideas in telecommunications, which are more amenable to instigating practices that lead to differential access and quality of service provision, based on the ability to pay. Net Neutrality is, however, more complex and nuanced than this basic dichotomisation. Even in contexts of common carriage found in telecommunications, the flow of data across the Internet has been the subject of intervention to slow or increase its speed in times of high network usage and for purposes of securing the most efficient flow of data possible. There is also a public interest aspect since for purposes of national security, protection of vulnerable groups and the thwarting of illegal behaviour, interventions in traffic traversing the Internet does take place, in the process deviating from the idea of pure 'non-interference' common carriage. The circumstances in which such activity is deemed acceptable and the extent and frequency of it, are thorny political problems to which there is unlikely to be reached a uniform, widely acceptable legal and regulatory solution.

However, moving beyond the unrealistic and inaccurate idea that the Internet existed in a pure state of 'neutrality' – which has been somehow contaminated by neo-liberal marketisation of electronic communication – can offer possibilities for social enrichment of digitally convergent online communication. The Internet of the 1980s and early 1990s has developed into an infrastructure with, at the time of writing, over 4 billion users (Statista 2018). The existence of faster and slower routes through this truly enormous global system of communication is inevitable. A key issue, therefore, is to create and preserve equal access rights and ensure an evolutionary understanding of basic minimum levels of service quality. Achieving the latter can set the context for policies that build upon a revised understanding of 'neutrality' as something that provides conditions of participatory equality and addresses conditions of disadvantage as being non-neutral in character. In this way, Net Neutrality can become a lynchpin communication policy matter, which unifies issues of access to the digital infrastructure and the core conditions of quality of service experienced by users within it. This can open the policy gates to achieving appropriate conditions of engagement with Internet content to deliver the cultural, educational, and deliberative benefits of a digitally converging global communications environment.

The three chapters in Part III of the volume all concern content issues, but they highlight similar tensions to those revealed in relation to infrastructure by the chapters in Part II, most notably clashes between vested interests and new technology challengers, and also conflicting perspectives on policy between neo-liberal and libertarian viewpoints, on the one side, and proponents of more interventionist approaches on the other. Chapter 5 has explored a similar clash of interests to that over net neutrality, this time in respect of copyright. The question of rights to ownership of content and abuses thereof has become one of the most contentious issues of the media convergence landscape. The task of finding a set of legal and policy solutions to copyright protection in the digital online era is rendered difficult by a series of issues in tension with each other. The extent and effect of efforts made by large corporate players to extend and deepen copyright protections can be viewed as a movement in the direction of restriction, foreclosure and stultification of digital media environments. On the other hand, it is difficult to gainsay the observation that an obsession with 'free' has come close to destroying the music business and is damaging other creative industries. Copyright protection that will be effective in the digital, online era can be seen as a crucial necessity in order to safeguard the incentive to create content and to maintain a functioning content market, thereby sustaining the creative industries and the livelihoods of all those who work in them. At the same time, often this conflict distils into a struggle between established and newer corporate interests in the media sector. Digital convergence – by creating a common platform for conflicts over copyright to be played out – has intensified these clashes as the corporate capitalism of the media evolves. There is certainly the potential that proprietary restrictions will be harmful in an online environment which, it is argued, benefits from a culture of innovation through liberal sharing and usage of ideas and techniques. A key issue is whether using online communications plat-forms for more extensive and intensive exchange and manipulation of information on the basis of free and open provision is ultimately a commercially and socially degenerative position.

Chapter 5 has taken the line that the digital exploitation of copyrighted content, both illegally through piracy and the facilitation thereof, and legally through 'free riding' by technology companies purporting to be acting as simple platforms or 'conduits' of communication (Levine 2011), if allowed to continue on the scales achieved, is likely to undermine severely the viability of media content producers. This may not necessarily be a critical matter for giant media companies, the 'Hollywood' interest deemed by critical political economists as the main exploiters and beneficiaries of an over-restrictive copyright regime. The chapter shows that deals can and have been struck between major content providers and the new technology companies (notably the 2014 Google/ Viacom settlement). However, effective copyright protection most cer-tainly is a critical issue for the wide tranche of smaller sized media content creators of various kinds which are so essential for maintaining plurality and vitality of content in the online era. It is important to appreciate that unfettered copying of digital content can have deleterious consequences for publicly valuable media content of an informational, educative and cultural nature, and those whose livelihoods are contingent on its sustained production. This core contradiction of convergence – that increased ability to share and creatively to copy might actually inhibit creativity and technological and sociocultural innovation in the long term – presents a key communications public policy dilemma, as yet under-addressed. Chapter 5 explores how copyright reform has been debated, and to some extent positive change introduced, in the United States and in Europe. It reveals that so far, on both sides of the Atlantic, legislative initiatives have been blocked by a combination of policy makers' concerns to promote the new technologies and widespread popular concerns about protecting privacy and Internet access as a human right, though in Europe, at least, there are growing demands to treat the technology companies as publishers rather than as platforms, pressure which may be serving to change their behaviour.

One of the most difficult challenges in the movement towards digital convergence has been a consideration of the extent of media concentration and the reasons behind it. The existence of plurality in media content is widely understood as a core constituent of well-functioning democratic life. As Chapter 5 has shown, digital convergence has a complex, often contradictory relationship with aspects of media concentration. On the one hand, barriers to entry have been lowered by the Internet, 'long tail' production and distribution has received a major boost, and indeed there has been a spectacular increase in media offers – with some democratising potential, at least. On the other hand, hard evidence points to the continuing problem of media concentration, with concentration of users on a number of popular websites and the continued corporate dominance of major players, most of whom have established an online presence for their pre-Internet media operations. The main conclusion to draw from this chapter is that the policy challenges presented by convergence in respect of media concentration are far from novel. The idea that new media technologies can offer the possibility of increased consumer choice has long been associated with new developments in radio and television historically. However, by dint of its very nature of bringing separate market phenomena together, digital convergence points to a more intense version of choice widening. This refers to media content of mass popularity but also that which is of multitudinous niche interest. Importantly, this resonates with the fundamental mission of public service broadcasting to cater for mass common, as well as minority interests. The key difference – though no less challenging to deliver – is that in the era of digital convergence this occurs in a (potentially) limitlessly capacious network environment, as opposed to a tightly capacity-constrained one. As Chapter 6 shows, convergence has therefore – understandably, if mistakenly – been deployed a key argument for the incremental, but far-reaching deregulation of media concentration rules that has accompanied a neo-liberal turn in media policy from the 1980s on, as well as leading to calls for diminishing the role of public service broadcasters, a theme explored in Chapter 7. Online network environments – not least through for example social media platforms – certainly provide capacity for unprecedented individual and group expression and interaction and in this sense enable a multiplicity of voices. Nevertheless, hard evidence, produced by scholars like Hindman and research organisations like Pew, suggests the predominance, in terms of weight of presence, of a much narrower range of individual and institutional voices in online environments. The means for gaining access to the web-based platforms of online content – search engines (e.g. Google, Bing), video-sharing websites (e.g. YouTube) and streaming services (e.g. Netflix, Amazon) – has also developed according to a near monopolistic market structure, that should at the very least raise concern to ensure that considerations of plurality remain constant and prominent features of media policy agendas. The chapter argues, therefore, that neo-liberal inspired deregulation is hardly the appropriate response to convergence and there continues to be a need for regulation and interventionist public policy, including subsidies to maintain plurality of media content, a theme developed in Chapter 7.

An underlying theme linking all three chapters in Part III of the volume is the importance of the long-established reputational staples of a well-functioning pluralistic media environment: professionalism, trustworthiness, balance and critical accountability. These staples of 'public service journalism' appear as important as ever in the context of the proverbial cornucopia of digital, online media content. However, as Chapter 6 has shown, despite its pluralism-enabling potential, the online world of digital convergence has in practice also, ironically, exhibited strong evidence of media concentration. A consistent and persistent feature of the media sector through its various phases is that excellent quality media content in all its forms is usually – though not always – expensive to produce. This feature of media markets, which has for many years created stimuli for market concentration to occur, is evident in the emergence of a small number of internationally dominant media players in online content and distribution. It is also evident in changes to news provision in the online world, where news content aggregators vie for the attention of both advertisers and readers alongside traditional newspaper and broadcast news providers seeking to develop presence in the online world. The close to zero cost of re-packaged and replicated information, offered in huge quantities for free and packaged loudly and colourfully for consumers, threatens to undermine and crowd out the creation of diverse, technically high quality, journalistic content thus representing a clear and present danger to content pluralism and, ultimately, the public interest, into the future.

In the fast changing, commercially-driven and individual consumer welfare-emphasising world of digital convergence, the continued relevance and validity of regulating and subsidising media to achieve a public interest purpose has been consistently called into question by commercial interests and advocates of neo-liberalism. As Chapter 7 has shown, this has been the case particularly with regard to generously funded public service journalism, conceived as having an extensive programme remit (i.e. covering a full range of programme genres). Yet, it is important to understand the distinctive character of the media industry as historically also having delivered, through commercial means, content with a strong public interest character. This was mandated through independent public authority in the case of television (e.g. the FCC in the USA, the IBA/ITC/Ofcom in the UK, the *Landesmedienanstalten* in Germany) and delivered through self-regulation and high standards of professionalism in the case of much print journalism. However, as Chapter 7 has shown, digital convergence has brought the disruption on a grand scale of these historically stable relationships, leading to two key consequences. First, a new, without exaggeration vast, commercially-underpinned media service environment has been created across the online world. The migration of readers and advertising revenues online has been a particularly daunting challenge to the traditional press sector, but new technology companies have also competed remarkably successfully against traditional broadcasters for the attention of viewers, and, as important, advertisers. Whether traditional broadcasters will be able to withstand the challenge of new technologies is as yet uncertain. On the one hand, they clearly face an awesome task as viewers – and with them advertising and subscription revenues – are attracted away by technology companies like Amazon and Netflix, offering streaming services, and from video-sharing sites, most notably YouTube. On the other hand, television viewing figures have remained surprisingly robust, with viewers taking advantage of time-shifting through digital video recording and the broadcasters' catch-up services such as the BBC's iPlayer, ITV Hub and All 4 Catch Up. One thing, however, is certain. The ensuing commercial maelstrom has intensified a drive to prioritise content with an almost exclusively commercial substance, the corollary of which is that commercially-provided public service broadcast content has dwindled in volume, hence, Ofcom's concern over a public service funding gap. In the news business too, journalistic outlets whose content is not predominantly commercial in character have struggled and even disappeared.

The second, related consequence is that digital convergence has pointed up the increasingly exposed position of public service media providers. For some, this has signalled their waning significance and relevance in a convergence era. From this perspective, the issue has become how, and how soon, these archaic features of the media environment should diminish or even disappear. For others, digital convergence has evoked a polar opposite response. Here, publicly funded public service media are considered more important than ever before, the key policy question being how they might be sustained and even expanded to meet the challenges of the digital, online environment. As regards 'public service journalism' that continues to be sustained commercially, such as in the struggling quality newspaper business and commercially funded public service broadcasting, most notably the UK's Channel 4, the key policy question is: through which means and institutional frameworks might publicly funded interventions feasibly occur to ensure the future survival of these vital serious high-quality content providers in the commercially hypercompetitive era of online digital convergence? As Chapter 7 has argued, this perspective sees media with a public purpose as providing an essential counter-weight to a predominantly marketised, internationalised media sector where is it realistically the case that law and regulation are less effective media policy tools than was hitherto the case. In an online social media world where hyperbole rubs shoulders with superficiality of treatment of complex social issues, public service media can provide a prominently positioned and trustworthy terrain for even-handed, reasoned national and international public awareness-raising and debate. In an increasingly cost-pressured media production environment, public service media can serve to invest in challenging, risky, diverse and socially relevant content and work towards maintaining universal access to an agreed suite of media services underpinned by the need to inform and educate content consumers of all characters, cultures and tastes.

ADDRESSING THE PROBLEMS OF MEDIA CONVERGENCE THROUGH MEDIA POLICIES

This volume has tackled the complex topic of how communications infrastructures and services have altered irrevocably as digitalisation has enabled new convergence possibilities. However, this process of change has repeatedly highlighted the only partial and often problematic state of convergence, despite a long history of governance which has developed in the constituent parts of what is now perhaps best labelled the mass and personal electronic communications environment. Much of the evidence provided in the previous chapters of this volume points to a sector rhetorically underpinned by visions of individual fulfilment and development delivered through growing consumerism and fast-paced market and service-based change. In such a predominant cultural landscape, the provision of media infrastructures and services through public action can seem outmoded, if not redundant. However, the volume has shown the dangers of adopting a solely market-envisioned view of the journey to media convergence. As a corollary, the current state of media convergence calls for the consideration of possible courses of action, designed through media policies, which are convergent in character and outlook. These policies should be underpinned by a recognition of the interconnected and often overlapping nature of media convergence. They should aim to understand better the connections between infrastructural enablement and content innovation and development. They should understand that public provision, protection and promotion of digital convergence infrastructure and content is a relevant and reasonable media policy goal which can contribute to the realisation of deep media convergence that goes beyond the too often articulated series of market rhetorical, straitjacketed policy approaches witnessed to date.

Regarding the development of communications infrastructure, the subject of Chapter 2, media policies should be underpinned by a realistic approach to understanding the sheer scale and extent of the job of network upgrading that is required. This can help to see past the hyperbole that has often surrounded the idea of network upgrade in successively used terms such as the Information Superhighway, the Information Society and Next Generation Networks. Here, the adoption of flexible policy approaches which combine private sector led investment with a stronger public sector vision and interventionism than has been hitherto the case is warranted. Specifically, policies for network upgrade must go beyond facilitation of market-based solutions where state aid is tolerated somewhat apologetically as a second best, sub-optimal, safety net. Neither should it be viewed as a first stage, pre-commercial, temporary policy solution read in the context of a neo-liberal market lens.

As shown in Chapter 3, the future of spectrum in a context of media convergence is one of the most contentious media policy issues at the time of writing. However, a progressive convergence media policy understanding of spectrum must continue to view it as a scarce public resource. In this way, the public interest uses of spectrum can remain at the forefront of media policy agendas as the technologies and markets of broadcasting and mobile communications evolve. Here careful and judiciously sanctioned use of spectrum at the international and national levels is imperative. Media policy actors must continue to examine what the best public use of the resource is. Here, the speed and extent of migration from broadcasting to IP-based networks is likely to be critical since this may provide more spectrum capacity for alternative uses. Similarly, the performance of the mobile communications sector in its use of allocated spectrum should be an ongoing concern of regulatory authorities for electronic communications given the contentious nature of the debate on the efficacy in public interest terms of allocating spectrum away from terrestrial broadcasting. These authorities should also undertake a comparative analysis by determining the public value generated historically and contemporaneously by terrestrial broadcast players in their occupation of the spectrum. Any reallocation of spectrum must not in any way compromise universality of coverage and access, something which should be viewed as an evolutionary concept in order to allow all users of the electronic communications system to take advantage of the opportunities for social welfare enhancement through the use of higher speed content-rich interactive communications. In particular, any changes to the allocation of spectrum away from broadcasters, both commercial and publicly funded, which hold a public service mission, should not stymy the development of progressive policies for media content, examples of which we refer to below. Here, media policy makers should develop policies which maximise the public utility to be derived from spectrum. This could involve a reconsideration of the nature of wirelessly provided services as delivering at least in part a public service function in terms of enriching digital citizenship in a convergence context, alongside them being services which are offered commercially on the basis of addressing customer demand in an individually tailored fashion. Realistically, such a radical re-think of the public utility and value of wireless networks is unlikely to be achieved in states with little or no public service media tradition, such as the USA, but might be more readily achievable elsewhere.

An expansionary and progressive perspective on the link between electronic communication network infrastructures and convergence services could be achieved by developing, radically, existing understandings of Net Neutrality. Drawing upon and taking forward the idea of intervention exposes the myth of neutrality and the paucity of a laissez faire strategy. Instead, the utility of selective intervention as a media policy tool can be understood in ways that could lead to the creation of policies whose intended effects could be to create a new and enlightened understanding of neutrality as an environment of equal communications opportunity and rights, that needs to be pursued and attained. This would challenge radically the idea of neutrality as a passive concept in policy terms and assert the need to intervene proactively in online communication environments to deliver enriched public utility which capitalises on the collapsing distinction between one-to-one and one-to-many communicative interactions. For this to occur in practice, a radical re-positioning of Net Neutrality policy has to occur to allow it to incorporate and re-work media policy ideas from the realm of broadcasting to focus on the attainment of equality of access and participation rather than non-interference. In short, media policy interventions in environments of digital convergence should be acknowledged as being potentially broad in their character and measures, undertaken with a wide variety of different targets that go far beyond safety net, second best strategies and which hold as their goal the maximisation of public utility of digital media networks and services.

Relating to issues raised in Part III of the volume, what precisely might convergence policy for media content look like in a boldly envisioned environment of this kind? As Chapter 5 has explained, copyright enforcement is a major challenge when digitalisation and the Internet have combined to make it so easy to exploit copyrighted content, legally as well as illegally, for commercial as well as for private individual benefit. There are undoubtedly very good reasons for some recasting of copyright law so that it operates in the digital online era as originally and always intended, namely to promote creativity and innovation. This might involve adoption of a more permissive approach to personal, non-commercial file copying, and an expansion of the parameters of fair use for creative purposes by the likes of artists, researchers, and public service institutions. The latter might themselves be encouraged to play a major role in the establishment of the 'creative commons' called for by critics of current copyright regimes (perhaps most famously by Lawrence

Lessig). There is certainly scope for reforming the process of licensing and selling rights to facilitate smaller, lower-value transactions and to encourage collective or 'blanket' licensing (Levine 2011). There is scope for measures to improve the functioning of the European copyright marketplace, promoting more cross-border access to content online, and wider opportunities for using copyrighted materials for research and for cultural heritage purposes, as the European Commission's copyright reform initiative envisages. Above all, imposing harsh penalties on individuals is hardly an acceptable approach to the problem when much more could be achieved against commercially motivated illegal websites and by making legal intermediaries take more responsibility for policing the content that is hosted on their platforms.

Chapter 5 shows that there appears to be mounting pressure, particularly in Europe, for new technology companies, like Google and its subsidiary YouTube, to be made more responsible, perhaps even to be treated as publishers rather than as platforms. This pressure on Internet intermediaries has gained momentum from concerns about social media platform providers' (Facebook, Twitter, etc.) responsibility for debasing the quality of political discourse and even, possibly, their being abused to interfere with democratic politics in the USA and Europe. There are indications too that this pressure on the technology giants, even if such legislation does not follow, may be motivating change While the more aggressive approach to piracy adopted in Europe may so far have delivered somewhat disappointing effect, the serious approach adopted to developing graduated response measures coupled with a policy discussion about making Internet intermediaries liable for the content they carry certainly has exerted pressure on the latter to take more responsibility for their activity. Chapter 5 has indicated that steps have been taken by the likes of Google/YouTube and Microsoft themselves to combat commercial copyright infringement as well as individual acts of piracy. However, as things stand at the time of writing, in Europe as in the United States, neo-liberal thinking and inhibitions about the need to promote the new technologies (and to defer to the new technology companies) has seen a concern for 'the free market' generally prevail over cultural and culture-industry interests, though this is far from being the whole story. The chapter has explained how a key obstacle to strengthening protection against copyright infringement, by involving technology companies more in policing and introducing the sanction of restricting access to the Internet, has also been presented by widespread popular concerns about protecting privacy and Internet access as a human right. Meanwhile, the fact remains that the Internet has encouraged copyright 'piracy' by individuals and 'free-riding' by giant technology companies on a scale that, in Robert Levine's (2011) words, promises to 'destroy the culture business'. At the time of writing, the way forward remains unclear. Like the Google/Viacom settlement it will almost certainly depend on more than regulation, but further regulatory steps will certainly need to be taken to address a problem that threatens to lead to cultural impoverishment in the digital, online future. Without effective copyright protection it is quite simply difficult to see how the market for quality content will continue to function.

Another key media policy priority for the digital, online era is to take action to help ensure that there should be a sufficient range of independent media voices with extensive reach and accessibility and that media consumption should not be too highly concentrated, ideally with citizens being exposed to and consuming news, information and sociocultural content from a pluralistic and diverse range of sources. Traditional remedies for limiting concentration focused on structural measures such as limits on shareholding, accumulations and/or market share in clearly defined 'relevant media markets': press, broadcasting, cross-media and so on. However, the sanction of divestment in cases where these limits were reached was in practice rarely ever in evidence. Restrictions on media ownership have always been open to challenge on the grounds of respect for values such as property rights and freedom of expression. Moreover, concentration has often been tolerated as a means to bolster national ownership of media industries, as in the case of small countries, in particular. But in the digital, online era, there are particular concerns about the viability of a restrictive approach. Media markets are fluid and converging, rendering it far more difficult to determine the relevant market for regulatory intervention, while forcing divestment might lead to an even greater diminution of pluralism in the context of media markets – newspaper markets in particular – that are seeing rapid disappearance of titles due largely to the Internet's impact both on advertising and on media consumption habits. It might actually make more sense to allow for an element of editorial concentration where that is likely to save newspapers. As seen, this has indeed been the regulators' approach in the USA and the UK. In the UK, News International has long used profits from its other titles to support the loss making *The Times*. How would forcing divestment on the Murdoch-controlled News International operation, as some have argued, help strengthen the sector which is experiencing decline approaching the US scale, with regional papers dying at a worrying rate and a loss-making national quality press which has already seen *The Independent* close down the non-digital, paper-based side of its operation? In 2011, the UK government removed local ownership rules precisely in order to enable partnerships between local newspapers, radio and ITV stations to help maintain a strong and diverse local media sector. Arguably the biggest problem with justiciable structural measures, is that the 'search for narrow, "objective" metrics has not been successful' (Crauford Smith and Tambini 2012: 35–63, 35). The easiest, and for neo-liberals the obvious, solution has been deregulation. Thus, since the first appearance of multichannel broadcasting (cable and satellite), the regulatory trend on both sides of the Atlantic has been towards removal of structural restrictions.

However, as Chapter 6 has also demonstrated, media concentration continues to be a problem in the digital, online world. The continued need for a precautionary approach should be clear. Even if there are growing difficulties in determining the relevant market, there needs to be a robust calculation that determines media power. Chapter 6 has pointed to the scale of media concentration, even in the Internet era, and argued that there remains a role for structural regulation. First, there are still clearly identifiable sectoral media markets and there are tried and tested methods for measuring media concentration in them. Second, as convergence renders these sector-specific controls obsolete, there are still approaches to cross-media regulation that can be deployed to measure concentrations of media power that potentially threaten plurality and diversity and pose a potentially unacceptable influence on society, culture and public opinion. Moreover, while there are clearly dangers associated with requiring companies to divest or in preventing consolidation in fragile markets like the press where preventing a take-over may mean losing a title, there are still behavioural obligations that can be laid on companies with significant media power. A company deemed by the regulator to have achieved a threshold of media power might be required to open up its media service to editorially independent, third-party journalism. The case of current German broadcasting regulation might serve as a model, where if the audience share of a television channel attains a 10 per cent threshold, the broadcaster is obliged to make available part of its airtime to an independent 'window service' chosen by the regulators. The main criterion for choosing the window service, which must amount to a minimum of 260 minutes per week, at least 75 minutes of which should be in prime time, is that it should contribute to pluralism and diversity, particularly in the fields of culture, education and information. This has provided a platform for independent productions and cooperative ventures with partners like the renowned investigative news magazines *Spiegel* and *Focus* (Humphreys 2015: 164). With little imagination, this model could be adapted to the converged media environment through application to all media enterprises deemed by regulators to have a significant audience and therefore potential influence on public opinion formation. As with other structural measures, the metric could be open to discussion.

Upon regulatory determination of a significant degree of media power, media companies with such power could be subjected to behavioural controls, such as the introduction of measures designed to ensure journalistic autonomy and the requirement for a number of public service obligations to be fulfilled by that company. Steps might also be taken to democratise powerful media companies. Legislation might be introduced to provide for editorial codes of practice or company statutes that would protect journalists' integrity and independence and even guarantee them a degree of industrial democracy. Legislation providing for this kind of 'internal press freedom' was discussed in (West) Germany during the 1970s but not in the end enacted because of fierce opposition from newspaper owners (Humphreys 1994: 108–9). Legislation might, for example, introduce a 'clause of conscience' which would increase protection of journalists' editorial integrity by making it costly for owners to sack them, through generous compensation provisions as in France. In Sweden, journalists have enjoyed the right to refuse to write a story that offends against a code of conduct agreed between the publishers' organisations and the journalists' union (Humphreys 1996: 108–10). A degree of internal pluralism and editorial independence from proprietorial control could be guaranteed by providing for pluralistically composed independent content advisory councils within the largest, most influential commercial broadcasting organisations (yet another idea from Germany). In sum, whether by statute or by codes of practice, ways might be found to limit undue proprietorial interference in journalism, to separate financial from editorial decisions, and, generally, to promote high professional standards of journalism.

One very obvious feature of media power is that provided by ownership or control of new media 'bottlenecks' or 'gateways'. Moreover, monopoly power over delivery and guidance/search systems is clearly not the only kind of bottleneck: monopoly control of rights is another form of 'bottleneck' media power to be entered into the regulatory equation. While sector-specific rules – for the press sector, and the broadcasting sector – might appear to be becoming less and less appropriate in the converging media landscape, the need to be aware of – and to address – ownership or control of media bottlenecks such as digital cable, satellite and terrestrial systems, EPGs, and market-dominant Internet intermediaries (ISPs, Google, YouTube), becomes more and more salient. Indeed, digital convergence has meant that media bottlenecks have become increasingly the focus of attention since those who control entry to – or movement along – the value chain for media content wield considerable (and potentially overweening) media power over the news, information and sociocultural material that citizens consume and by extension therefore over public opinion. At the same time, it is apparent that – potentially at least – awesome new media power is being acquired over content by new bottleneck-controllers of the means to access content. The media policy solution might appear to be to rely on competition law combined with what is called 'conditional access regulation', whereby bottleneck controllers are required to provide access to both content providers and end-users on fair and non-discriminatory terms, and this has indeed been the general thrust of media policy at national and EU level over the past two decades that media convergence has been on the agenda (since, for instance, the EU's 1999 Communications Review, or the UK's 2001 Broadcasting Act). However, as Thomas Gibbons (2004) has explained, there are currently shortfalls in bottleneck regulation; the bundling of programming packages – pay-TV services offering a 'package' of channels instead of the option to buy à la carte – has not been addressed.

Much debate has surrounded the bottleneck power of Google. While there are no grounds for suspecting that Google uses its search algorithms for any editorial purposes that may impinge on public opinion and democratic pluralism, there is certainly the potential. So far there has been one notable intervention against the Internet intermediary for allegedly exploiting its bottleneck control, albeit on grounds of competition policy rather than pluralism concerns. Google's 90 per cent dominance of the European Internet search market has led to concerns about abuse of dominant market position. While market dominance itself is not against EU law, abuse of dominant market position certainly is. Since 2010 Brussels competition authorities have investigated allegations that Google's search engine had favoured its own services over those of rivals. On three occasions, the anti-trust case appeared close to settlement, but on each the settlements were aborted amid suspicions that Google was foot-dragging and cries of protest from Google's opponents. In April 2015, Competition Commissioner Margrethe Vestager finally filed formal charges against Google, accusing it of displaying its Google Shopping channel more prominently than rival offerings. On 27 June 2017 the Commission announced a €2.42 billion ($2.7 bn; £2.1 bn) fine on Google after a ruling that the company had indeed abused its own market power by promoting its own shopping comparison service at the top of search results. This was the European competition authority's largest penalty to date against a company for market distortion. The ruling also demanded that Google end its anti-competitive practices within 90 days or face a further penalty (Kelion 2017).

As Chapter 5 has indicated, there are also demands to treat Internet intermediaries like Google as publishers rather than as platforms. Indeed, the case for doing so has drawn considerable strength recently from concern over the manner in which the likes of Facebook and Twitter have allegedly damaged political discourse and even allowed interference in the political process. This raises a wider question. How amenable are the new media to regulation? On the one hand, stricter regulation would not be a straightforwardly easy task. The multiplication of distribution outlets for media products introduced by waves of new media – first cable and satellite, then digitalisation and the Internet – makes it futile to argue for a simple continuation into the digital age of the traditional far-reaching kind of regulation of the electronic media. Already, before the globalising Internet, the development of international satellite TV made it possible for broadcasters to circumvent over-stringent regulation by basing up-linking of their services from locations with the laxest regulatory requirements. In the digital age, as media services have converged with telecommunications and the Internet, a decrease in the amount and scope of regulation of private commercial media has been inevitable. For Internet operators, self-regulation backed up by law for serious offenses such as extreme pornography and incitement to racial hatred are widely regarded as the only form of regulation that has appeared viable. Yet there is an obvious rebuttal to any such over-technologically deterministic perspective. In fact, the Internet has not so easily escaped regulation, as Goldsmith and Wu (2006) have documented engagingly and comprehensively. They argue convincingly that even in non-authoritarian contexts, the destiny of the Internet lies in the hands of policy makers and politicians, particularly those in powerful polities, like the USA and the European Union, as indeed the latter's aforementioned action against Google (and it has similarly acted against Amazon over tax) over competition issues have shown.

Lastly, to counterbalance private commercial accumulations of media power that by dint of the international nature of the online world escape easy regulation, it will be necessary to maintain strong, well-resourced public-service broadcasters which have an extensive – rather than minimal – programme remit and which are given the means to develop into public service media for the Internet era. Their internally pluralistic services should serve as a vital counterbalance to a commercial sector that lacks sufficient external pluralism (being highly concentrated). The flagship role of key PSBs like the BBC is crucial, but the UK's commitment to the principle of public service plurality is merit-worthy – and the means should be found to maintain commitment to other PSBs, like Channel 4. Chapter 7 develops this line of argument and argues, in addition, that new kinds of public support for media pluralism need to be considered. Subsidies should be considered for crisis-ridden newspapers, for launching new online ventures, for independent producers, regional production, community radio and TV and so on. There should be a 'technology-neutral' approach to subsidising 'public service journalism'. This could be financed by raising an industry levy on the profits of those commercial companies which enjoy market power in the advertising and pay-TV markets. Relatedly, a way of sharing the public support (subsidy) going to the media sector, would be public–private partnerships. This could help new Internet start-ups and provide a means to help alleviate the crisis of the press sector as it transitions to the digital era. Notably, in the UK, it has been suggested that the BBC might cooperate with beleaguered local newspapers (though critics have seen this as an unwelcome and competition-threatening expansion of the BBC's remit). Above all, as Chapter 7 has argued, so long as it is not funded by 'top-slicing' (taking a portion of) their licence fee income, the idea of the introduction – alongside existing PSBs – of a new PSP-type public service institution, which would disburse funds on a transparent and contestable basis, has considerable promise. Digital convergence requires policies that will ensure the continued fulfilment of public service journalistic functions and the provision of public service content in a technology neutral way. In the age of digital convergence, public service communication should not be conceived as something only related to broadcasting.

CONCLUSION: INTEGRATING MEDIA POLICY AND GOVERNANCE FOR DEEPER MEDIA CONVERGENCE

This volume has made a journey through the many years in which media convergence of one kind or another has developed across a range of different issue areas. Fundamentally, it is clear that both the problems and the possibilities of digital media convergence require a quite radical shift in perspective and its subsequent translation into more detailed, robust and better resourced set of media policies than have been in place to date. It is undeniably the case that media convergence, by dint of the fact that it involves formerly disparate technical, economic, cultural, social and political phenomena coming together is innately complex. However, this complexity should be a spur and even an inspiration to develop effective policy action rather than a stimulus to obfuscate and retreat in respect of the raft of matters which this volume has shown to be germane to current and future social well-being and experience.

The online world, through the development of the Internet, has been the key site for the manifestation of the technologies, services and content of convergence across digitalised media. However, the Internet is a now a global communications phenomenon and it has been well documented how policies developed at the national level, based on assumptions of national jurisdiction, cannot be completely effective. This feature of the Internet should be acknowledged and incorporated into policy actions for digital convergence, rather than used as an excuse for policy inactivity. The risk of reduced policy effectiveness in a digital media environment should be acknowledged and understood as a feature that 'comes with the territory' of media convergence. There are two key ways in which this risk can be leveraged. First, given the innately global nature of much of the online world, there should be developed international policy exchange fora for media convergence to help understand the problems of convergence and the different perspectives taken from it. This could facilitate policy development and learning at the global level on convergence media policy. Such activity could be developed in a multi-stakeholder environment like the Internet Governance Forum, which, though much criticised for not having decision-taking power, in this less formal information exchange mode could prove effective with a more realistic weight of expectation placed upon it than has been the case to this point. Second, as has been noted in the volume, the reduced ability of, for example, the media policy tool of regulatory governance to be effective on its own, points to the potential utility of combinative policy action. Given the complex, multi-layered nature of media convergence, it would seem logically symmetrical to design media policy package-based solutions which could combine technical, legal, regulatory, fiscal, and educative tools. Whilst this may seem a potentially messy and ineffective response to convergence, whilst requiring innovativeness and flexibility in thinking and implementation, it is one likely to yield the most fruitful outcomes. As noted throughout this volume, the idea of intervention should replace that of withdrawal and laissez faire, or at least have more prominence than it has had hitherto. Here, a route to effective policy making for digital convergence should be a fundamental consideration of the compatibilities and incompatibilities of the traditions of computing, telecommunications, publishing and broadcasting. This volume has shown that even after decades of movement towards convergence, there still appears significant sectoral separatism. Only when a more intense and, in principle, accommodative attempt is made to understand what each component of electronic communications can provide in assisting the evolution of convergence, can a proper set of insights be applied to ensure that the advantages and opportunities in each historical sector – in terms of organisational perspective, and cultural and operational values – are realised. In constructing policies for convergence, considerations of infrastructure and content should be undertaken in unison. Whilst adding complexity, this has the potential to be a more cost-effective route to securing a way to ensure appropriate policy solutions. Given that the key convergence infrastructure is the Internet, ensuring its technical proficiency and security, as well as affordable access to it, are indispensable elements of convergence media policy. Beyond that, policies for the development of socially, as well as commercially, beneficial media content should be created. Here, an underpinning idea should be the primacy to be afforded to the human being above and beyond technical artefacts. The development apace of artificial intelligence and an increasingly algorithmically driven online world makes this an absolute policy requirement.

Convergence content policies are undoubtedly the least well developed and most urgent aspect of what should constituent a progressive policy for media convergence. An underpinning feature of them should be acceptance of the primacy of the public interest. Foregrounding the public interest is likely to broaden and enrich an environment of media convergence which presently lacks the historically strong public dimension once found in the quarters of broadcasting, telecommunication and journalism publishing. Bringing this forward and renewing it in the online world should be done unapologetically and with gusto. Ultimately, the public interest should supersede that of commerce as a matter of principle, even though, in reality, they are likely to be co-terminus in significant part due to the deeply embedded nature of twenty-first century electronic capitalism, a situation unlikely to change in the foreseeable future. Finally, holding policy goals and aspirations for media convergence will amount to little without a development and expansion – as opposed to a financial re-working at current levels – in the funding mechanisms and amounts available for publicly funded media in a convergence world. This volume has made reference to innovations, such as the public service publisher. The ubiquitous, highly lucrative nature of much of digital commerce also points to the potential utility of leveraging revenue through some form of digital taxation system. This could underpin a necessarily complex, though ultimately progressive, governance of media convergence to evolve with effective purpose in the coming decades.

References

Aaronovitch, D. (2012), 'There's nothing noble in this Wiki blackout', *The Times*, Thursday, 19 January, p. 21.

ACT, AER, ENPA, EPC and VPRT (2009), *Joint Letter to Commissioner Kroes on the Revision of the Broadcasting Communication*, Brussels: ACT, AER, ENPA, EPC and VPRT.

Ala Fossi, M. and M. Bonet (2016), 'Clearing the skies: European spectrum policy and future challenges of DTT in Finland and Spain', *International Journal of Digital Television*, 7 (3), 363–377.

Allan, S. and E. Thorsen (eds) (2009), *Citizen Journalism: Global Perspectives*, New York: Peter Lang.

Anderson, C. (2004), 'The Long Tail', *Wired*, October 2004.

Anderson, C. (2006), *The Long Tail: Why the Future of Business is Selling Less of More*, New York: Hyperion.

Anderson, C. (2009a), *Free*, London: Random House Business Books.

Anderson, C. (2009b), *The Longer Long Tail: How Endless Choice is Creating Unlimited Demand*, London: Random House Business Books.

APWPT (2014), 'European Commission Endangers Cultural and Creative Industries and Freedom of the Press', APWPT Press Release, 5 September, accessed 5 April 2018 at: https://www.apwpt.org/downloads/apwpt-pr_lamy-rep_of_eu_com05092014.pdf.

ARD (2015), 'ARD response to the public consultation on the Lamy Report: The future use of the UHF TV broadcasting band', accessed 5 January 2018 at: https://ec.europa.eu/digital-single-market/en/news/results-lamy-report-public-consultation-700mhz-spectrum-band (organisations' contributions).

Armstrong, M. and H. Weeds (2007), 'Public service broadcasting in the digital world', in Paul Seabright and Jurgen von Hagen (eds), *The Economic Regulation of Broadcasting Markets: Evolving Technology and Challenges for Policy*, Cambridge: Cambridge University Press, pp. 81–149.

Assemblée Nationale (2009), *Projet de Loi Relatif à la Protection Pénale de la Propriété Littéraire et Artistique sur Internet*, 22 September.

Association of European Radios (AER) (2014), 'European Commission – Public consultation on the future use of the UFH Terrestrial broadcasting band: The Lamy Report – AER Comments', accessed 23 March

2018 at: https://ec.europa.eu/digital-single-market/en/news/results-lamy-report-public-consultation-700mhz-spectrum-band (organisations' contributions).

Aufderheide, P. (1999), *Communications Policy and the Public Interest: The Telecommunications Act of 1996*, New York: Guilford Press.

Bagdikian, B.H. (1983), *The Media Monopoly*, Boston: Beacon Press.

Bagdikian, B.H. (2004), *The New Media Monopoly*, Boston: Beacon Press.

Baker, C.E. (2007), *Media Concentration and Democracy: Why Ownership Matters*, Cambridge: Cambridge University Press.

Baker, J. (2014), 'Net neutrality: EU's three headed beast now at war with itself', *The Register*, 26 November, accessed 20 March 2015 at: http://www.theregister.co.uk/2014/11/26/net_neutrality_eus_three headed_beast_now_at_war_with_itself/.

Baker, J. (2015), 'EU annoys industry and activists with net neutrality proposal', *The Register*, 5 March, accessed 20 March 2015 at: http://www.theregister.co.uk/2015/03/05/net_neutrality_eu-ministers_proposals_treated_with_suspicion/.

Barnett, S. and J. Townend (eds) (2015), *Media Power and Plurality: From Hyperlocal to High Level Policy*, Basingstoke: Palgrave Macmillan, Palgrave Global Media Policy and Business Series.

Barnett, S., G.N. Ramsay and I. Gaber (2012), 'From Callaghan to the credit crunch: Changing trends in British television 1975–2009, report funded by the Leverhulme Trust, University of Westminster, London.

Barron, A. (2011), '"Graduated response" *a l'Anglaise*: Online copyright infringement and the Digital Economy Act 2010', *Journal of Media Law*, 3 (2), 305–47.

Barwise, P. (2009), 'New forms of funding for PSB', speech to a seminar organized by the Federation of Entertainment Unions, 22 June 2009, accessed 24 November 2017 at: https://www.bectu.org.uk/news/315.

Barwise, P. and R.G. Picard (2014), *What If There Were No BBC Television?*, Oxford: Reuters Institute for the Study of Journalism.

Barwise, P. et al. (2015), 'Incorporating social value into spectrum allocation', DCMS, November, accessed 5 January 2018 at: https://www.gov.uk/government/publications/incorporating-social-value-into-spectrum-allocation-decisions.

BBC (2007), BBC response to 'A new approach to public service content in the digital media age', accessed 23 March 2018 at: http://www.ofcom.org.uk/consult/condocs/pspnewapproach/responses/bbc.pdf.

BBC (2017), 'US halts internet "six strikes" anti-piracy scheme', *BBC News*, posted 31 January 2017, accessed 5 December 2017 at http://www.bbc.co.uk/news/technology-38808719.

BECTU (2007), Ofcom: 'A new approach to public services content in the digital media age', BECTU comments, accessed 23 March 2018 at: http://www.ofcom.org.uk/consult/condocs/pspnewapproach/responses/bectu.pdf.

Belli, L. (2013), 'Network neutrality and human rights – an input paper', in L. Belli and P. De Filippi (eds), *The Value of Network Neutrality for the Internet of Tomorrow: Report of the Dynamic Coalition on Network Neutrality*, accessed 12 September 2016 at: https://hal.archives-ouvertes.fr/hal-01026096, pp. 11–25.

Benkler, Y. (2006), *The Wealth of Networks: How Social Production Transforms Markets and Freedom*, New Haven, CT: Yale University Press.

Body of European Regulators in Electronic Communications (BEREC) (2011), 'A Framework for Quality of Service in the Scope of Net Neutrality', Brussels, BoR (11) 53, 8 December, accessed 5 April 2018 at: http://berec.europa.eu/doc/berec/bor/bor11_53_qualityservice.pdf.

Body of European Regulators in Electronic Communications (BEREC) (2012a), 'Differentiation practices and related competition issues in the scope of Net Neutrality', Brussels, BoR (12) 31, 29 May.

Body of European Regulators in Electronic Communications (BEREC) (2012b), 'BEREC guidelines for quality of service in the scope of Net Neutrality', Brussels, BoR (12) 32, 29 May.

BNE et al. (2015), 'Support to the NOC position adopted by several regional organisations for the frequency range 470-694/698 MHz' Document – E XXX 2015, 30 October, accessed 4 January 2018 at: H:\IAM\1.CLIENTS\BNE2015\09.MARKETINGANDCOMMS\WEB SITE\UPLOADS\INFORMATIONTOUPLOAD\WRC-15-EV1_1510 27_FINAL.DOCX.

Brevini, B. (2013), *Public Service Broadcasting Online: A Comparative European Policy Study*, Basingstoke: Palgrave Macmillan.

Bridge, M. (2017a), 'Internet giants fail to tackle growth in illegal streaming', *The Times*, Saturday, 29 July, p. 17.

Bridge, M. (2017b), 'Fake news storm marks "beginning of the end" for social media giants', *The Times*, Friday, 29 December, p. 19.

British Entertainment Industry Radio Group (BEIRG) (2015), 'European Commission consultation. British Entertainment Industry Radio Group. Public Consultation on the future use of the UHF TV broadcasting band – the Lamy Report', accessed 23 March 2018 at: https://ec.europa.eu/digital-single-market/en/news/results-lamy-report-public-consultation-700mhz-spectrum-band (organisations' contributions).

Brown, I. and C. Marsden (2013), *Regulating Code – Good Governance and Better Regulation in the Information Age*, Cambridge, MA: MIT Press.

BT (2015), 'BT's response to the EC public consultation "Results of the work of the high level group on the future use of the UHF band (470–790 MHz) (Report by Pascal Lamy)', 8 April, accessed 5 January 2018 at: https://ec.europa.eu/digital-single-market/en/news/results-lamy-report-public-consultation-700mhz-spectrum-band (organisations' contributions).

Budde (2016), '2016 Australia – The National Broadband Network – moving into 2017', accessed 8 November 2017 at: https://www.budde.com.au/Research/2016-Australia-The-National-Broadband-Network-Moving-into-2017.

Campaign for Press and Broadcasting Freedom (CPBF) (2007), *Response to Ofcom's Document: A New Approach to Public Service Content in the Digital Media Age. The Potential Role of the Public Service Publisher*, London: CPBF.

Carey, W.L. (1974), 'Federalism and corporate law; reflections upon Delaware', *Yale Law Review*, 83, 663–669.

Castells, M. (2013 [2009]), *Communication Power*, Oxford: Oxford University Press, second edition.

Cave, M. and P. Crocioni (2007), 'Does Europe need network neutrality rules?', *International Journal of Communication*, 1, 669–679.

Cawley, A. and P. Preston (2006), 'Broadband and digital "content" in the EU-25: Recent trends and challenges', *Telematics and Informatics*, 24 (4), 259–271.

Center for Democracy and Technology (2006), 'Preserving the essential Internet', June, accessed 20 September 2013 at: https://net.educause.edu/ir/library/pdf/EPO0653.pdf.

CEPT (2015), 'Final report from CEPT of WRC-15', unpublished document.

Ceruzzi, P. (2003), *A History of Modern Computing*, Boston: The MIT Press.

Channel Four Television Corporation (2007), *Channel 4 Response to the Ofcom Consultation: A New Approach to Public Service Content in the Digital Media Age – the Potential Role of the Public Service Publisher*, April 2007.

Clark, D.D. (2007), 'Network neutrality: Words of power and 800-pound gorillas', *International Journal of Communication*, 1, 701–708.

Clark, J. and P. Aufterheide (2009), 'Public media 2:0: Dynamic, engaged publics', report from the Future of Public Media Project, funded by the Ford Foundation, Washington, DC, American University, Center for Social Media, accessed 8 December 2017 at: https://www.scribd.com/document/12650140/Public-Media-2-0-Dynamic-Engaged-Publics.

Coates, S. (2015), 'Osborne: BBC must curb online ambitions', *The Times*, 6 July, p. 1.

220   *Regulation, governance and convergence in the media*

Coates, S. (2017), 'Prosecute web giants for abuse, May urged: New law would treat social media as publishers', *The Times*, Tuesday, 12 December, p. 1 (main headline).

Collins, R. (1994), *Broadcasting and Audio-visual Policy in the European Single Market*, London: John Libbey.

Compaine, B.M. (2005), 'The media monopoly myth: How new competition is expanding our sources of information and entertainment', paper for New Millennium Research Council, accessed 22 January 2012 at: http://newmillenniumresearch.org/archive/Final_Compaine_Paper_050205.pdf.

Compaine, B.M. and D. Gomery (2000), *Who Owns the Media? Competition and Concentration in the Mass Media Industry*, 3rd edition, Mahwah, NJ: Lawrence Erlbaum Associates.

Conseil Constitutionel (2006), *Décision n° 2006-540 DC du 27 juillet 2006, |Loi relative au droit d'auteur et aux droits voisins dans la société de l'information*, accessed 25 March 2015 at: http://www.conseil-constitutionnel.fr/conseil-con..cision-n-2006-540-dc-du-27-juillet-2006.1011.html.

Cottle, S. (2008), 'Reporting demonstrations: The changing media politics of dissent', *Media, Culture and Society*, 30 (6), 853–872.

Council of Europe (2004), 'Transnational media concentrations in Europe', report prepared by the Media Division, Directorate General of Human Rights, Strasbourg, November 2004.

Crauford Smith, R. and D. Tambini (2012), 'Measuring media plurality in the United Kingdom: Policy choices and regulatory challenges', *Journal of Media Law*, 4 (1), 35–63.

Crisafis, A. (2009), 'Nicolas Sarkozy pledges €600m state aid to newspapers', *The Guardian Online*, posted 23 January, accessed 17 October 2017 at: https://www.theguardian.com/media/2009/jan/23/sarkozy-pledges-state-aid-to-newspapers.

Crisafis, A. (2010), 'Nicolas Sarkozy's internet police warn 100,000 illegal downloaders', *The Guardian Online*, posted 29 December, accessed 24 February 2012 at: http://www.guardian.co.uk/world/2010/dec/29/sarkozy-internet-police-warn-downloaders.

Curran, J. (2012a), 'Rethinking internet history' in James Curran, Natalie Fenton and Des Freedman (eds), *Misunderstanding the Internet*, London & New York: Routledge, pp. 34–65.

Curran, J. (2012b), 'Reinterpreting the internet' in James Curran, Natalie Fenton and Des Freedman (eds), *Misunderstanding the Internet*, London & New York: Routledge, pp. 3–33.

Curran, J., N. Fenton and D. Freedman (2012), *Misunderstanding the Internet*, London and New York: Routledge.

Dahlberg, L. (2005), 'The corporate colonization of online attention and the marginalization of critical communication', *Journal of Communication Inquiry*, 29 (2), 160–180.

Dean, J. (2015), 'Google faces $6.6 bn fine in Brussels competition inquiry', *The Times*, Thursday 16 April, p. 19.

Dean, J. (2017), 'Disney fights tech giants with $66 bn Fox takeover', *The Times*, Friday, 15 December, p. 51.

Deibert, R. (2000), 'International plug 'n play? Citizen activism, the internet, and global public policy', *International Studies Perspectives*, 1 (3), 255–272.

Department of National Heritage (1995), *Media Ownership: The Government's Proposals*, White Paper, CM 2872. London: HMSO.

DIGITALEUROPE (2014), 'DIGITALEUROPE response to the consultation on the Lamy Report on the future use of the UHF TV broadcasting band', Brussels, 1 April, accessed 5 January 2018 at: https://ec.europa.eu/digital-single-market/en/news/results-lamy-report-public-consultation-700mhz-spectrum-band (organisations' contributions).

DigitalUK (2015), 'Response to consultation: Lamy Report: the future use of the UHF TV broadcasting band', 12 April, accessed 5 January 2018 at: https://ec.europa.eu/digital-single-market/en/news/results-lamy-report-public-consultation-700mhz-spectrum-band (organisations' contributions).

DLA Piper (2009), 'EU study on the legal analysis of a single market for the information society – new rules for a new age?', DLA Piper, November.

Downes, L. (2015), 'Did the national broadband plan spur innovation?', *Washington Post*, accessed 10 November 2017 at: https://www.washingtonpost.com/nres/innovations/wp/2015/03/23/did-the-national-broadband-plan-spur-innovation/?utm_term=.2854c2bbb7e0.

Downie Jr, L. and M. Schudson (2009), 'The reconstruction of American journalism', *Columbia Journalism Review*, 19 October, accessed 23 July 2010 at: http://www.journalism.columbia.edu/cs/ContentServer/jrn/1212611716674/page/1212611716651/JRNSimplePage2.htm.

Doyle, G. (2002), *Media Ownership*, London: Sage.

Dwyer, T. (2010), *Media Convergence*, Maidenhead: Open University Press.

eBizMBA (2015), 'Top 15 most popular news websites', accessed 21 May 2015 at http://www.ebizmba.com/articles/news-websites.

EBU (2014), *Delivery of Broadcast Content over LTE Networks*, Technical Report 027, Geneva, July, accessed 5 April 2018 at: https://tech.ebu.ch/docs/techreports/tr027.pdf.

EBU (2015), 'EBU response to the public consultation on the Lamy Report: The future use of the UHF TV broadcasting band',

26 November, accessed 5 January 2018 at: https://ec.europa.eu/digital-single-market/en/news/results-lamy-report-public-consultation-700mhz-spectrum-band (organisations' contributions).

ECC (2014), *Long Term Vision for the UHF Band*, ECC Report 224, 28 November, accessed 6 April 2018 at: http://www.erodocdb.dk/Docs/doc98/official/pdf/ECCREP224.PDF.

ECC (2017), 'What we do', 23 October, accessed 5 January 2018 at: https://cept.org/ecc/what-we-do.

The Economist (2012), 'Newspapers versus google: taxing times', *The Economist*, 10 November, accessed 17 July 2017 at: https://www.economist.com/news/international/21565928-newspapers-woes-grow-some-are-lobbying-.

The Economist (2017a), 'Funnel vision', *The Economist*, 28 October, pp. 65–66.

The Economist (2017b), 'Rupert stops the presses', *The Economist*, 25 November, pp. 67–68.

Edelvold Berg, C. (2011), 'Sizing up size on TV markets: Why David would lose to Goliath', in Gregory Ferrell Lowe and Christian S. Nissen (eds), *Small Among Giants: Television Broadcasting in Smaller Countries*, Gothenburg: University of Gothenburg, NORDICOM, pp. 57–89.

EDRi (2013), 'Net neutrality threatened by the Commission's draft regulation', accessed 12 September 2016 at: https://edri.org/edrigramnumber11-17net-neutrality-ec-regulation/.

Elstein, D. (2008), 'How to fund public service content in the digital age', in Timothy Gardam and David Levy (eds), *The Price of Plurality: Choice, Diversity and Broadcasting Institutions in the Digital Age*, Oxford: Reuters Institute for the Study of Journalism, pp. 86–90.

Elstein, D., D. Cox, B. Donoghue, D. Graham and G. Metzger (2004), *Beyond the Charter: The BBC After 2006*, report by The Broadcasting Policy Group, London, accessed 6 November 2017 at: https://archive.org/stream/BeyondTheCharter/Beyond%20the%20Charter#page/n1/mode/2up.

Enders Analysis (2012), 'Media ownership rules', 30 April, submission to the *Leveson Inquiry*, accessed December 2017 at: http://webarchive.nationalarchives.gov.uk/20140122192333/http://www.levesoninquiry.org.uk/wp-content/uploads/2012/07/Annex-1-to-Submission-by-Claire-Enders-Enders-Analysis.pdf.

Ericsson (2015), 'Spectrum decisions at WRC-15, a step towards the networked society', 3 December, accessed 5 January 2018 at: https://www.ericsson.com/en/news/2015/12/spectrum-decisions-at-wrc-15-a-step-towards-the-networked-society.

Ermert, M. (2017), 'Intermediaries could be made liable in EU copyright legislation', *Intellectual Property Watch*, 14 July, accessed 17 July 2017 at: https://www.ip-watch.org/2017/.../intermediaries-made-liable-eu-copyright-legislation.

Eskelinen, H., L. Frank and T. Hirvonen (2008), 'Does strategy matter? A comparison of broadband rollout policies in Finland and Sweden', *Telecommunications Policy*, 32 (6), 412–421.

ETNO (2015), 'ETNO response to the "Public consultation on the Lamy Report: The future use of the UHF TV broadcasting band"', April.

European Commission (1988), *Green Paper on Copyright and the Challenge of Technology – Copyright Issues Requiring Immediate Action*, COM (88) 172 final, Brussels, 7 June 1988.

European Commission (1992), *Pluralism and Media Concentration in the Internal Market*, Green Paper, COM (92) 480, Brussels, 23 December 1992.

European Commission (1994a), *Europe and the Global Information Society: Recommendations to the EC*, 'The Bangemann Report', Brussels: European Commission.

European Commission (1994b), *Follow-up to the Consultation Process Relating to the Green Paper on 'Pluralism and Media Concentration in the Internal Market – An Assessment of the Need for Community Action*. COM (94) 353, Brussels, 5 October 1994.

European Commission (1996), *Draft Proposal for a Directive on Media Pluralism*, Directorate-General for the Internal Market (XV), Brussels, July.

European Commission (1997a), *Green Paper on the Convergence of the Telecommunications, Media and Information Technology Sectors, and the Implications for Regulation: Towards an Information Society Approach*,COM (97) 623, Brussels, 3 December 1997.

European Commission (1997b), *Proposal for a Directive on 'Media Ownership in the Internal Market'*, Working document of the Directorate-General for the Internal Market (XV), Brussels, 1 February 1997.

European Commission (2001), *Communication from the Commission on the Application of State Aid Rules to Public Service Broadcasting*, Official Journal of the European Communities 2001/C 320/04, Brussels, 15 November.

European Commission (2007), *Media Pluralism in the Member States of the European Union*, SEC (2007) Brussels, 32, 16 January 2007, accessed 6 December 2017 at: http://ec.europa.eu/information_society/media_taskforce/doc/pluralism/media_pluralism_swp_en.pdf.

European Commission (2009a), *Community Guidelines for the Application of State Aid Rules in Relation to the Rapid Deployment of Broadband Networks*, Brussels, 19 May.

European Commission (2009b), 'Commission declaration on net neutrality' (2009/C 308/02), OJC 308/2, 18 December.

European Commission (2010a), 'Digital agenda: Commission outlines action plan to boost Europe's prosperity and well-being'. Brussels, 19 May, IP/10/581.

European Commission (2010b), 'Digital agenda for Europe: Key initiatives', memo/10/200, Brussels, 19 May.

European Commission (2010c) *Commission Staff Working Document. Analysis of the application of Directive 2004/48/EC of the European Parliament and the Council of 29 April 2004 on the enforcement of intellectual property rights in the Member States*, SEC (2010) 1589 final, Brussels, 22 December 2010.

European Commission (2011), 'The open internet and net neutrality in Europe', Communication from the Commission to the European Parliament, the Council, the Economic and Social Committee and the Committee of the Regions, COM (2011) 222 final, Brussels, 19 April.

European Commission (2013a), *Preparing for a Fully Converged Audiovisual World: Growth, Creation and Values*, COM (2013) 231 final, Brussels, 24 April.

European Commission (2013b), *Proposal for a regulation of the European Parliament and of the Council laying down measures concerning the European single market for electronic communications and to achieve a Connected Continent, and amending Directives 2002/20/EC, 2002/21/EC and 2002/22/EC and Regulations (EC) No 1211/2009 and (EU) No 531/2012*, COM (2013) 627 final, 2013/0309 (COD), Brussels, 11 September.

European Commission (2015), *Proposal for a Council Decision on the position to be adopted, on behalf of the European Union, in the International Telecommunication Union (ITU) World Radiocommunication Conference 2015 (WRC- 15)*, 2015/0119 (NLE), COM (2015) 234 final, Brussels, 29 May.

European Commission (2016), *Proposal for a Decision of the European Parliament and of the Council on the use of the 470-790 MHz frequency band in the Union*, COM (2016) 43 final, Brussels, 2 February.

European Commission (2017a), 'Connectivity for a European Gigabit Society', 19 October, accessed 5 April 2018 at: https://ec.europa.eu/digital-single-market/en/policies/improving-connectivity-and-access.

European Commission (2017b), 'About 5G-PPP', accessed 10 November 2017 at: https://5g-ppp.eu.

European Council (1991), *Council Directive 91/250/EEC of 14 May 1991 on the legal protection of computer programs*, Luxembourg: Official Journal L 122, 17 May 1991, pp. 0042–0046.

European Council (1992), *Council Directive 92/100/EEC of 19 November 1992 on rental right and lending right and on certain rights related to copyright in the field of intellectual property*, Luxembourg: Official Journal L 346, 27 November 1992, pp. 61–66.

European Council (1993a), *Council Directive 93/83/EEC of 27 September 1993 on the coordination of certain rules concerning copyright and rights related to copyright applicable to satellite broadcasting and cable retransmission*, Luxembourg: Official Journal L 248, 6 October 1993 pp. 0015–0021.

European Council (1993b), *Council Directive 93/98/EEC of 29 October 1993 harmonizing the term of protection of copyright and certain related rights*, Luxembourg: Official Journal L 290, 24 November 1993, pp. 9–13.

European Council (1996), *Council Directive 96/9/EC of 11 March 1996 on the protection of data bases*, Luxembourg: Official Journal L 077, 27 March 1996.

European Council (2001), *Council Directive 2001/29/EC on the harmonisation of certain aspects of copyright and related rights in the Information Society*, Luxembourg: Official Journal L 167/10, 26 June 2001.

European Federation of Journalists (EFJ) (2005), *Media Power in Europe: The Big Picture of Ownership*, Brussels: European Federation of Journalists, accessed 6 December 2017 at: http://www.ifj.org/fileadmin/images/EFJ/EFJ_documents/Reports/Media_Power_in_Europe.pdf.

European Parliament and Council (1995), *Directive 95/46/EC of the European Parliament and of the Council of 24 October 1995 on the Protection of Individuals with Regard to the Processing of Personal Data and on the Free Movement of Such Data*, Brussels, OJL281/31, 23 November.

European Parliament and Council (2000), *Directive 2000/31/EC of the European Parliament and of the Council of 8 June 2000 on certain legal aspects of information society services, in particular electronic commerce, in the Internal Market ('Directive on electronic commerce')*, Official Journal of the European Communities, L 178, 17 July 2000.

European Parliament and Council (2001a), *Regulation (EC) No 45/2001 of the European Parliament and of the Council of 18 December 2000 on the protection of individuals with regard to the processing of personal data by the Community institutions and bodies and on the free movement of such data*, Official Journal of the European Communities, L 8/1, 12 January 2001.

European Parliament and Council (2001b), *Directive 2001/29/EC of the European Parliament and of the Council of 22 May 2001 on the harmonisation of certain aspects of copyright and related rights in the information society*, Luxembourg: Official Journal of the European Communities, L 167, 22 June 2001.

European Parliament and Council (2002a), *Directive of the European Parliament and Council on a Common Regulatory Framework for Electronic Communications Networks and Services (Framework Directive)*, Brussels, 4 February, PE-CONS 3672/01.

European Parliament and Council (2002b), *Decision of 7 March 2002 on a regulatory framework for radio spectrum policy in the European Community (Radio Spectrum Decision)*, Brussels, 24 April, OJL108/1-6.

European Parliament and Council (2002c), *Directive 2002/22/EC of 7 March 2002 on universal service and users' rights relating to electronic communications networks and services (Universal Service Directive)*, 24 April, OJL108/51-77.

European Parliament and Council (2004a), *Directive 2004/38/EC of 29 April 2004 on the right of citizens of the Union and their family members to move and reside freely within the territory of the Member States amending Regulation (EEC) No 1612/68 and repealing Directives 64/221/EEC, 68/360/EEC, 72/194/EEC, 73/148/EEC, 75/34/EEC, 75/35/EEC, 90/364/EEC, 90/365/EEC and 93/96/EEC*, 30 April, OJL158/77-123.

European Parliament and Council (2004b), *Directive 2004/48/EC of the European Parliament and Council of 29 April 2004 on the Enforcement of Intellectual Property Rights*, Official Journal of the European Communities, L 157, 30 April 2004.

European Parliament and Council (2009a), *Directive 2009/140/EC of the European Parliament and of the Council of 25 November 2009 amending Directives 2002/21/EC on a common regulatory framework for electronic communications networks and services, 2002/19/EC on access to, and interconnection of, electronic communications networks and associated facilities, and 2002/20/EC on the authorisation of electronic communications networks and services*, Official Journal of the European Union, L 337, 18 December 2009.

European Parliament and Council (2009b), *Directive 2009/136/EC of the European Parliament and of the Council of 25 November 2009 amending Directive 2002/22/EC on universal service and users' rights relating to electronic communications networks and services, Directive 2002/58/EC concerning the processing of personal data and the protection of privacy in the electronic communications sector and Regulation (EC) No 2006/2004 on cooperation between national authorities responsible for the enforcement of consumer protection laws*, Official Journal of the European Union, L 337, 18 December 2009, pp. 11–36.

European Parliament and Council (2010), *Directive 2010/13/EU of 10 March 2010 on the coordination of certain provisions laid down by law, regulation or administrative action in Member States concerning the provision of audiovisual media services (Audiovisual Media Services Directive)*, OJL95/1-24, 15 April.

European Parliament and Council (2014), *Directive 2014/61/EU of the European Parliament and of the Council of 15 May 2014 on measures to reduce the cost of deploying high-speed electronic communications networks*, Official Journal of the European Union, L 155/1, 23 May 2014.

European Parliament and Council (2015), *Regulation (EU) 2015/2120 of the European Parliament and of the Council of 25 November 2015 laying down measures concerning open internet access and amending Directive 2002/22/EC on universal service and users' rights relating to electronic communications networks and services and Regulation (EU) No 531/2012 on roaming on public mobile communications networks within the Union*, Official Journal of the European Union, L 310/1, 25 November 2015.

European Parliament and Council (2017), *Decision (EU) 2017/899 of 17 May 2017 on the use of the 470-790 MHz frequency band in the Union*, OJL138/131-137, 25 May.

European Parliament Committee on Legal Affairs (2017), *Draft report on the proposal for a directive of the European Parliament and the Council on copyright in the Single Market*, 10 March, EP Committee on Legal Affairs, Rapporteur: Therese Comodini Cachia, 2016/0280 (COD).

Falch, M. (2007), 'Penetration of broadband services – The role of policies', *Telematics and Informatics*, 24 (4), 246–258.

Falch, M. and A. Henten (2010), 'Public private partnerships as a tool for stimulating investments in broadband', *Telecommunications Policy*, 34 (9), 496–504.

FCC (2010), 'Connecting America: The national broadband plan', 17 March, accessed 19 December 2017 at: https://www.fcc.gov/general/national-broadband-plan.

FCC (2016), 'FCC releases sixth 'Measuring broadband America' report, FCNews from the Federal Communications Commission, Washington, 1 December.

Feijoo, C., J. Gomez-Barroso and E. Bohlin (2011), 'Public support for the deployment of next generation access networks: Common themes, methodological caveats and further research', *Telecommunications Policy*, 35 (9–10), 791–793.

Ferrell Lowe, G. and C.S. Nissen (eds) (2011), *Small Among Giants: Television Broadcasting in Smaller Countries*, Gothenbug: Nordicom, University of Gothenburg.

Financial Times (2017), 'Big media deals do not ensure a Disney ending', editorial, *The Financial Times*, Friday 15 December, p. 10.

Flew, T., P. Iosifidis and J. Steemers (eds) (2016), *Global Media and National Policies: The Return of the State*, Basingstoke: Palgrave Macmillan.

Foster, R. and K. Meek (2009), *Paying for Public Service Content: A Role for Spectrum Pricing. A report by Human Capital for the BBC*, A report by Human Capital for the BBC, September 2009, accessed 5 November 2017 at: http://static1.1.sqspcdn.com/static/f/1321365/16982409/1332252200827/human_capital.pdf?token=Lm9ZgoI2n%2FzzLuBhVPzxQlNf1CY%3D.

Foundation for Information Policy Research (n.d.), *Implementing the EU Copyright Directive*, accessed 19 February 2016 at: http://www.fipr.org/copyright/guide/eucd-guide.pdf.

Frean, A. (2017), 'Social media should pay for taking news stories', *The Times*, Thursday 3 August, p. 42.

Freedman, D. (2008), *The Politics of Media Policy*, Cambridge: Polity.

Freedman, D. (2009), 'The public service publisher – an obituary', *Journal of British Cinema and Television*, 6 (1), 103–121.

Freedman, D. (2012a), 'Web 2.0 and the death of the blockbuster economy', in James Curran, Natalie Fenton and Des Freedman (eds), *Misunderstanding the Internet*, London and New York: Routledge, pp. 69–94.

Freedman, D. (2012b), 'Outsourcing internet regulation', in James Curran, Natalie Fenton and Des Freedman (eds), *Misunderstanding the Internet*, London and New York: Routledge, pp. 95–120.

Fuchs, C. (2014), *Social Media: A Critical Introduction*, London: Sage.

Garrahan, M. (2017), 'Disney agrees $66 bn deal to buy Murdoch's 21st Century Fox assets', *Financial Times*, main headline, Friday 15 December 2017, p. 1.

Gibbons, T. (2004), 'Control over technical bottlenecks – a case for media ownership law?', in Susanne Nikoltchev (ed.), *Regulating Access to Digital Television: Technical Bottlenecks, Vertically Integrated Markets and New Forms of Media Concentration*, Strasbourg: European Audiovisual Observatory, Iris Special, pp. 59–67.

Gibbons, T. and P. Humphreys (2012), *Audiovisual Regulation under Pressure: Comparative Cases from North America and Europe*, London and New York: Routledge.

Gibson, O. and R. Wray (2006), 'Regulator presses on with plan for new digital operator', *The Guardian*, 21 December, p. 27.

Gilder, G. (1990), *Life After Television: The Coming Transformation of Media and American Life*, New York/London: W.W. Norton & Company.

Given, J. (2010), 'Take your partners: Public–private interplay in Australian and New Zealand plans for next generation broadband', *Telecommunications Policy*, 34 (9), 540–549.

Goldsmith, J. and T. Wu (2006), *Who Controls the Internet: Illusions of a Borderless World*, New York: Oxford University Press.

Goodman, J. (2006), *Telecommunications Policy: Making in the European Union*, Cheltenham, UK and Northampton MA, USA: Edward Elgar Publishing.

Gowers, A. (2006), *Gowers Review of Intellectual Property*, London: HM Treasury.

Gowing, N. (2011), 'Time to move on: New media realities – new vulnerabilities of power', *Media, War and Conflict*, 4 (1), 13–19.

Grant, P. and C. Wood (2004), *Blockbusters and Trade Wars: Popular Culture in a Globalized World*, Vancouver/Toronto: Douglas and McIntyre.

GSMA (2015), 'GSMA commends allocation of additional spectrum for mobile broadband at WRC-15', Press release 27 November, accessed 5 January 2018 at: https://www.gsma.com/newsroom/press-release/gsma-commends-allocation-of-additional-spectrum-for-mobile-broadband-at-wrc-15/.

Guardian editorial (2015), 'The BBC: Digital Overload', *The Guardian*, 15 June 2006, p. 32.

Guardian Media Group (2007), *Guardian Media Group Response to Ofcom Consultation: A New Approach to Pubic Service Content in the Digital Media Age*.

Hallin, D.C. and P. Mancini (2004), *Comparing Media Systems: Three Models of Media and Politics*, Cambridge, UK, and New York, USA.

Harcourt, A.J. (2005), *The European Union and the Regulation of Media Markets*, Manchester: Manchester University Press.

Hargreaves, I. (2011), *Digital Opportunity: A Review of Intellectual Property and Growth*, London: Department for Business, Innovation and Skills, accessed 17 March 2015 at: https://www.gov.uk/government/publications/digital-opportunity-review-of-intellectual-property-and-growth.

Herman, E.S. and N. Chomsky (2002 [1988]), *Manufacturing Consent: The Political Economy of the Mass Media*, New York: Pantheon.

Hern, A. (2014), 'EU divided on issue of net neutrality', *The Guardian*, 27 November, accessed 19 March 2015 at: http://www.theguardian.com/technology/2014/nov/27/european-commission-net-neutrality/.

Heyman, R. and J. Pierson (2013), 'Blending mass self-communication with advertising in Facebook and LinkedIn: Challenges for social media and user empowerment', *International Journal of Media and Cultural Politics*, 9 (3), 229–246.

Hindman, M. (2009), *The Myth of Digital Democracy*, Princeton: Princeton University Press.

Hindman, M., K. Tsioutsiouliklis and J.A. Johnson (2003), '"Googlearchy": How a few heavily-linked sites dominate politics on the Web', paper presented at the Annual Meeting of the Midwest Political Science Association, Chicago, IL, 31 March.

Hooper, R. and R. Lynch (2012), *Copyright Works: Streamlining Copyright Licensing for the Digital Age*, London: Intellectual Property Office, accessed 17 March 2015 at: http://www.copyrighthub.co.uk/Documents/dce-report-phase2.aspx.

Horrigan, J. and M. Duggan (2015), 'Barriers to broadband adoption: Cost is now a substantial challenge for many non-users', Pew Research Center, Internet and Technology, 21 December, accessed 10 November 2017 at: http://www.pewinternet.org/2015/12/21/3-barriers-to-broadband-adoption-cost-is-now-a-substantial-challenge-for-many-non-users/.

Horten, M. (2012), *The Copyright Enforcement Enigma: Internet Politics and the 'Telecoms Package'*, Basingstoke: Palgrave Macmillan.

House of Commons Culture, Media and Sport Committee (2007), *Public Service Content, First Report of Session 2007-8*, 15 November 2007, HC 36-I, accessed 23 March 2018 at: https://publications.parliament.uk/pa/cm200708/cmselect/cmcumeds/36/36i.pdf.

House of Commons, Culture, Media and Sports Committee (2013), *Supporting the Creative Economy*, Third Report of the Session 2013-14, House of Commons, 11 September, accessed 23 March 2018 at: https://publications.parliament.uk/pa/cm201314/cmselect/cmcumeds/674/674.pdf.

House of Lords (2010), *Communications Committee First Report, The British Film and Television Industries*, January 2010, accessed 24 November 2014 at: http://www.publications.parliament.uk/pa/ld200910/ldselect/ldcomuni/37/3702.htm.

Hugenholtz, B. et al. (2006), *The Recasting of Copyright & Related Rights for the Knowledge Economy*, Final Report, The Institute for

Information Law, University of Amsterdam, the Netherlands, November 2006, accessed 18 February 2016 at: http://ec.europa.eu/internal_market/copyright/docs/studies/etd2005imd195recast_report-2006.pdf.

Humphreys, P. (1994), *Media and Media Policy in Germany*, Oxford: Berg.

Humphreys, P. (1996), *Mass Media and Media Policy in Western Europe*, Manchester: Manchester University Press.

Humphreys, P. (2006), 'Press subsidies in the context of the information society. Historical perspectives, modalities, concept and justification' in Isabel Fernàndez Alonso, Miquel de Moragas, José Joaquín Blasco Gil and Núria Almiron (eds), *Press Subsidies in Europe*, Barcelona: Generalitat de Catalunya/INCOM/UAB, pp. 38–55.

Humphreys P. (2008), 'Redefining public service media: A comparative study of France, Germany and the UK', paper presented at the Fourth Annual Conference of RIPE, Public Service Media in the 21st Century: Participation, Partnership and Media Development, hosted by the Zweites Deutsches Fernsehen and the two universities of Mainz, Germany, accessed 11 December 2017 at http://www.uta.fi/jour/ripe/papers/Humphreys_P.pdf.

Humphreys, P. (2009), EU state aid rules, public service broadcasters' online media engagement and public value tests: The German and UK cases compared', *Interactions: Studies in Communication and Culture*, 1 (2), 171–184.

Humphreys, P. (2011), 'A political scientist's contribution to the comparative study of media systems in Europe: A response to Hallin and Mancini', in Natascha Just and Manuel Puppis (eds), *Trends in Communication Policy Research: New Theories, Methods and Subjects*, Bristol: Intellect.

Humphreys, P. (2015), 'Transferable media pluralism policies from Europe', in Steven Barnett and Judith Townend (eds), *Media Power and Plurality: From Hyperlocal to High-Level Policy*, Basingstoke: Palgrave Macmillan, pp. 151–169.

Humphreys, P. and M. Lang (1998), 'Regulating for media pluralism and the pitfalls of Standortpolitik: The re-regulation of German broadcasting ownership laws', *German Politics*, 7 (2), 176–201.

Humphreys, P. and S. Simpson (2005), *Globalisation, Convergence and European Telecommunications*, Cheltenham, UK and Northampton, MA, USA: Edward Elgar Publishing.

Humphreys, S. (2013), 'Predicting, securing and shaping the future: Mechanisms of governance in online social environments', *International Journal of Media and Cultural Politics*, 9 (3), 247–258.

International Telecommunication Union (2017), 'World Radiocommunication Conferences', accessed 23 March 2018 at: http://www.itu.int/en/ITU-R/conferences/wrc/Pages/default.aspx.

Iosifidis, P. (ed.) (2007), *Public Television in the Digital Era: Technological Challenges and New Strategies for Europe*, Basingstoke: Palgrave Macmillan.

Iosifidis, P. (ed.) (2010), *Reinventing Public Service Communication: European Broadcasters and Beyond*, Basingstoke: Palgrave Macmillan.

Iosifidis, P. (2011), *Global Media and Communication Policy*, Basingstoke: Palgrave Macmillan.

ITV (2007), *Response to Ofcom's Document: A New Approach to Public Service Content in the Digital Media Age. The Potential Role of the Public Service Publisher*, London: ITV.

Jenkins, H. (2008), *Convergence Culture: Where Old and New Media Collide*, New York: New York University Press.

Just, N. and M. Puppis (2012), 'Communications policy research: Looking back, moving forward', in Natascha Just and Manuel Puppis (eds), *Trends in Communications Policy Research – New Theories, Methods and Subjects*, Bristol: Intellect Publishers, pp. 9–30.

Katholieke Universiteit Leuven ICRI, Jönköping International Business School, MMTC, Central European University and Ernst & Young Consultancy, Belgium (2009), *Independent Study on Indicators for Media Pluralism in the Member States: Towards a Risk-Based Approach, Report Prepared for the European Commission*, Directorate-General Information Society and Media, SMART 007A2007-002. Contract No: 30-CE-0154276/00-76, Leuven, Belgium, July 2009, accessed 11 December 2017 at: http://ec.europa.eu/information_society/media_taskforce/pluralism/study/index-en.htm.

Kaye, J. and S. Quinn (2010), *Funding Journalism in the Digital Age*, New York: Peter Lang.

Keating, D. (2015), 'Ansip slams Council position on phone roaming charges', *European Voice*, 24 March, accessed 25 March 2015 at: http://www.europeanvoice.com/article/ansip-slams-council-position-on-phone-roaming-charges/?utm_source=email&utm_medium=alert&utm_campaign=Ansip+slams+Council+position+on+phone+roaming+charges.

Kelion, L. (2017), 'Google hit with record EU fine over shopping service', accessed on 5 April 2018 at: http://www.bbc.co.uk/news/technology-40406542.

Keynote (2010), *The Publishing Industry 2010*.

Klinenberg, E. (2007), *Fighting for Air; The Battle to Control America's Media*, New York: Metropolitan Books, Henry Holt and Company.

Kruger, L. (2013), 'The national broadband plan goals: Where do we stand?', CRS Report for Congress, Congressional Research Service, 7-5700, R43016, 19 March.

Lamy, P. (2014), *Report to the EC: Results of the Work of the High Level Group on the Future use of the UHF Band* (470–790), accessed 10 January 2016 at: https://ec.europa.eu/digital-single-market/en/news/public-consultation-lamy-report-future-use-uhf-tv-broadcasting-band.

LaRose, R. et al. (2014), 'Public broadband investment priorities in the US: An analysis of the Broadband Technologies Opportunities Program', *Government Information Quarterly*, 31, 53–64.

Lentz, B. (2013), 'Excavating historicity in the US net neutrality debate', *Communication, Culture and Critique*, 6 (4), 568–597.

Lessig, L. (2004), *Free Culture: The Nature and Future of Creativity*, London and New York: Penguin Books.

Lessig, L. (2006), *Code Version 2.0*, New York: Basic Books.

Lessig, L. (2011), *Republic, Lost: How Money Corrupts Congress – and a Plan to Stop It*, New York and Boston: Twelve Books.

Lessig, L. and R.W. McChesney (2006), 'No tolls on the internet', *The Washington Post*, Thursday, 8 June, accessed 12 March 2015 at: http://www.washingtonpost.com/wp-dyn/content/article/2006/06/07/AR20060607021.

Leveson, Lord Justice B.H. (2012), *An Inquiry into the Culture, Practices and Ethics of the Press. Executive Summary*, November, presented to Parliament pursuant to section 26 of the Inquiries Act 2005, accessed 26 July 2017 at: https://www.gov.uk/government/uploads/system/uploads/attachment_data/file/229039/0779.pdf.

Levine, R. (2011), *Free Ride. How the Internet is Destroying the Culture Business and How the Culture Business can Fight Back*, London: The Bodley Head.

Levy, D. (1999), *Europe's Digital Revolution: Broadcasting Regulation, the EU and the Nation State*, London and New York: Routledge.

Li, G. (2012), 'The return of public investment in telecommunications: Assessing the early challenges of the national broadband network policy in Australia', *Computer Law & Security Review*, 28 (2), 220–330.

Linge, N. and A. Sutton (2015), *30 Years of Mobile Phones in the UK*, Stroud: Amberley Publishing.

Littoz-Monnet, A. (2007), *The European Union and Culture; Between Economic Regulation and European Cultural Policy*, Manchester; Manchester University Press.

Lovink, G. (2011), *Networks Without a Cause*, Cambridge: Polity Press.

Lutz, A. (2012), 'These 6 Corporations Control 90% of the Media in America', *Business Insider*, accessed 10 March 2016 at: http://

www.businessinsider.com/these-6-corporations-control-90-of-the-media-in-america-2012-6?IR=T.

MacDonald, R., G. Cannella and J. Ben-Avie (2013), 'Net neutrality: Ending network discrimination in Europe', in Luca Belli and Primavera De Filippi (eds), *The Value of Network Neutrality for the Internet of Tomorrow, Report of the Dynamic Coalition on Network Neutrality*, pp. 11–25, accessed 12 September 2016 at: https://hal.archives-ouvertes.fr/hal-01026096.

Majone, G. (1996), *Regulating Europe*, London and New York: Routledge.

Mansell, R. (2016), 'Media convergence policy issues', *Oxford Research Encyclopedia of Communication*, November. DOI: 10.1093/acrefore/9870190228613.013.62.

Mansell, R. (2017), 'Inequality and digitally mediated communication: Divides, contradictions and consequences', *Javnost – the Public*, 24 (2), 146–161.

Marsden, C. (2010), *Net Neutrality: Towards a Co-Regulatory Solution*, London: Bloomsbury Academic.

Marsden, C. (2017), *Network Neutrality: From Policy to Law to Regulation*, Manchester: Manchester University Press.

Marsden, C. and L. Belli (2015), 'Not Neutrality but "Open Internet" a L'Europeenne', accessed 15 March 2016 at: http://blogs.lse.ac.uk/mediapolicyproject/2015/10/29/not-neutrality-but-open-internet-a-la-europeenne/.

Marshallsea, T. (2017), 'How Australia's A$49bn internet network came to be ridiculed', BBC.co.uk, 27 October, accessed 10 November 2017 at: http://www.bbc.co.uk/news/world-australia-41577003.

May, C. (2000), *A Global Political Economy of Intellectual Property Rights. The New Enclosures?*, London and New York: Routledge.

Mayer Schoberger, V. and K. Cukier (2013), *Big Data: A Revolution That Will Transform How We Live, Work and Think*, New York: Mifflin Harcourt Books.

McChesney, R.W. (1993), *Telecommunications, Mass Media, and Democracy: The Battle for the Control of US Broadcasting*, New York: Oxford University Press.

McChesney, R.W. (2004), *The Problem of the Media: US Communication Politics in the 21st Century*, New York: Monthly Review Press.

McChesney, R.W. and J. Nichols (2010), *The Death and Life of American Journalism: The Media Revolution that Will Begin the World Again*, Philadelphia, PA, USA: Nation Books.

McChesney, R.W. (2013), *Digital Disconnect: How Capitalism is Turning the Internet Against Democracy*, New York/London: The New Press.

McCourt, D. (2007), 'Hollywood feels the pull of internet television', *Financial Times*, 17 April, p. 15.

McDiarmid, A. and M. Shears (2013), 'The importance of Internet neutrality to protecting human rights online', in Luca Belli and Primavera De Filippi (eds), *The Value of Network Neutrality for the Internet of Tomorrow, Report of the Dynamic Coalition on Network Neutrality*, pp. 26–35, accessed 23 March 2018 at: https://hal.archives-ouvertes.fr/hal-01026096.

McQuire, S. (2008), *The Media City: Architecture and Urban Space*, London: Sage.

Media Reform Coalition (2014), 'The elephant in the room: a survey of media ownership and plurality in the United Kingdom', accessed 5 December 2017 at: http://www.mediareform.org.uk/wp-content/uploads/2014/04/ElephantintheroomFinalfinal.pdf.

Mediaset (2015), 'Public consultation on the Lamy Report: the future use of the UHF TV broadcasting band – Mediaset's response', accessed 5 January 2018 at: https://ec.europa.eu/digital-single-market/en/news/results-lamy-report-public-consultation-700mhz-spectrum-band (organisations' contributions).

Menon, S. (2011), 'The evolution of the policy objectives of South Korea's broadband convergence network from 2004 to 2007', *Government Information Quarterly*, 28 (2), 280–289.

Meyer, D. (2016), 'EU lawmakers are about to try making Google pay for Google News', *Fortune*, accessed 17 July 2017 at: http://fortune.com/2016/08/31/eu-google-ancillary-copyright/.

Michalis, M. (2016), 'New networks, old market structures? The race to next generation networks in the EU and calls for a new regulatory paradigm', in Seamus Simpson, Manuel Puppis and Hilde Van den Bulck (eds), *European Media Policy for the Twenty-First Century. Assessing the Past, Setting Agendas for the Future*, London: Routledge, pp. 139–160.

Micklethwait, J. and A. Wooldridge (2004), *The Right Nation: Why America is Different*, London: Penguin.

Ministère de la Culture et de la Communication (2013), *Décret n° 2013-596 du 8 juillet 2013 supprimant la peine contraventionnelle complémentaire de suspension de l'accès à un service de communication au public en ligne et relatif aux modalités de transmission des informations prévue à l'article L. 331-21 du code de la propriété intellectuelle*, Journal Officiel n° 0157, July 2013, p. 11428, texte n° 60.

Mission O. (2007), 'Le developpement et la protection des oeuvres culturalles sur les nouveaux reseaux', report for the minister de la culture et de la communication, November 2007, accessed 25 March

2015 at: http://www.culture.gouv.fr/culture/actualites/index-olivennes 231107.htm.

Moe, H. (2010), 'Governing public service broadcasting: "Public value tests" in different national contexts', *Communication, Culture & Critique*, 3, 207–223.

Montagnini, M.L. and M. Borghi (2008), 'Promises and pitfalls of the European copyright law harmonization process', in David Ward (ed.), *The European Union and the Culture Industries: Regulation and the Public Interest*, Aldershot: Ashgate, pp. 213–240.

Moore, M. (2017a), 'Editor accuses web giants of theft from journalists', *The Times*, Thursday 16 November, p. 15.

Moore, M. (2017b), 'Google axes one-click rule on news sites', *The Times*, Business pages, Tuesday, 3 October, p. 47.

Moore, M. (2017c), 'Licence fee cash to fund children's shows on ITV', *The Times*, Saturday, 30 December, p. 32.

Moran, M. (2003), *The British Regulatory State: High Modernism and Hyper-Innovation*, Oxford: Oxford University Press.

Morrison, S. (2008), 'Plurality and the sustainability of the British production industry' in Tim Gardam and David A.L. Levy (eds), *The Price of Plurality: Choice, Diversity and Broadcasting Institutions in the Digital Age*, Oxford: Reuters Institute for the Study of Journalism, pp. 91–94.

Mueller, M. (2010), *Networks and States – the Global Politics of Internet Governance*, Boston: MIT Press.

Murgia, M. (2017), 'Google plans to share revenues with news publishers', *FT.Com*, 22 October, accessed 6 December 2017 at: https://www.ft.com/content/5609bbfe-b4cf-11e7-aa26-bb002965bce8.

Musiani, F. and M. Loeblich (2013), 'Net neutrality from a public sphere perspective', in Luca Belli and Primavera De Filippi (eds), *The Value of Network Neutrality for the Internet of Tomorrow, Report of the Dynamic Coalition on Network Neutrality*, pp. 36–45, accessed 12 September 2016 at: https://hal.archives-ouvertes.fr/hal-01026096.

Musiani, F. and M. Loeblich (2016), 'The net neutrality debate from a public sphere perspective' in Seamus Simpson, Manuel Puppis and Hilde Van Den Bulck (eds) *European Media Policy for the 21st Century – Assessing the Past, Setting Agendas for the Future*, London: Routledge, pp. 161–174.

Napoli, P.M. (2015), 'Media ownership and the political economy of research in US policymaking', in Steven Barnett and Judith Townend (eds), *Media Power and Plurality: From Hyperlocal to High-Level Policy*, Basingstoke: Palgrave Macmillan, pp. 101–115.

Negroponte, N. (1995), *Being Digital*, London: Hodder and Stoughton.

Nerssessian, J. (2015), 'BBC website a threat to papers, minister says', *Independent*, 28 October, p. 7.

Newman, N. (2017), *Journalism, Media and Technology Trends and Predictions 2017*, Oxford: Reuters Institute for the Study of Journalism, p. 2, accessed 1 November 2017 at: https://reutersinstitute.politics.ox.ac.uk/sites/default/files/2017-04/Journalism%2C%20Media%20and%20Technology%20Trends%20and%20Predictions%202017.pdf.

Nichols, J. and R.W. McChesney (2009), 'The death and life of great American newspapers', *The Nation*, 18 March, accessed 6 December 2017 at: http://www.thenation.com/print/article/death-and-life-great-american-newspapers.

Nielson, R.K. with G. Linnebank (2011), *Public Support for the Media: A Six-Country Overview of Direct and Indirect Subsidies*, Oxford: Reuters Institute for the Study of Journalism.

Noam, E. (2009), *Media Ownership and Concentration in America*, Oxford University Press.

Nokia (2015), 'Nokia response to the public consultation on the future use of the UHF TV broadcasting band: the Lamy Report', accessed 5 January 2018 at: https://ec.europa.eu/digital-single-market/en/news/results-lamy-report-public-consultation-700mhz-spectrum-band (organisations' contributions).

Nora, S. and A. Minc (1980), *The Computerisation of Society – A Report to the President of France*, Boston: MIT Press.

Nordicity (2011), *Analysis of Public Support for Broadcasting and Other Culture in Canada*, report prepared for the Canadian Broadcasting Corporation/La SociétéRadio-Canada, April 2011, accessed 11 December 2017 at: http://www.nordicity.com/media/20121112jzxkpxjc.pdf.

NTIA (2015), 'WRC-Archive' accessed 4 January 2018 at: https://www.ntia.doc.gov/category/wrc-15-archive.

O'Brien, K. (2013), 'Telecoms want 'net neutrality' applied more widely', *New York Times*, 17 June.

Ofcom (2004), *Ofcom Review of Public Service Broadcasting. Phase 2 – Meeting the Digital Challenge*, London: Ofcom, accessed 17 December 2017 at: https://www.ofcom.org.uk/__data/assets/pdf_file/0030/36669/psb_phase2.pdf.

Ofcom (2005), *Review of Public Service Television. Phase 3. Competition For Quality*, London: Ofcom, accessed 17 December 2017 at: https://www.ofcom.org.uk/__data/assets/pdf_file/0017/15911/psb3.pdf.

Ofcom (2007), *A New Approach to Public Service Content in the Digital Media Age. The Potential Role of the Public Service Publisher*, London: Ofcom, accessed 11 December 2017 at: https://www.ofcom.org.uk/__data/assets/pdf_file/0028/51877/newapproach.pdf.

Ofcom (2009), *Ofcom's Second Public Service Broadcasting Review: Putting Viewers First*, 21 January 2009, accessed 11 December 2017 at: https://www.ofcom.org.uk/__data/assets/pdf_file/0016/51325/psb2 statement.pdf.

Ofcom (2010), *Report on Public Interest Test on the Proposed Acquisition of British Sky Broadcasting plc by News Corporation*, 31 December, accessed December 2017 at: https://www.ofcom.org.uk/__ data/assets/pdf_file/0017/81413/public-interest-test-report.pdf.

Ofcom (2017), *News Consumption in the UK 2016*, published 29 June 2017, p. 26, accessed 15 November 2017 at: https://www.ofcom. org.uk/__data/assets/pdf_file/0017/103625/news-consumption-uk-2016. pdf.

Olmstead, K., A. Mitchell and T. Rosenstiel (2011), *Navigating News Online*, Washington, DC: Pew Research Center.

Orange (2015), 'Orange response to the public consultation on the Pascal Lamy Report: The future use of the UHF TV broadcasting band', accessed 5 January 2018 at: https://ec.europa.eu/digital-single-market/ en/news/results-lamy-report-public-consultation-700mhz-spectrum-band (organisations' contributions).

PACT (2007), *Response to Ofcom's Discussion Paper on PSP*. March 2007.

Patry, W. (2009), *Moral Panics and the Copyright Wars*, Oxford: Oxford University Press.

Peha, J.M., W.H. Lehr and S. Wilkie (2007), 'The state of the debate on network neutrality', *International Journal of Communication*, 1, 709–716.

PEW (2012), The Pew Center's Project for Excellence in Journalism, *The State of the News Media 2012: An Annual Report on American Journalism*, accessed 19 May 2015 at: http:/stateofthemedia.org.

PEW (2015), The Pew Research Center, *Digital: Top 50 Online News Entities*, accessed 15 March 2016 at: www.journalism.org/media-indicators/digital-top-50-online-news-entities-2015.

PEW (2016), Pew Research Center, *The State of the News Media*, Washington, DC, posted 13 June, accessed 31 October 2017 at: https://assets.pewresearch.org/wp-content/uploads/sites/13/2016/06/301 43308/state-of-the-news-media-report-2016-final.pdf.

PEW (2017), *Home Broadband Use over Time*, accessed 10 November 2017 at: http://www.pewinternet.org/fact-sheet/internet-broadband/.

Pickard, V. (2014), *America's Battle for Media Democracy: The Triumph of Corporate Libertarianism and the Future of Media Reform*, New York: Cambridge University Press.

Picot, A. and C. Wernick (2007), 'The role of government in broadband access', *Telecommunications Policy*, 31, 660–674.

Preston, P. and A. Cawley (2008), 'Broadband development in the European Union to 2012: A virtuous circle scenario', *Futures*, 40 (9), 812–821.

Prindle, G.M. (2003), 'No competition: How radio consolidation has diminished diversity and sacrificed localism', *Fordham Intellectual Property, Media and Entertainment Journal*, 14 (1), 279–325.

Prosser, T., D. Goldberg and S. Verhulst (1996), 'The impact of new communications technologies on media concentration and pluralism, academic study commissioned by Council of Europe's committee of experts on media concentrations and pluralism', University of Glasgow, School of Law, August 1996.

Ralph, A. (2017), 'Guardian makes $44m loss as it fights rise of online competitors', *The Times*, Wednesday, 26 July, p. 40.

RCC (2013), 'Preliminary position of the RCC administrations on agenda items of the World Radiocommunications Conference 2015', 25 April, Annex 2 to Decision 3/9.

RCC (2015), 'Position of the RCC administrations on agenda items of the World Radiocommunications Conference 2015', 12 August, document number: WRC-15-IRWSP-15/1-E.

Reda, J. (2017a), 'Extra copyright for news sites', 13 December, accessed 3 January 2018 at: https://juliareda.eu/eu-copyright-reform/extra-copyright-for-news-sites/.

Reda, J. (2017b), 'Estonian Council presidency questions extra copyright for news snippers, but endorses censorship machines', 31 August, accessed 3 January 2018 at https://juliareda.eu/2017/08/council-presidency-copyright/.

Remeikis, A. (2017), 'Most voters believe NBN will fail to meet Australia's needs', *The Guardian*, 30 October, accessed 8 November 2017 at: https://www.theguardian.com/australia-news/2017/oct/31/most-voters-believe-nbn-will-fail-to-meet-australias-needs-guardian-essential-poll.

Robinson, J. (2010), 'What's its recipe for success?' *Media Guardian*, 15 November.

RSPG (2015), 'Opinion on a long term strategy on the future use of the UHF band (470–790 MHz) in the EU', RSPG15-595 final, Brussels, 15 February.

Ruddick, G. (2017a), 'UK government considers classifying Google and Facebook as publishers', *The Guardian Online*, 11 October, accessed 5 December 2017 at: https://www.theguardian.com/technology/2017/oct/11/government-considers-classifying-google-facebook-publishers.

Ruddick, G. (2017b), 'Ofcom chair raises prospect of regulation for Google and Facebook', *The Guardian Online*, accessed 5 December

2017 at: https://www.theguardian.com/media/2017/oct/10/ofcom-patricia-hodgson-google-facebook-fake-news.

Ruhle, E., I. Brusic, J. Kittl Jorg and M. Ehrler (2011), 'Next Generation Access (NGA) supply side interventions: An international comparison', *Telecommunications Policy*, 35 (9–10), 794–803.

Rusbridger, A. (2009), 'Why journalism matters', London: Media Standards Trust, speech, accessed 15 November 2017 at: http://mediastandardstrust.org/wp-content/uploads/downloads/2010/08/Why-Journalism-Matters-Alan-Rusbridger.pdf.

Rushe, D. (2015), 'US regulator backs net neutrality demand', *The Guardian*, Friday, 27 February, p. 20.

Rushe, D. and L. Gambino (2017), 'US regulator scraps net neutrality rules that protect open internet', *The Guardian*, Friday, 15 December, accessed 4 January 2018 at: https://www.theguardian.com/technology/2017/dec/14/net-neutrality-fcc-rules-open-internet.

Sabatier, P.A. (1998), 'An advocacy coalition framework of policy change and the role of policy-oriented learning therein', *Policy Sciences*, 21, 129–168.

Satellite and Cable Broadcasters' Group (SCBG) (2007), *Ofcom Consultation. Public Service Publisher. Submission by the Satellite and CableBroadcasters' Group*, 21 March 2007.

Scharpf, F. (1997), 'Introduction: The problem-solving capacity of multi-level governance', *Journal of European Public Policy*, 4 (4), 520–538.

Scharpf, F. (1999), *Governing in Europe: Effective and Democratic?* Oxford: Oxford University Press.

Sherman, J. (2017), 'Guardian considers returning to its northern roots', *The Times* (Jill Sherman is the media editor), Wednesday 5 April, p. 13.

Shin, D-H. and J. Jung (2012), 'Socio-technical analysis of Korea's broadband convergence network: Big plans, big projects, big prospects?' *Telecommunications Policy*, 36 (7), 579–593.

Shirky, C. (2008), *Here Comes Everybody: The Power of Organizing without Organizations*, London: Penguin.

Shirky, C. (2010), *Cognitive Surplus: Creativity and Generosity in a Connected Age*, London: Penguin.

Simpson, S. (2004), 'Explaining the Commercialisation of the Internet: a neo-Gramscian Contribution', *Information, Communication and Society*, 7 (1), 50–69.

Simpson, S. (2010), 'Effective communications regulation in an era of convergence? The case of premium rate telephony and television in the UK' *Convergence*, 16 (2), 217–233.

Simpson, S. (2012), 'New approaches to the development of tele-communications infrastructures in Europe? The evolution of European Union policy for next generation networks', in Natascha Just and

Manuel Puppis (eds), *Trends in Communications Policy Research: New Theories, Methods and Subjects*, Bristol: Intellect Books, pp. 335–354.

Simpson, S. (2017), 'European Union telecommunications policy', in *Oxford Research Encyclopedia of Communication*, Oxford: Oxford University Press, Online Publication Date: October. DOI: 10.1093/acrefore/9780190228613.013.128.

Sims, M. (2012), 'Editorial: WRC tips the scales', *PolicyTracker*, 24 February, accessed 3 February 2016 at: https://www.policytracker.com/headlines/editorial-wrc-tips-the-scales.

Skogerbø, E. (1997), 'The press subsidy system in Norway. Controversial past – unpredictable future?, *European Journal of Communication*, 12 (1), 99–118.

Sky (2015), 'Sky's response to Pascal Lamy's report to the European Commission on the future use of the UHF band (470–790 MHz), accessed 5 January 2015 at: https://ec.europa.eu/digital-single-market/en/news/results-lamy-report-public-consultation-700mhz-spectrum-band (organisations' contributions).

Smyth, J. (2017), 'Australia struggles to deliver national broadband plan. Politics, poor technology and high costs hit costs hit A$49bn NBN rollout', *Financial Times*, 26 September, accessed 10 November 2017 at: http://www.ft.com/content/bob3c2fc-9d32-11e7-8cd4-932067fbf946.

Spillane, C. (2017), 'Publishers to get power to sue internet platforms', *Politico*, 3 August 2017, accessed 5 December 2017 at: https://www.politico.eu/article/publishers-spar-with-internet-platforms-over-copyright-fight-yahoo-google/.

Standeford, D. (2014a), 'US struggles to agree WRC-15 position on UHF band', *PolicyTracker*, 30 January, accessed 3 February 2017 at: https://www.policytracker.com/headlines/broadcast-wireless-sectors-fail-to-agree-on-draft-us-wrc-15-position-on-uhf-band.

Standeford, D. (2014b), 'EU High Level Group divided on future use of 470–790 MHz', *PolicyTracker*, 1 September, accessed 3 February at: https://www.policytracker.com/headlines//eu-high-level-group-fails-to-agree-on-future-use-of-490-790-mhz.

Standeford, D. (2014c), 'Ofcom to oppose shifting 470-694 MHz band to mobile use', *PolicyTracker*, 1 July, accessed 3 February 2017 at: https://www.policytracker.com/headlines/ofcom-to-oppose-shifting-470-694-mhz-band-to-wireless-uses.

Standeford, D. (2015a), 'European regulators and telcos set out WRC-15 wishlist', *PolicyTracker*, 3 November, accessed 3 February 2017 at: https://www.policytracker.com/headlines/european-telecoms-operators-set-out-wrc-15-wishlist.

Standeford, D. (2015b), 'UK recommends mechanism for valuing social benefits of spectrum', *PolicyTracker*, 1 December, accessed 3 February

2017 at: https://www.policytracker.com/headlines/social-value-in-spectrum-allocation.

Statista (2018), 'Global digital population as of January 2018', accessed 5 April 2018 at: https://www.statista.com/statistics/617136/digital-population-worldwide/.

Stempel, J. (2014), 'Google, Viacom settle landmark YouTube lawsuit', *Reuters*, Technology News, 18 March, accessed 5 September 2017 at: http://www.reuters.com/article/us-google-viacom-lawsuit/google-via com-settle-landmark-youtube-lawsuit-idUSBREA2H11220140318.

Streeter, T. (1996), *Selling the Air: A Critique of the Policy of Commercial Broadcasting in the United States*, Chicago: University of Chicago Press.

Strover, S. and S. McDowell (2014), 'Broadband redux 2013', *Government Information Quarterly*, 31, 50–52.

The Sunday Times (2015), 'Brussels hammers the tech giants', 19 April, Focus, p. 5.

Sweeney, M. (2012), 'Ofcom outlines new anti-piracy rules; draft code details "three strikes" policy for illegal downloaders to come into effect from March 2014', *Guardian Online*, 26 June, accessed 3 March 2016 at: http://www.theguardian.com.technology/2012/jun/26/ofcom-outline.

Sweeney, M. (2016), 'UK ad market booms but newspapers lose £155m in print advertising', *Guardian Online*, 26 April, accessed 30 December 2017 at: https://www.theguardian.com/media/2016/apr/26/uk-ad-market-booms-but-newspapers-lose-155m-in-print-advertising.

Telefonica (2015), 'Telefonica S.A. response to the public consultation on the future use of the UHF TV broadcasting band: the Lamy Report', accessed 5 January 2018 at: https://ec.europa.eu/digital-single-market/en/news/results-lamy-report-public-consultation-700mhz-spectrum-band (organisations' contributions).

TI (2015), 'The Danish telecom industry response to the hearing of the Lamy Report: the future use of the UHF TV broadcasting band', 10 April, accessed 5 January 2018 at: https://ec.europa.eu/digital-single-market/en/news/results-lamy-report-public-consultation-700mhz-spectrum-band (organisations' contributions).

The Times (2015), 'Playing monopoly', editorial, 16 April.

The Times (2018), 'Zero-sum game', editorial, 15 March.

Titcombe, J. (2017), 'Google and Microsoft agree crackdown on illegal downloads', *The Telegraph*, Technology, 20 February, accessed 25 September 2017 at: http://www.telegraph.co.uk/technology/2017/02/20/google-microsoft-agree-anti-piracy-code-crackdown-illegal-down loads.

Toffler, A. (1980), *The Third Wave*, New York: Bantam Books.

UK Film Council (2007), *Ofcom A New Approach to Public Service Content in the Digital Media Age. The Potential Role of the Public Service Publisher. Response to Consultation*, March 2007.

US Government (2015), 'United States of America – Proposals for the work of the conference', accessed 4 January 2018 at: https://www.ntia. doc.gov/files/ntia/publications/ai_1.1_470-698_mhz_usa_proposal_2014-03-10.pdf.

Ward, D. (2004), *Mapping Study of Media Concentration in Ten European Countries*, Hilversum: Commissariaat voor de Media, accessed 6 December 2017 at: http://citeseerx.ist.psu.edu/viewdoc/download?doi=10.1.1.691.2674&rep=rep1&type=pdf.

Watson, J. (2007), 'Can you out a value on spectrum?', *PolicyTracker*, 1 June, accessed February 2017 at: https://www.policytracker.com/headlines//can-you-put-a-social-value-on-spectrum.

Watson, J. (2012), 'Moving broadcasting from 700MHz will be a challenging business', *PolicyTracker*, 4 October, accessed 3 February 2017 at: https://www.policytracker.com/headlines/moving-broad casting-from-700-mhz-will-be-a-challenging-business.

Watson, J. (2014), 'Sweden reallocates 700MHz band for mobile use', *PolicyTracker*, 3 April, accessed 3 February 2017 at: https://www. policytracker.com/headlines/sweden-reallocates-700-mhz-band-for-mobile-use.

WBU (2015), 'World broadcasting unions reaffirms joint support to DTT after WRC-15', accessed 5 January 2018 at: http://nabanet.com/wp-content/uploads/2017/08/PRESS-RELEASE-The-WBUs-Reaffirm-Joint-Support-to-DTT-after-WRC-15.pdf.

Weberling, J. (2011), *Mapping Digital Media: Case Study: German Public Service Broadcasting and Online Activity*, Open Society Foundations, No. 13.

WhiteSpace Alliance (2015), 'Response to Lamy Report Public Consultation on 700MHz spectrum band', accessed on 15 January 2016 at: https://ec.europa.eu/digital-single-market/en/news/results-lamy-report-public-consultation-700mhz-spectrum-band (organisations' contributions).

Withers, K. (2009), *Mind the Funding Gap: The Potential of Industry Levies for Continued Funding of Public Service Broadcasting*, London: Institute of Public Policy Research, an IPPR report for the media unions BECTU and the NUJ.

WSG (2015), 'Frequencies for the creative sector gain future regulatory certainty after World Radio Conference, welcomes the Wider Spectrum Group', 2 December, accessed 5 January 2018 at: http://www.pearle. ws/en/positionpapers/detail/92.

Wu, T. (2003), 'Network neutrality, broadband discrimination', *Journal of Telecommunications and High Technology Law*, 2, 141–176.

Wu, T. (2010), *The Master Switch: The Rise and Fall of Information Empires*, London: Atlantic Books.

Wyatt, E. (2011), 'House approves a measure to block the FCC's rule on Net Neutrality', *New York Times*, 9 April, accessed 25 November 2013 at: http://query.nytimes.com/gst/fullpage.html?res=990CE3D81339F93 AA35757C0A9679D8B63&ref=netneutrality.

Wyatt, E. (2013), 'Verizon-FCC court fight takes on regulating the Net', *New York Times*, 8 September, accessed 5 January 2018 at: http:// www.nytimes.com/2013/09/09/business/verizon-and-fcc-net-neutrality-battle-set-in-district-court.html.

Yang, J.L. and N. Easton (2009), 'Obama & Google (a love story)', *Fortune Magazine*, October 26, accessed 30 December 2017 at: http://archive.fortune.com/2009/10/21/technology/obama_google.fortune/ index.htm.

Yip, D. (2015), 'Brussels open to mobile downlink in lower UHF band', *PolicyTracker*, 9 December, accessed 3 February 2017 at: https:// www.policytracker.com/headlines/wireless-broadband-could-still-be-allowed-to-share-lower-uhf-frequencies.

Youell, T. (2014a), 'Americas may struggle to agree common position for WRC-15', *PolicyTracker*, 13 January, accessed 5 January 2018 at: https://www.policytracker.com/headlines/faultines-emerge-as-the-americas-struggle-to-prepare-a-common-position-ahead-of-the-wrc-15.

Youell, T. (2014b), 'Broadcasters' report rejects co-primary allocation of UHF', *PolicyTracker*, 11 November, accessed 3 February 2017 at: https://www.policytracker.com/headlines/turning-off-dtt-could-cause-net-cost-the-eu-as-much-as20ac40-billion-according-to-new-study.

Youell, T. (2014c), 'Creating order out of chaos in Europe's 470-690MHz band', *PolicyTracker*, 7 March, accessed 3 February 2017 at: https:// www.policytracker.com/headlines/making-order-out-of-chaos-in-the-european-470-mhz-2013-694-mhz-band.

Youell, T. (2015a), 'US negotiators reaffirm commitment to global mobile allocation for 470-694/8 MHz band', *PolicyTracker*, 9 November, accessed 3 February 2017 at: https://www.policytracker.com/ headlines/fcc-commissioners-re-affirm-commitment-to-global-allocation-of-470-2013-694-8-mhz-for-mobility.

Youell, T. (2015b), 'WRC-15 chair urges delegates to overcome differences on IMT identification', *PolicyTracker*, 20 November, accessed 3 February 2017 at: https://www.policytracker.com/headlines/chair-of-wrc-15-urges-delegates-to-take-their-finger-off-the-trigger-on-imt-identification.

Youell, T. (2015c), 'Mobile operators to focus on sub-1GHz spectrum for 5G', *PolicyTracker*, 24 March, accessed 3 February 2017 at: https://www.policytracker.com/headlines/mobile-operators-agree-that-5g-will-mostly-rely-on-exclusive-licensed-spectrum.

Youell, T. (2015d), 'Europe formally agrees to oppose IMT identification of UHF spectrum below 700 MHz band', *PolicyTracker*, 24 June, accessed 3 February 2017 at: https://www.policytracker.com/headlines/europe-formally-agrees-to-oppose-imt-identification-for-imt-below-700-mhz-band.

Youell, T. (2015e), 'What are the prospects for 470-694 MHz in Region 1 at WRC-15?, *PolicyTracker*, 5 November, accessed 3 February 2017 at: https://www.policytracker.com/headlines/europe2019s-policymakers-enter-wrc-negotiations-wanting-to-defend-470-2013-694-mhz-broadcasting-allocation-while-mobile-industry–talks-of-mobile-broadband-dividend-from-potential-reallocation.

Youell, T. (2015f), 'Will it be second time lucky for the European Commission?', *PolicyTracker*, 11 June, accessed 3 February 2017 at: https://www.policytracker.com/free-content/blogs/toby-youell/will-it-be-second-time-lucky-for-the-european-commission.

Youell, T. (2015g), 'German 700MHz band spectrum stuck at bear reserve price', *PolicyTracker*, 3 June, accessed 3 February 2017 at: https://www.policytracker.com/free-content/blogs/toby-youwell/german-700-mhz-band-spectrum-stuck-at-near-reserve-price.

Index

Quality of service guidelines (and net neutrality) xiii, 86–7, 91, 218

Radio (broadcasting, station, etc.) xiii, 7, 13, 38, 55–9, 60, 62, 65, 67, 69, 71, 134–8, 142, 151, 155, 168, 191, 200, 209, 213, 216, 218, 239
Radio Conference Subcommittee (RCS) 57
Radio Spectrum Decision (EU) 65, 226
Readerships 165, 171, 189
Reagan, President Ronald 137, 139, 162, 174
Recording Industry Association of America (RIAA) xiii, 111, 129
Regional Commonwealth in the field of Communications (RCC) xiii, 59
'Regulatory state' 22, 236
Relevant market, see Concentration
Republicans (US) 82–4, 110, 162
Retransmission fees 187
Reuse fees 187
Reuters Institute 179, 181, 189, 191, 217, 222, 236–7
Richards, Ed 182
Rudd, Kevin 47
Rural Utilities Service (RUS, US) xiii, 43
Rusbridger, Alan 175, 240
Russia 59

'Safe harbour' (copyright enforcement) 107, 109, 111, 116, 118
Samsung 58
Sarkozy, President Nicolas 120, 175, 220
Satellite (TV, broadcaster – ing, communication) xi, xii, xiii, 6, 19, 34, 55–6, 58, 69, 71, 112–13, 115, 134, 141–2, 151, 160–1, 170, 177, 184, 186, 188–9, 209–10, 212, 225, 240

Satellite and Cable Broadcasters' Group (SCBG) xiii, 184, 188, 240
Scandinavia 174
Schools 39, 43–4
Schudson, Michael 166–8, 190, 221
Scott Trust 173
Search engines (also see Google, Yahoo!, AOL and Bing) 106, 118–19, 125, 151–2, 156, 160, 187, 201
Sector-specific regulation (media concentration) 27–8, 130, 154
Security
  National 13, 55, 137, 198
  Internet/network/online 15, 79, 80, 86, 92, 215
Self-regulation 151, 202, 212
Senate,
  French 121
  US, also see Congress 83, 110
Sepulveda, Daniel 59
Services Ancillary to Broadcasting/Programme making (SAB/SAP) 60, 74
Services of General Economic Interest (SGEI) xiii, 39, 40
Set Top Box 45, 160
Share trading 51
Share of reference approach (to cross-media concentration regulation) 156
Significant Market Power (net neutrality, media concentration) xiii, 35, 88, 90, 96, 142, 146, 157
Simpson, Seamus vi-ix, 6, 7, 19, 34, 38–9, 53, 97, 116, 231, 235–6, 240–41
Sky (also see BSkyB) 69, 156, 170, 186, 188, 238, 241
'Smart phones', also see mobile communication 46, 55, 175
Smith, Lamar S. 110
SnapChat 16, 75
Socialist Party, PS (France) xiii, 121–2, 129, 141